DATA COMMUNICATIONS & NETWORKING

Gahlot

CYBER TECH PUBLICATIONS
4264/3, Ansari Road, Darya Ganj, New Delhi-110002(India)
Ph.: 011-23244078, 011-43559448 Fax: 011-23280028
E-Mail: cyberpublicationsdelhi@yahoo.com
E-mail: cybertechpublications@gmail.com
Website: www.cybertechpublications.com

DATA COMMUNICATIONS & NETWORKING

Gahlot

First Edition 2016

ISBN: 978-81-7884-409-1

Published by:
G.S. Rawat for Cyber Tech Publications
CYBER TECH PUBLICATIONS
4264/3, Ansari Road, Darya Ganj, New Delhi-110002(India)
Ph.: 011-23244078, 011-43559448 Fax: 011-23280028
E-Mail: cyberpublicationsdelhi@yahoo.com
E-mail: cybertechpublications@gmail.com
Website: www.cybertechpublications.com

Contents

Preface

The term "electronic banking" or "e-banking" covers both computer and telephone banking. Using computer banking, a charity's computer either dials directly into its bank's computer or gains access to the bank's computer over the internet. Using telephone banking, the charity controls its bank accounts by giving the bank instructions over the telephone. Both computer and telephone banking involve the use of passwords which give access to the charity's accounts. Internet banking is changing the banking industry and is having the major effects on banking relationships. Banking is now no longer confined to the branches were one has to approach the branch in person, to withdraw cash or deposit a cheque or request a statement of accounts. In true Internet banking, any inquiry or transaction is processed online without any reference to the branch (anywhere banking) at any time.

Providing Internet banking is increasingly becoming a "need to have" than a "nice to have" service. The net banking, thus, now is more of a norm rather than an exception in many developed countries due to the fact that it is the cheapest way of providing banking services. Using these methods, banking transactions can be actioned 24 hours a day. Computer banking allows a charity, for instance, to view recent transactions, print out statements and transfer funds between accounts and make payments. Many banks also have the facility for a charity to set up, amend or cancel standing orders. Electronic banking also allows payments to be made to the charity, i.e. acceptance of credit card donations.

—*Author*

1

An Overview on Electronic and Internet Banking

INTRODUCTION

Internet banking is changing the banking industry and is having the major effects on banking relationships. Banking is now no longer confined to the branches were one has to approach the branch in person, to withdraw cash or deposit a cheque or request a statement of accounts. In true Internet banking, any inquiry or transaction is processed online without any reference to the branch (anywhere banking) at any time. Providing Internet banking is increasingly becoming a "need to have" than a "nice to have" service. The net banking, thus, now is more of a norm rather than an exception in many developed countries due to the fact that it is the cheapest way of providing banking services. The precursor for the modern home online banking services were the distance banking services over electronic media from the early '80s (the term online became popular in the late '80s). These services used the videotex system. In the US the first bank to offer these services did so in 1981 and by 1985 at least 37 banks offered videotex banking services. Because of the commercial failure of videotex these banking services never became popular except in France where the use of videotex (Minitel) was subsidised by the telecom provider. Online banking (or Internet banking) allows customers to conduct financial transactions on a secure website operated by their retail or virtual bank, credit union or building society. With cybercafes and kiosks springing up in different cities access to the Net is going to be easy. Internet banking (also referred as e banking) is the latest in this series of technological wonders in the recent past involving use of Internet for delivery of banking products & services. Even the Morgan Stanley Dean Witter Internet research emphasised that Web is more important for retail financial services than for many other industries.

Features

Online banking solutions have many features and capabilities in common, but traditionally also have some that are application specific.

The common features fall broadly into several categories

- Transactional (e.g., performing a financial transaction such as an account to account transfer, paying a bill, wire transfer... and applications... apply for a loan, new account, etc.)
    - o Electronic bill presentment and payment - EBPP
    - o Funds transfer between a customer's own checking and savings accounts, or to another customer's account
    - o Investment purchase or sale
    - o Loan applications and transactions, such as repayments
- Non-transactional (e.g., online statements, check links, cobrowsing, chat)
    - o Bank statements
- Financial Institution Administration - features allowing the financial institution to manage the online experience of their end users
- ASP/Hosting Administration - features allowing the hosting company to administer the solution across financial institutions

Features commonly unique to business banking include

- Support of multiple users having varying levels of authority
- Transaction approval process
- Wire transfer

Features commonly unique to Internet banking include

- Personal financial management support, such as importing data into a personal finance program such as Quicken, Microsoft Money or TurboTax. Some online banking platforms support account aggregation to allow the customers to monitor all of their accounts in one place whether they are with their main bank or with other institutions.

Security

Protection through single password authentication, as is the case in most secure Internet shopping sites, is not considered secure enough for personal online banking applications in some countries. Basically there exist two different security methods for online banking.

- The PIN/TAN system where the PIN represents a password, used for the login and TANs representing one-time passwords to authenticate transactions. TANs can be distributed in different ways, the most popular one is to send a list of TANs to the online banking user by postal letter. The most secure way of using TANs is to generate them by need using a security token. These token generated TANs depend on the time and a unique secret, stored in the security token (this is called two-factor authentication or 2FA). Usually online banking with PIN/TAN is done via a web browser using SSL secured connections, so that there is no additional encryption needed.
- Signature based online banking where all transactions are signed and encrypted digitally. The Keys for the signature generation and encryption can be stored on smartcards or any memory medium, depending on the concrete implementation.

Attacks

Most of the attacks on online banking used today are based on deceiving the user to steal login data and valid TANs. Two well known examples for those attacks are phishing and pharming. Cross-site scripting and keylogger/Trojan horses can also be used to steal login information. A method to attack signature based online banking methods is to manipulate the used software in a way, that correct transactions are shown on the screen and faked transactions are signed in the background.

Countermeasures

There exist several countermeasures which try to avoid attacks. Digital certificates are used against phishing and pharming, the use of class-3 card readers is a measure to avoid manipulation of transactions by the software in signature based online banking variants. To protect their systems against Trojan horses, users should use virus scanners and be careful with downloaded software or e-mail attachments. In 2001 the FFIEC issued guidance for multifactor authentication (MFA) and then required to be in place by the end of 2006.

WHITHER INTERNET BANKING

In India, a number of banks have either gone for Internet Banking or are on the verge of going for it. The system I am talking about is different from what was possible up to now - off line information or few limited services. I am talking about the type that enables the customer to transact business on line in real time.

The decision to implement an Internet banking solution for your bank should not be based on the "we-too-have-it" factor (an economist will call it Mr. Jones' effect). Before you decide for Internet based delivery channel you should consider a variety of factors. The first and the foremost being the business justification for it. In any case the RBI is going to need it (duly passed by your board of directors) before you get permission for it.

A channel management software has a wide range of possible configurations. It may range from the simple Internet Banking channel to a full range of channels - ATMs, POSs, Kiosks, mobile banking (SMS and IVR), TVs and so on. Many new channels may be coming in. At the simplest, it will cost you about two crores of rupees. Apparently, you should have a careful assessment of whether you should go in for an Internet based banking system or not.

I am not suggesting that you should consider it from the narrow viewpoint of your spread on additional business generated Vs the rate of return on your capital investment. You will have to take into account the following factors:

1. Possibility of new business generated.

2. Additional floating funds expected from new as well as the existing customers.
3. Expansion in the geographical reach of your business (Please note, the markets are opening and expanding).
4. Your plans to integrate with other banks or the total banking system (RBI has started the implementation of RTGS. An internal real-time transaction system combined with the Real Time Gross Settlement System of the RBI will be a miraculous achievement for the Indian banking customer).
5. The image value. The image of a tech-savvy bank, especially if you are targeting Generation X.
6. The chances of your customers shifting loyalty if you do not modernise.

You may have two objections to my above statements:

a. It is just not possible to quantify the above factors.
b. If you take into account these factors, especially points 2 through 6, almost every bank will have a strong case for delivery channel management system for banking.

I may not agree with you on point 'a' but on point 'b' I have to agree. But, if that is the case, why should you spend time and money on analysing these. Time and money do not come for free. There are reasons for it. For one, if you have built a detailed business case for it with projected figures, your Internet banking team knows where to push and for what objective. This is the first requirement for any successful investment. For another, when you analyse your business relevance to the Internet Banking, with points 2 to 6 in mind, you will realise that your investment in the Internet Banking is not complete with buying and installing the SW and the HW. You must have a plan for generating new customers, new deposits, new borrowers, a plan to utilise the floats efficiently as soon as they are available. You will need an entirely new set of procedures (which responds with e-speed), a new set of mentality, a new behaviour pattern, and a new service image. And all this will need investment - investment in Process Redesign, in Process Change Management, in training the personnel, in new recruitment, in marketing the concept not only to the external clients but, before this, to the internal clients - the employees-, and so on.

This all may sound so obvious and so simple. My experience with the banks suggests that the bankers who may readily spend 4- 5 crores of rupees on buying and implementing a channel management system of the most modern type, will not invest 20 -30 lakhs of rupees on these activities. The problem of the proverbial last mile! For them the project ends with the successful UAT. My strong recommendation is that let your project begin with the completion of UAT. As a banker you are not interested in the technology. Your objective is business - the business of banking. And your project will start with the end of the technological side of the project.

So, if you want to go for a channel management system or simply Internet banking system, go for it. But plan your investment not only in the hardware and software and the firewall. Have a complete business plan including all the aspects as stated above, with required investments. Then only will your business be able to reap the benefits of this investment.

SOME HIDDEN COSTS

Rather these are unforeseen costs, some of which you normally fail to see at the beginning when you are planning your budget. I am listing some of the more obvious expenditure items that are left out at the time of initial budgeting. Individually, these appear to be small; together they become a substantial part of the total cost. And if you miss out on these, your wisdom in estimation is going to be questioned later on.

1. Hardware and Software for Backup System and Test System
2. Firewall System - Hardware, OS, Software
3. Firewall for back up system
4. Encryption mechanism
5. Web Server Certificates.
6. Leased line and backup connection costs
7. Security policy design, validation and auditing costs.
8. Disaster Recovery Centre (DRC) costs

9. Risk Management and Contingency Plan
10. Costs of hiring / buying computers for project implementation and UAT.
11. Costs involved in hiring consultant(s) for techno-legal planning.
12. Process Change Management
13. Setting up new Data Centre or expanding the existing one
14. Leased line and encryption of data between Data Centre and DRC.
15. New support resources and their training.
16. Telephone bills, Transport and hotel charges for consultants.
17. Additional costs due to people working late, working on holidays and weekends.

The list is only indicative and not comprehensive. Besides each one of these items has its own detail workouts. My intention here is only to alert to you to minimise surprises. For, even after covering all the areas you can think of, you will have quite a few of them.

BUDGETING FOR E-BANKING

One of the problems that afflict any information technology project is the cost escalation. When you are planning to implement an IT project you must take a detailed look at the costs involved. If not calculated properly, the cost calculation can overshoot by 100 to 200 percent. And if the project is in crores of rupees, one can not overemphasise the consequences. Important banking projects these days -such as centralised core banking, Internet Banking, Treasury etc. easily come in this price range.

In this article I will discuss some of the areas that cause cost surprises in major IT project implementation.

Product SW Cost Structure: The cost structure in any proposal from a vendor, will have three components. There will be a one time license fee which the vendor will charge you. Another, major component is the annual maintenance charge or the Annual License Fee. This can vary from 10 to 20 percent of the software cost. This usually includes all the enhancements of the product that the vendor will release from time to time. And the third will be the professional service charges. Service charges will be applicable to all activities in which the professional of the vendor will be working on your project. The last component is most prone to cost surprises.

Professional Service Charges: In the contract of implementation and support this rate will be marked as per-day fee for vendor professionals, allowance and hotel charges (if applicable). Whenever you want to implement a core banking system, treasury system or internet banking system, it will have to be approved by your Board of Directors, simply because of the financial implication. And imagine the impact when you find that your entire budget is over and the project is only 50 percent complete.

The main culprit here is the professional fee for consultants. It is not always necessary that the vendor engineers are the most proficient ones. In fact most of the vendors send only the second or third line of consultants / engineers for implementation projects. This means that while the vendor consultants are refining their skills on their product, you keep paying more and more. Or you become their training ground. Besides, the professional service effort is always an estimated effort, you can not bind the vendor once the work agreement is signed off. In situations where the system integration has to be done between two different systems, such as in the case of Internet banking or treasury systems, which have to be connected to the core banking system using APIs (Application Programming Interface), the risk of cost escalation on this account increases many folds.

The one way out seems to be to provide for a fixed charge for professional services. Most probably you will have selected the product through a quotation process form a number of vendors. And you can insist on a fixed charge for the professional services, else the quotation has no meaning. Another alternative is to have a man-days budget with a variation cap incorporated in the contract.

Be a Good Customer

If you manage to achieve a professional services cost cap, you will need to show some discipline You will need to be a good customer.

The worst area where banks let vendors down and compel them to be dishonest is the decision making process. When a project is launched, manpower resources are committed to it. These resources are highly paid besides having huge overhead costs. The decision making process in most of the banks is such that in spite of the budget having been approved for the project, for every decision - be it for a business requirements specifications or be it for an item of expenditure- days and sometimes weeks are lost. This will throw any project plan and manpower budget out of gear. And a vendor who has calculated and committed the price quotation on a reasonably tight budget, will incur heavy losses. Hence, if you manage to get a fixed manpower budget in the contract, please have a foolproof decision making and expenditure sanction machinery in place for the project. A decision should not be delayed because someone in the bank is sick or is out on a honeymoon.

The essence here is that unless you find a way to control the professional services charge for your project, your entire financial estimates for the project is at the risk of going for a toss. At the same time if vendor commits you a fixed professional service charge, and you do not support him with an efficient decision making system for the project, the vendor will have no option but to abandon the project mid-way. Both the conditions have equally unpleasant consequences for you.

NET AND MOBILE BANKING

The regulatory body has not yet sanctioned virtual bank, in abroad there are banks like EGG Bank or NET Bank, which only have a virtual presence without any physical branches. Net Banking is conducting ones banking or bank account online through a computer and a net connection. The system is updated immediately after every transaction automatically. In other words it is said that it is updated 'on-line, real time'. Through netbanking one can check the status of his/her account, place queries and also can be facilitated with a wide range of transactions simultaneously.

Net Banking has three basic features. They are as follows:

- The banks offer only relevant informations about their products and services to the mass.
- Few banks provide interaction facility between the banks and its customers.
- Banks are coming up with arrangements of utility payments, like telephone bills, electricity bills, etc.

The current statistics show that hardly 10 per cent of Indian customers uses the internet for banking. Among all the facilities provided, the maximum of them uses only for checking balance or requesting for a cheque book. Very few customers uses the advance interactive services provided by the banks.

According to HDFC and ICICI Bank, 17 per cent of ICICI customers use the Internet for banking and 10 per cent of HDFC customers prefer it.

Cost of Installation of Services

For basic features, the cost for providing such services to the banks come around Rs 40 lakh to Rs 50 lakh. For the third level service or sophisticated services, the investments mount to the tune of Rs 4 crore to Rs 5 crore. These investments is just a fraction if compared to the operations of the bank using physical infrastructure.

MOBILE BANKING

"The account that travels with you". This is needed in today's fast business environment with unending deadlines for fulfillment and loads of appointments to meed and meetings to attend. With mobile banking facilities, one can bank from anywhere, at anytime and in any condition or anyhow. The system is either through SMS or through WAP. (Check out for SMS Banking under different head)

Mobile Banking is the hottest area of development in the banking sector and is expected to replace the credit/debit card system in future. In past two years, mobile banking users has increased three times if we compare the use of either debit card or credit card. Moveover 85-90% mobile users do not own credit cards.

Mobile banking uses the same infrastructure like the ATM solution. But it is extremely easy and inexpensive to implement. It reduces the cost of operation for bankers in comparison to the use of ATMs.

Using compact HTML and WAP technologies, the following operations can be conducted through advanced mobile phones which can is further viewed on channels such as the Internet via the Channel Manager.

- Bill payments

- Fund transfers
- Check balances
- Any many more which is also available in SMS Banking

In countries like Korea, two SIM Card is used in mobile phones. One for the telephonic purpose and the other for banking. Bank account data is encrypted on a smart-card chip. About 3.3 million transactions were reported by Bank of Korea in 2004.

SMS BANKING

Businesses are in move. So is to be your money. You may have to thank the banks which are providing banking at the send-of-your-sms. The technology is at its highest level to move your money while you are on the move. If you are having non-WAP enabled mobile handset, you can use the facility of SMS services. The following operations can be easily used by the service provider:

- Balance enquiry
- Last three transactions
- Cheque payment status
- Cheque book request
- Statement request
- Demat - Free Balance Holding
- Demat - Last two Transactions
- Bill Payment

The SMS facility brings peace of mind to customers and opens doors to many more technological possibilities and innovative services. It is very similar to how an ATM works.

To use ATM, a card is necessary and to use SMS service, a mobile phone is needed. In both the cases, secret number is necessary to access.

SMS banking is also very much safe. First, one authenticates the mobile number with the authentications key. Second, the customer uses secret Mobile Personal Iddentification Number (MPIN).

A new concept has been developed by Bank of Punjab Ltd. They call it "Mobile Wallet". With the support of this technology, a customer can make payment and receive payment of account of buy/sell (merchants) through SMS.

In this system, a buyer sends a message for buying and the bank in return sends a message confirming the purchase both to the merchant as well as to the buyer. Debit card number is the key field which is used for the authenticity of the customer.

The processes of the service are simplified as under:

- Customer has to send "REG(one space)(Account Number)(one space)(Debit Card Number)" as an SMS to bank's mobile number 9810999992 for registration. For e.g. "REG 06SB11052122 5047531105000109109" Bank will confirm the registration with the return message.
- After that customer will visit nearest branch to collect the service brochure and get it filled.
- Registration will be a one time process.Once registered, customer would be able to buy things from any of the registered merchant of the bank.
- Customer need to send "PAY(one space)(merchant code)(one space)(amount)(one space)(Debit card number)" as an SMS on bank's mobile number 9810999992. For e.g for making a payment of Rs. 56.16 to merchant BOPSTC from card no. 5047531105000109109, Send the following message "PAY BOPSTC 56.16 5047531105000109109"
- The transaction will be validated online and immediately funds will be transferred from customer account to merchant account.
- Bank would send transaction confirmation as an message to both merchant and customer(buyer).
- An SMS report will be sent to both merchant & buyer everyday stating the total number of transaction & total amount of transaction made during previous one day.

Note :- There is obviously a limit to the volume of transactions now.

SOME USEFUL TIPS

Generally with 3 invalid login attempts, SMS Banking services are locked. Immediately contact the branch for unlocking the services. In case one forgets the password, obtain a new password from the branch. To log out, choose the "Log out" option in the handset and SMS Banking session ends.

Services Provided by Net Banking

Queries

- Check Balance
- See Statement
- Inquire about cheqae status
- Ask for a Statement
- Ask for a Cheque Book
- Inquire about Fixed Deposit
- Inquire about TDS details
- See Demat Account
- Update profile

Transactions

- Stop a Cheque
- Pay Bills
- Ask for a Demand Draft
- Transfer funds between your accounts
- Transfer funds to a third party
- Request for a new Fixed Deposit
- Shop Online
- Pay Bank Credit Card Dues

Advantages of Net Banking

- It removes the traditional geographical barriers as it could reach out to customers of different countries/legal jurisdiction. This has raised the question of jurisdiction of law/supervisory system to which such transactions should be subjected.
- It has added a new dimension to different kinds of risks traditionally associated with banking, heightening some of them and throwing new risk control challenges.

- Security of banking transactions, validity of electronic contract, customers' privacy, etc., which have all along been concerns of both bankers and supervisors have assumed different dimensions given that Internet is a public domain, not subject to control by any single authority or group of users.
- It poses a strategic risk of loss of business to those banks who do not respond in time to this new technology, being the efficient and cost effective delivery.

BANKING SERVICES FOR NRIS IN INDIA

Almost all the Indian Banks provide services to the NRIs. There are different types of accounts for them. They are:

- Non-Resident (Ordinary) Account - NRO A/c
- Non-Resident (External) Rupee Account - NRE A/c
- Non-Resident (Foreign Currency) Account - FCNR A/c

a.An Indian resident who is earning forign exchange can also maintain Foreign Currency account in the country with an authorised dealer bank but only to the maximum limit of 50% of such foreign exchange earnings under the Exchange Earners Foreign Currency Account (EEFC) Scheme.

Some of the FAQs given below will make it easy to understand the services provided by banks to the NRIs.

TOP BANKS IN INDIA

With the advancement of technology and the birth of competition, banks are in the race of becoming the best in the country. With an eye upon customer satisfaction policy they are providing best of the best services with the minimum hazards. Banks like ABN AMRO introduced banking with a coffee.

It made a tie-up with one of the best coffee bar in the country, Barista and remained open till late evening for customers with a setup of a coffee bar in the premises. Few banks have introduced world ATM card to make travellers across the globe more safe and secure. What else. Internet and Phone Banking is the call of the day for banks.

In this race towards the best, we have selected top 20 banks in the country from all segment. It is not the ranking of banks but only for general information about the top banks in India.

Indian Banks Association

The Indian Banks Association (IBA) was formed on the 26th September, 1946 with 22 members. Today IBA has more than 156 members comprising of Public Sector banks, Private Sector banks, Foreign banks having offices in India, Urban Co-operative banks, Developmental financial institutions, Federations, merchant banks, mutual funds, housing finance corporations, etc.

The Functioning of IBA

- To promote sound and progressive banking principles and practices.
- To render assistance and to provide common services to members.
- To organise co-ordination and co-operation on procedural, legal, technical, administrative and professional matters.
- To collect, classify and circulate statistical and other information.
- To pool together expertise towards common purposes such as reduction in costs, increase in efficiency, productivity and improve systems, procedures and banking practices.
- To project good public image of banking through publicity and public relations.
- To encourage sports and cultural activities among bank employees.

The Offices of IBA

The Organisational Structure of IBA

The Managing Committee manages the affairs, business and funds of IBA. The managing Committee is elected by the Ordinary members of the Association, and is the highest management and policy making body of the Association.

The Chairman of the Association heads upon the working of the Association. He provides guidelines to the Association. The administrative head of IBA is the Chief Executive of IBA. He is also the Secretary to the Managing Committee. He leads a team of executives, officers and other staff members. IBA constitutes standing committees/task forces/ small groups/ committees of experts from member banks for the examining of various aspects relating to industry level issues to get solutions. Recommendations of these groups/committees, are communicated to members with the approval of the managing committee or taken up with the concerned authorities for action.

PROXY BANKING IN INDIA

Indian villages were miles away from mutual funds, insurance and even equity trading. Thanks to Internet Kiosk and the ATM duo which has made it possible for rural India. This kiosk has been set up by ICICI Bank in partnership with network n-Logue Communications in remote villages of Southern part of the country.

This is known as Proxi Banking. With the help of fibre optic cables, this kiosk works on wireless in local loop technology.

Reasons for Setting-up of Proxi Banking

- 58% of rural households still do not have bank accounts.
- Only 21% of rural households have access to credit from a formal source.
- 70% of marginal farmers do not have deposit account.
- 87% households have no formal credit.
- Only 1% rural househlods rely on a loan from a financial intermediary. · The loans take between 24 to 33 weeks to get sanctioned.
- Consumers bribe officials to get loans approved which varies between 10 and 20 per cent of the loan amount.
- Branch banking in rurals is a loss-making.

Benefits to Rurals

- Small loans given for buying buffaloes.
- Loans for setting up a tea shop.
- Life and non-life insurance provided.
- Weather insurance given to farmers.

- Insurance policies sold to farmers like groundnut, castor, soya, paddy crop, etc.

The Proxy Banking is an innovative approach to rural lending and will add to the government's expanding base of kisan credit cards and the good old guidelines for agricultural lending.

Bank of India was founded in 1906 in Mumbai. It became the first Indian bank to open a branch outside India in London in 1946 and the first to open a branch in continental Europe at Paris in 1974.

2

Guidance on Electronic Banking

INTRODUCTION

This guidance is aimed principally at small and medium-sized charities and answers the questions we are most often asked by charities about electronic banking.

Much of the guidance is concerned with best practice advice on electronic banking. Section 5 deals with the legal power needed to adopt electronic banking This part of the guidance does not apply to charitable companies. However, the best practice advice applies to all charities using electronic banking, regardless of their legal structure.

Common terms

"e" – a prefix meaning "electronic" as in, for example, e-mail, e-banking or e-commerce.

BACS (Banks Automated Clearing System) – This is an electronic payment system allowing funds to be moved between bank accounts electronically. For instance, in a charity this may be used to pay staff on the payroll and to pay suppliers.

PC – Personal computer

Governing document – means any document that sets out the charity's purposes and, usually, how it is to be administered. It may be a trust deed, a constitution, memorandum and articles of association, rules, conveyance, will, Royal Charter, Scheme of the Commissioners or, in relation to an appeal, the published terms of the appeal inviting donations.

Trustees – means charity trustees. Charity trustees are the people who are responsible for the general control and management of the administration of the charity. In the charity's governing document they may be called trustees, managing trustees, committee members, governors or directors, or they may be referred to by some other title.

1. What is electronic banking?

The term "electronic banking" or "e-banking" covers both computer and telephone banking. Using computer banking, a charity's computer either dials directly into its bank's computer or gains access to the bank's computer over the internet. Using telephone banking, the charity controls its bank accounts by giving the bank instructions over the telephone. Both computer and telephone banking involve the use of passwords which give access to the charity's accounts.

Using these methods, banking transactions can be actioned 24 hours a day. Computer banking allows a charity, for instance, to view recent transactions, print out statements and transfer funds between accounts and make payments. Many banks also have the facility for a charity to set up, amend or cancel standing orders. Electronic banking also allows payments to be made to the charity, i.e. acceptance of credit card donations. Most charities that use electronic banking will also continue to use some of the elements of more traditional methods of banking, such as a chequebook.

Electronic banking services differ between the different banks and building societies. If trustees decide that they want to use electronic banking then they should shop around for the most suitable package for their charity.

2. What is the Charity Commission's view about electronic banking for charities?

With changing bank technology more and more charities are likely to consider moving away from paper based banking methods; many charities have already done so. Broadly speaking our view is that the trustees of a charity will be justified in deciding to use electronic banking if:

- they can identify overall advantages for the charity in doing so;
- they put in place adequate financial controls; and
- they have, or can acquire, the necessary legal power.

It is important that any decision to adopt electronic banking be made with the benefits and advantages to the charity in mind. It is not right to move to electronic banking just because it seems fashionable or because the charity's bank wants it to change (the motive for this might be to help the bank to reduce its own costs, rather than to provide a better service for the charity).

With electronic banking we would expect the same level of internal financial controls as we would with the more traditional forms of banking. There should continue to be clear segregation of duties to prevent any single person from being able to control substantial resources or obtaining unauthorised access to information; and there should be proper approval at, or delegated from, trustee level for movements and payments from bank accounts. Further advice on internal financial controls can be found in our publication CC8.

3. What are the advantages and potential difficulties of electronic banking?

Advantages

- For trustees who give their own time to charities it means that they can carry out charity banking out of working hours in the evenings and at weekends. Trustees are able to carry out transactions 24 hours a day, 7 days a week and will no longer be restricted to bank opening hours.
- Trustees can instantly see what is happening with the charity's money rather than waiting for statements to be sent.
- There is no time spent queuing or journey time to travel to and from the bank for trustees or employees of the charity.
- It might be especially useful to charities that have branches. Paragraphs 51 to 55 of the Statement of Recommended Practice on Accounting and Reporting by Charities (Charities SORP 2000) emphasise that annual accounts must incorporate details of branch finances. Electronic banking enables individual branches to have their own local accounts but enables the main charity to access information regarding the bank balances of each branch. This may help the trustees to exercise greater control over

branch finances and may enable the funds of all the branches to be added together to secure a more favourable rate of interest.

Potential difficulties

- Unless the charity already owns computer equipment there will be an initial financial outlay to establish computer banking. This will involve the purchase and maintenance of a computer and the establishment of a telephone line.
- To use telephone banking there is the cost of the telephone call to the bank, although these are usually charged at a local rate.
- For charities that have more than a basic computer banking service there may be a charge for the services of the bank.
- Computer banking requires some personal computer skills although banks and building societies are making efforts to make their software as "user friendly" as they can.
- A charity may have used the same banking systems for many years and find a new arrangement initially more complicated to understand and operate. It will also mean having to adapt and to modify existing internal financial controls.
- The need for an indemnity – see section 6 below

4. Is electronic banking as secure as more traditional methods of banking?

Electronic banking services are used increasingly by small and large organisations all over the world. Organisations and banks have a vested interest in making sure that electronic banking is as secure as possible.

Banks have a password system for both computer and telephone banking. With telephone banking all telephone calls are recorded, so checks can be made if there are queries about a transaction. Care has to be taken by a charity to ensure that only trusted people have access to the passwords.

Systems can operate hierarchical passwords so that some people are given "read only" access (i.e. the ability to read information but not to change it or add to it), while others may be able to suggest changes which then need to be activated by a supervisor.

Some banks or building societies will offer arrangements where two or more people each have to enter their own password or personal number before transactions are effected. Some banks allow larger organisations to purchase a plastic card reader: when a payment or transfer has to be made each official can swipe their card (connected to their PC) and then enter a personal number to release the payment. In this way, one official cannot effect a transaction without other officials being made aware of it and being required to authorise it. Some banks have plans to bring in systems that involve electronic signatures or other advanced identification systems.

Whatever arrangements a charity uses, the trustees should prevent any one individual from being able to control significant resources.

5. Does a charity need any particular legal power to adopt electronic banking?

The Trustee Act 2000 gives trustees the power to delegate specified functions. One of these is the function of carrying out decisions that the trustees have taken.

Trustees can establish whatever banking arrangements they consider appropriate, subject to the proper level of financial controls, to carry out their decisions. These arrangements can include an account which is operated electronically. In their instructions to the bank or building society the trustees should clearly identify the scope of the authority of the person or persons who the trustees have authorised to operate the account. The trustees should continue to monitor and review the arrangements and remain free to cancel or amend the arrangements or authorise others to operate the account for them.

The powers conferred by the Trustee Act 2000 apply to unincorporated charities but not to charitable companies. The powers which the Act confers are in addition to any powers conferred on the trustees by the charity's governing document. Trustees are not allowed to make use of the powers in the Trustee Act if the charity's governing document specifically prohibits the use of electronic banking or restricts trustees to conventional banking arrangements. If the governing document of a charity contains such a prohibition or restriction, trustees should approach us for advice on amending their governing document.

6. Do trustees have to sign an indemnity before their charity can use electronic banking?

A bank will usually ask a charity or its trustees to give the bank an indemnity before it agrees to provide an electronic banking service. The indemnity will typically say that the charity or its trustees agree to cover the bank for all costs and losses it sustains arising from use of the electronic banking facility (except where the costs or losses have come about because of the bank's own error or negligence).

We recognise that most banks or building societies will not offer electronic banking to a charity unless the charity or its trustees agree to give this type of indemnity.

However, charity trustees need to give careful consideration as to whether or not to give such an indemnity. The reason why the banks seek an indemnity is because the risks of misuse of the account are greater in the case of electronic banking than in the case of conventional banking. The indemnity will have the effect of relieving the bank from responsibilities to which it would have been subject had the account been a conventionally operated trust account.

Under conventional banking arrangements, a bank would have to make good a loss to the charity if it debited the charity's account on the basis of a cheque or other written instruction which had been forged - unless the bank could show that the trustees had, by their negligence, facilitated the forgery. In electronic banking arrangements, the effect of the indemnity would be that the bank would only have to make good a loss caused by an unauthorised instruction if the trustees could show that the bank had been negligent.

Whilst under conventional banking arrangements a bank can be liable to make good a loss to a charity's account if it gives effect to an instruction from the trustees which it knows or should have known involved a breach of trust, under electronic banking arrangements the indemnity would relieve the bank of this sort of responsibility.

No system of controls, however elaborate, can guarantee that a charity will be totally protected against abuse. Trustees often express concern about the extent of their personal liability in the event of any loss to the charity through misappropriation or misapplication of funds. Having sufficiently rigorous controls provides not only the protection for the charity property but also the best defence against a charge of failing to protect the charity's funds and thereby being in breach of trust. If funds are lost through trustees neglecting their duty of care they could be held personally liable to repay to the charity the funds lost. However, reasonable internal financial controls will reduce the risks associated with electronic banking and hence the risk of a claim being made under an indemnity.

Identity Theft Red Flags and Address Discrepancies

The federal financial institution regulatory agencies and the Federal Trade Commission (agencies) are soliciting comments on the attached Notice of Proposed Rulemaking (NPRM) titled "Identity Theft Red Flags and Address Discrepancies" that was published in the *Federal Register* on July 18, 2006. The NPRM implements sections 114 and 315 of the Fair and Accurate Credit Transactions Act of 2003, which requires the agencies to issue regulations and guidelines.

The regulations that the agencies are jointly proposing under section 114 would require each financial institution and creditor to develop and implement a written identity theft prevention Program (program) that includes policies and procedures for detecting, preventing and mitigating identity theft in connection with account openings and existing accounts. The program is required to be risk based and must be tailored to the size and complexity of each financial institution or creditor and the nature and scope of its activities.

The proposed regulations include guidelines listing patterns, practices, and specific forms of activity that raise a "red flag" signaling a possible risk of identity theft.

An institution or creditor would be required to incorporate into its program those red flags from the guidelines that are relevant to detecting the risks of identity theft to its customers or its own safety and soundness. Given the changing nature of identity theft, an institution or creditor also would be required to incorporate additional red flags on an ongoing basis from its own experiences, supervisory guidance, and other methods of identity theft the institution or creditor has identified. Under the proposed regulations, the program must include policies and procedures for verifying the identity of persons opening new accounts, detecting any red flags that are relevant to its operations, and implementing a mitigation strategy appropriate to the identified level of risk.

The proposed regulations implementing section 114 also would require credit card and debit card issuers to develop policies and procedures to assess the validity of a request for a change of address followed closely by a request for an additional or replacement card.

Additional proposed regulations implementing section 315 would require users of consumer reports, such as banks that use credit reports, to develop reasonable policies and procedures regarding notices of address discrepancies they receive from a consumer reporting agency (CRA).

If a user of a consumer report receives notice from a CRA that a consumer's address it has provided to obtain the report "substantially differs" from the consumer's address in the CRA's file, the user must provide the CRA with an address for the consumer that the user has reasonably confirmed to be accurate.

Authentication in an Internet Banking Environment

The Federal Financial Institutions Examination Council (FFIEC) has issued the attached guidance, "Authentication in an Internet Banking Environment." This updated interagency guidance, which replaces the FFIEC's *Authentication in an Electronic Banking Environment,* issued in 2001, specifically addresses the need for risk-based assessment, customer awareness, and security measures to authenticate customers using a financial institution's Internet-based services.

This guidance applies to both retail and commercial customers and does not endorse any particular technology. National banks should use this guidance when evaluating and implementing authentication systems and practices whether they are provided internally or by a technology service provider. Although this guidance is focused on the risks and risk management techniques associated with the Internet delivery channel, the principles are applicable to all forms of electronic banking activities.

Consistent with the *FFIEC Information Technology Examination Handbook,* Information Security Booklet December 2002, financial institutions should periodically:

- Ensure that their information security program:
  - Identifies and assesses the risks associated with Internet-based products and services;
  - Identifies risk mitigation actions, including appropriate authentication strength; and
  - Measures and evaluates customer awareness efforts;
- Adjust, as appropriate, their information security program in light of any relevant changes in technology, the sensitivity of their customer information, and internal or external threats to information; and
- Implement appropriate risk mitigation strategies.

Examiners should begin to assess national banks' progress in meeting the expectations outlined in the guidance and, thereafter, monitor ongoing conformance as needed during the risk-based supervisory process. Banks are expected to have achieved conformance with the guidance by year-end 2006.

Proper Disposal of Consumer Information

The attached final rule, issued jointly by the federal bank and thrift regulatory agencies, was published in the *Federal Register* on December 28, 2004 (69 FR 77610).

The rule requires financial institutions to adopt measures for properly disposing of consumer information derived from credit reports.

The final rule implements section 216 of the Fair and Accurate Credit Transactions Act of 2003 (FACT Act) by amending the Interagency Guidelines Establishing Standards for Safeguarding Customer Information (retitled by this rulemaking as the Interagency Guidelines Establishing Standards for Information Security). *See, e.g.*, part 30, Appendix B (national banks).

The final rule effectively requires a financial institution to dispose of "consumer information" in a manner consistent with the requirements in the guidelines that currently apply to the disposal of "customer information."

Under the final rule, financial institutions must make adjustments to their information security programs to properly dispose of "consumer information" that is not already protected as "customer information." This would include information from credit reports about a financial institution's employee or about a consumer whose application for a product or service is denied.

In addition, the final rule establishes a new part 41 to house the OCC's Fair Credit Reporting Act regulations, including a section requiring the proper disposal of consumer information that cross-references the guidelines.

The final rule will take effect on July 1, 2005.

3

INTERNET BANKING

INTRODUCTION

Internet Banking allows the Banks (and other Financial Service providers) to overcome the tradeoff between content and reach. With the use of Internet, banks can provide their services to a much wider audience then they could do without it. Even before the coming of Internet, competition had shifted from products to services. This was due, in large part, to the advent of Private Sector Banks. Two distinct trends can be discerned in the realm of Internet Banking. On one hand, Banks and Financial Institutions are trying to enter into new areas and consolidate their hold on the entire financial sector.

On the other hand, new Dot Coms are entering the financing business and challenging the banks. It could be said that two opposite things are happening at the same time. The banks, via their consolidation moves are trying to preserve their strongholds, while the Dot Coms are trying to fragment the market by providing superior services. Banks and Financial Institutions are trying to leverage their Brands and their position in the industry. While, the Dot Coms are using their competency in superior service design and experience of competing in this highly unstable environment. All the players share the same objectives: acquiring customers, providing them with new financial information, services, and products, and doing so in a way that enhances the value proposition of their products and services.

Before the entry of these banks, the retail banking was more of a commodity with hardly any differentiation on the basis of products or services. Banks offered similar products and similar service. But the new private sector banks changed the scenario by differentiating on the basis of service. They started providing Telephone based banking and introduced the concept of home banking. The superior service being provided by these banks was the main reason for their rapid growth. But their reach was limited due to logistics of setting up branches and increasing the reach of their service. Any attempt to increase the branch network would have increased their overheads and any attempt to widen the areas being served by a branch was likely to lead to deterioration in the service levels. In other words, these banks were caught in a dilemma as they faced the Reach and content tradeoff. With the advent of Internet these banks have been able to overcome this tradeoff. By using the Internet, these banks can expand their reach as well as maintain the standards of their services. *This booklet provides guidance to bankers and examiners on identifying and controlling the risks associated with Internet banking activities. It is one of a series of specialized booklets in the* "Internet banking" refers to systems that enable bank customers to access accounts and general information on bank products and services through a personal computer (PC) or other intelligent device.

Internet banking products and services can include wholesale products for corporate customers as well as retail and fiduciary products for consumers. Ultimately, the products and services obtained through Internet banking may mirror products and services offered through other bank delivery channels. Some examples of wholesale products and services include:

- Cash management.
- Wire transfer.
- Automated clearinghouse (ACH) transactions.
- Bill presentment and payment.

Examples of retail and fiduciary products and services include:

- Balance inquiry.
- Funds transfer.
- Downloading transaction information.

- Bill presentment and payment.
- Loan applications.
- Investment activity.
- Other value-added services.

Other Internet banking services may include providing Internet access as an Internet Service Provider (ISP). The OCC has determined that a national bank subsidiary may provide home banking services through an Internet connection to the bank's home banking system and, incidental to that service, may also provide Internet access to bank customers using that service (see OCC Interpretive Letter No. 742, the "Apollo" letter). Historically, banks have used information systems technology to process checks (item processing), drive ATM machines (transaction processing), and produce reports (management information systems). In the past, the computer systems that made the information systems operate were rarely noticed by customers. Today, Web sites, electronic mail, and electronic bill presentment and payment systems are an important way for banks to reach their customers.

National banks have experimented with various forms of online banking for many years. Some of the early experiments involved closed systems where the customers accessed banks through a dial-in or cable TV connection. These systems limited a bank's potential customer base because they required out-of area customers to either incur long-distance charges on their phone bills or subscribe to a particular cable TV service to access the bank. With the widespread growth of the Internet, customers can use this technology anywhere in the world to access a bank's network. The Internet, as an enabling technology, has made banking products and services available to more customers and eliminated geographic and proprietary systems barriers. With an expanded market, banks also may have opportunities to expand or change their product and service offerings.

TYPES OF INTERNET BANKING

Understanding the various types of Internet banking products will help examiners assess the risks involved. Currently, the following three basic kinds of Internet banking are being employed in the marketplace:

- Informational — This is the basic level of Internet banking. Typically, the bank has marketing information about the bank's products and services on a stand-alone server. The risk is relatively low, as informational systems typically have no path between the server and the bank's internal network. This level of Internet banking can be provided by the bank or outsourced. While the risk to a bank is relatively low, the server or Web site may be vulnerable to alteration. Appropriate controls therefore must be in place to prevent unauthorized alterations to the bank's server or Web site.
- Communicative — This type of Internet banking system allows some interaction between the bank's systems and the customer. The interaction may be limited to electronic mail, account inquiry, loan applications, or static file updates (name and address changes).

  Because these servers may have a path to the bank's internal networks, the risk is higher with this configuration than with informational systems. Appropriate controls need to be in place to prevent, monitor, and alert management of any unauthorized attempt to access the bank's internal networks and computer systems. Virus controls also become much more critical in this environment.
- Transactional — This level of Internet banking allows customers to execute transactions. Since a path typically exists between the server and the bank's or outsourcer's internal network, this is the highest risk architecture and must have the strongest controls. Customer transactions can include accessing accounts, paying bills, transferring funds, etc.

Internet Banking Risks

Internet banking creates new risk control challenges for national banks. From a supervisory perspective, risk is the potential that events, expected or unexpected, may have an adverse impact on the bank's earnings or capital.

The OCC has defined nine categories of risk for bank supervision purposes. The risks are credit, interest rate, liquidity, price, foreign exchange, transaction, compliance, strategic, and reputation. These categories are not mutually exclusive and all of these risks are associated with Internet banking.

Credit Risk

Credit risk is the risk to earnings or capital arising from an obligor's failure to meet the terms of any contract with the bank or otherwise to perform as agreed. Credit risk is found in all activities where success depends on counterparty, issuer, or borrower performance. It arises any time bank funds are extended, committed, invested, or otherwise exposed through actual or implied contractual agreements, whether on or off the banks balance sheet. Internet banking provides the opportunity for banks to expand their geographic range. Customers can reach a given institution from literally anywhere in the world. In dealing with customers over the Internet, absent any personal contact, it is challenging for institutions to verify the bonafides of their customers, which is an important element in making sound credit decisions. Verifying collateral and perfecting security agreements also can be challenging with out-of-area borrowers. Unless properly managed, Internet banking could lead to a concentration in out-of-area credits or credits within a single industry. Moreover, the question of which state's or country's laws control an Internet relationship is still developing.

Effective management of a portfolio of loans obtained through the Internet requires that the board and management understand and control the bank's lending risk profile and credit culture. They must assure that effective policies, processes, and practices are in place to control the risk associated with such loans. *See* the "Loan Portfolio Management," booklet of the for a more complete discussion of credit risk.

Interest Rate Risk

Interest rate risk is the risk to earnings or capital arising from movements in interest rates. From an economic perspective, a bank focuses on the sensitivity of the value of its assets, liabilities and revenues to changes in interest rates. Interest rate risk arises from differences between the timing of rate changes and the timing of cash flows (repricing risk); from changing rate relationships among different yield curves affecting bank activities (basis risk); from changing rate relationships across the spectrum of maturities (yield curve risk); and from interest-related options embedded in bank products (options risk). Evaluation of interest rate risk must consider the impact of complex, illiquid hedging strategies or products, and also the potential impact that changes in interest rates will have on fee income. In those situations where trading is separately managed, this refers to structural positions and not trading portfolios. Internet banking can attract deposits, loans, and other relationships from a larger pool of possible customers than other forms of marketing. Greater access to customers who primarily seek the best rate or term reinforces the need for managers to maintain appropriate asset/liability management systems, including the ability to react quickly to changing market conditions.

Liquidity Risk

Liquidity risk is the risk to earnings or capital arising from a bank's inability to meet its obligations when they come due, without incurring unacceptable losses. Liquidity risk includes the inability to manage unplanned changes in funding sources. Liquidity risk also arises from the failure to recognize or address changes in market conditions affecting the ability of the bank to liquidate assets quickly and with minimal loss in value. Internet banking can increase deposit volatility from customers who maintain accounts solely on the basis of rate or terms. Asset/liability and loan portfolio management systems should be appropriate for products offered through Internet banking. Increased monitoring of liquidity and changes in deposits and loans may be warranted depending on the volume and nature of Internet account activities.

Price Risk

Price risk is the risk to earnings or capital arising from changes in the value of traded portfolios of financial instruments. This risk arises from market making, dealing, and position taking in interest rate, foreign exchange, equity, and commodities markets.

Banks may be exposed to price risk if they create or expand deposit brokering, loan sales, or securitization programs as a result of Internet banking activities. Appropriate management systems should be maintained to monitor, measure, and manage price risk if assets are actively traded.

Foreign Exchange Risk

Foreign exchange risk is present when a loan or portfolio of loans is denominated in a foreign currency or is funded by borrowings in another currency. In some cases, banks will enter into multi-currency credit commitments that permit borrowers to select the currency they prefer to use in each rollover period. Foreign exchange risk can be intensified by political, social, or economic developments. The consequences can be unfavorable if one of the currencies involved becomes subject to stringent exchange controls or is subject to wide exchange-rate fluctuations. Foreign exchange risk is discussed in more detail in the "Foreign Exchange," booklet of the Internet Banking. Banks may be exposed to foreign exchange risk if they accept deposits from non-U.S. residents or create accounts denominated in currencies other than U.S. dollars. Appropriate systems should be developed if banks engage in these activities.

Transaction Risk

Transaction risk is the current and prospective risk to earnings and capital arising from fraud, error, and the inability to deliver products or services, maintain a competitive position, and manage information. Transaction risk is evident in each product and service offered and encompasses product development and delivery, transaction processing, systems development, computing systems, complexity of products and services, and the internal control environment.

A high level of transaction risk may exist with Internet banking products, particularly if those lines of business are not adequately planned, implemented, and monitored. Banks that offer financial products and services through the Internet must be able to meet their customers' expectations. Banks must also ensure they have the right product mix and capacity to deliver accurate, timely, and reliable services to develop a high level of confidence in their brand name. Customers who do business over the Internet are likely to have little tolerance for errors or omissions from financial institutions that do not have sophisticated internal controls to manage their Internet banking business. Likewise, customers will expect continuous availability of the product and Web pages that are easy to navigate. Software to support various Internet banking functions is provided to the customer from a variety of sources. Banks may support customers using customer-acquired or bank-supplied browsers or personal financial manager (PFM) software. Good communications between banks and their customers will help manage expectations on the compatibility of various PFM software products.

Attacks or intrusion attempts on banks' computer and network systems are a major concern. Studies show that systems are more vulnerable to internal attacks than external, because internal system users have knowledge of the system and access. Banks should have sound preventive and detective controls to protect their Internet banking systems from exploitation both internally and externally. *See* OCC Bulletin 99-9, "Infrastructure Threats from Cyber-Terrorists" for additional information.

Contingency and business resumption planning is necessary for banks to be sure that they can deliver products and services in the event of adverse circumstances. Internet banking products connected to a robust network may actually make this easier because back up capabilities can be spread over a wide geographic area. For example, if the main server is inoperable, the network could automatically reroute traffic to a back up server in a different geographical location. Security issues should be considered when the institution develops its contingency and business resumption plans. In such situations, security and internal controls at the back-up location should be as sophisticated as those at the primary processing site. High levels of system availability will be a key expectation of customers and will likely differentiate success levels among financial institutions on the Internet. National banks that offer bill presentment and payment will need a process to settle transactions between the bank, its customers, and external parties. In addition to transaction risk, settlement failures could adversely affect reputation, liquidity, and credit risk.

Compliance Risk

Compliance risk is the risk to earnings or capital arising from violations of, or nonconformance with, laws, rules, regulations, prescribed practices, or ethical standards. Compliance risk also arises in situations where the laws or rules governing certain bank products or activities of the bank's clients may be ambiguous or untested. Compliance risk exposes the institution to fines, civil money penalties, payment of damages, and the voiding of contracts. Compliance risk can lead to a diminished reputation, reduced franchise value, limited business opportunities, reduced expansion potential, and lack of contract enforceability. Most Internet banking customers will continue to use other bank delivery channels. Accordingly, national banks will need to make certain that their disclosures on Internet banking channels, including Web sites, remain synchronized with other delivery channels to ensure the delivery of a consistent and accurate message to customers.

Federal consumer protection laws and regulations, including CRA and Fair Lending, are applicable to electronic financial services operations including Internet banking. Moreover, it is important for national banks to be familiar with the regulations that permit electronic delivery of disclosures/notices versus those that require traditional hard copy notification. National banks should carefully review and monitor all requirements applicable to electronic products and services and ensure they comply with evolving statutory and regulatory requirements.

Advertising and record-keeping requirements also apply to banks' Web sites and to the products and services offered. Advertisements should clearly and conspicuously display the FDIC insurance notice, where applicable, so customers can readily determine whether a product or service is insured. Regular monitoring of bank Web sites will help ensure compliance with applicable laws, rules, and regulations. *See* the "Consumer Compliance Examination" booklet of the , OCC Bulletin 94-13, "Nondeposit Investment Sales Examination Procedures," and OCC Bulletin 98-31, "Cuidance on Electronic Financial Services and Consumer Compliance" for more information.

Application of Bank Secrecy Act (BSA) requirements to cyberbanking products and services is critical. The anonymity of banking over the Internet poses a challenge in adhering to BSA standards. Banks planning to allow the establishment of new accounts over the Internet should have rigorous account opening standards. Also, the bank should set up a control system to identify unusual or suspicious activities and, when appropriate, file suspicious activity reports (SARs).

The BSA funds transfer rules also apply to funds transfers or transmittals performed over the Internet when transactions exceed $3,000 and do not meet one of the exceptions. The rules require banks to ensure that customers provide all the required information before accepting transfer instructions. The record keeping requirements imposed by the rules allow banks to retain written or electronic records of the information. The Office of Foreign Asset Control (OFAC) administers laws that impose economic sanctions against foreign nations and individuals. This includes blocking accounts and other assets and prohibiting financial transactions. Internet banking businesses must comply with OFAC requirements. A bank needs to collect enough information to identify customers and determine whether a particular transaction is prohibited under OFAC rules. *See* the *FFIEC Information Systems Examination* (*IS*) for a discussion of OFAC.

Strategic Risk

Strategic risk is the current and prospective impact on earnings or capital arising from adverse business decisions, improper implementation of decisions, or lack of responsiveness to industry changes. This risk is a function of the compatibility of an organization's strategic goals, the business strategies developed to achieve those goals, the resources deployed against these goals, and the quality of implementation. The resources needed to carry out business strategies are both tangible and intangible. They include communication channels, operating systems, delivery networks, and managerial capacities and capabilities. The organization's internal characteristics must be evaluated against the impact of economic, technological, competitive, regulatory, and other environmental changes.

Management must understand the risks associated with Internet banking before they make a decision to develop a particular class of business. In some cases, banks may offer new products and services via the Internet. It is important that management understand the risks and ramifications of these decisions. Sufficient levels of technology and MIS are necessary to support such a business venture. Because many banks will compete with financial institutions beyond their existing trade area, those engaging in Internet banking must have a strong link between the technology employed and the bank's strategic planning process.

Before introducing a Internet banking product, management should consider whether the product and technology are consistent with tangible business objectives in the bank's strategic plan. The bank also should consider whether adequate expertise and resources are available to identify, monitor, and control risk in the Internet banking business.

The planning and decision making process should focus on how a specific business need is met by the Internet banking product, rather than focusing on the product as an independent objective. The bank's technology experts, along with its marketing and operational executives, should contribute to the decision making and planning process. They should ensure that the plan is consistent with the overall business objectives of the bank and is within the bank's risk tolerance. New technologies, especially the Internet, could bring about rapid changes in competitive forces. Accordingly, the strategic vision should determine the way the Internet banking product line is designed, implemented, and monitored.

Reputation Risk

Reputation risk is the current and prospective impact on earnings and capital arising from negative public opinion. This affects the institution's ability to establish new relationships or services or continue servicing existing relationships. This risk may expose the institution to litigation, financial loss, or a decline in its customer base.

Reputation risk exposure is present throughout the organization and includes the responsibility to exercise an abundance of caution in dealing with customers and the community. A bank's reputation can suffer if it fails to deliver on marketing claims or to provide accurate, timely services. This can include failing to adequately meet customer credit needs, providing unreliable or inefficient delivery systems, untimely responses to customer inquiries, or violations of customer privacy expectations.

A bank's reputation can be damaged by Internet banking services that are poorly executed or otherwise alienate customers and the public. Well designed marketing, including disclosures, is one way to educate potential customers and help limit reputation risk. Customers must understand what they can reasonably expect from a product or service and what special risks and benefits they incur when using the system. As such, marketing concepts need to be coordinated closely with adequate disclosure statements. A national bank should not market the bank's Internet banking system based on features or attributes the system does not have. The marketing program must present the product fairly and accurately.

National banks should carefully consider how connections to third parties are presented on their Web sites. Hypertext links are often used to enable a customer to link to a third party. Such links may reflect an endorsement of the third party's products or services in the eyes of the customer. It should be clear to the customer when they have left the bank's Web site so that there is no confusion about the provider of the specific products and services offered or the security and privacy standards that apply. Similarly, adequate disclosures must be made so that customers can distinguish between insured and noninsured products.

National banks need to be sure that their business continuity plans include the Internet banking business. Regular testing of the business continuity plan, including communications strategies with the press and public, will help the bank ensure it can respond effectively and promptly to any adverse customer or media reactions.

Risk Management

Financial institutions should have a technology risk management process to enable them to identify, measure, monitor, and control their technology risk exposure. Examiners should refer to OCC Bulletin 98-3, "Technology Risk Management" for additional guidance on this topic. Risk management of new technologies has three essential elements:

- The planning process for the use of the technology.
- Implementation of the technology.
- The means to measure and monitor risk.

The OCC's objective is to determine whether a bank is operating its Internet banking business in a safe and sound manner. The OCC expects banks to use a rigorous analytic process to identify, measure, monitor, and control risk. Examiners will determine whether the level of risk is consistent with the bank's overall risk tolerance and is within the bank's ability to manage and control.

The risk planning process is the responsibility of the board and senior management. They need to possess the knowledge and skills to manage the bank's use of Internet banking technology and technology-related risks. The board should review, approve, and monitor Internet banking technology-related projects that may have a significant impact on the bank's risk profile. They should determine whether the technology and products are in line with the bank's strategic goals and meet a need in their market. Senior management should have the skills to evaluate the technology employed and risks assumed. Periodic independent evaluations of the Internet banking technology and products by auditors or consultants can help the board and senior management fulfill their responsibilities.

Implementing the technology is the responsibility of management. Management should have the skills to effectively evaluate Internet banking technologies and products, select the right mix for the bank, and see that they are installed appropriately. If the bank does not have the expertise to fulfill this responsibility internally, it should consider contracting with a vendor who specializes in this type of business or engaging in an alliance with another provider with complementary technologies or expertise.

Measuring and monitoring risk is the responsibility of management. Management should have the skills to effectively identify, measure, monitor, and control risks associated with Internet banking. The board should receive regular reports on the technologies employed, the risks assumed, and how those risks are managed. Monitoring system performance is a key success factor. As part of the design process, a national bank should include effective quality assurance and audit processes in its Internet banking system. The bank should periodically review the systems to determine whether they are meeting the performance standards.

Internal Controls

Internal controls over Internet banking systems should be commensurate with an institution's level of risk. As in any other banking area, management has the ultimate responsibility for developing and implementing a sound system of internal controls over the bank's Internet banking technology and products. Regular audits of the control systems will help ensure that the controls are appropriate and functioning properly. For example, the control objectives for an individual bank's Internet banking technology and products might focus on: C Consistency of technology planning and strategic goals, including efficiency and economy of operations and compliance with corporate policies and legal requirements.

- Data availability, including business recovery planning.
- Data integrity, including providing for the safeguarding of assets, proper authorization of transactions, and reliability of the process and output.
- Data confidentiality and privacy safeguards.
- Reliability of MIS.

Once control objectives are established, management has the responsibility to install the necessary internal controls to see that the objectives are met. Management also has the responsibility to evaluate the appropriateness of the controls on a cost-benefit basis. That analysis may take into account the effectiveness of each control in a process, the dollar volume flowing through the process, and the cost of the controls. Examiners will need to understand the bank's operational environment to evaluate the proper mix of internal controls and their adequacy. According to the Information Systems Audit and Control Association (ISACA) the basic internal control components include:

- Internal accounting controls — Used to safeguard the assets and reliability of financial records. These would include transaction records and trial balances
- Operational controls — Used to ensure that business objectives are being met. These would include operating plans and budgets to compare actual against planned performance.
- Administrative controls — Used to ensure operational efficiency and adherence to policies and procedures. These would include periodic internal and external audits.

ISACA separates internal controls into three general categories. The three control categories can be found in the basic internal controls discussed above.

- Preventive Controls — Prevent something (often an error or illegal act) from happening. An example of this type of control is logical access control software that would allow only authorized persons to access a network using a combination of a user ID and password.
- Detective Controls — Identify an action that has occurred. An example would be intrusion detection software that triggers an alert or alarm.

- Corrective Controls — Correct a situation once it has been detected. An example would be software backups that could be used to recover a corrupted file or database.

Banks or service providers offering transaction-based Internet banking products need to have a high level of controls to help manage the bank's transaction risk. Examples of these controls could include:

- Monitoring transaction activity to look for anomalies in transaction types, transaction volumes, transaction values, and time-of-day presentment.
- Monitoring log-on violations or attempts to identify patterns of suspect activity including unusual requests, unusual timing, or unusual formats.
- Using trap and trace techniques to identify the source of the request and match these against known customers.

Internet Banking 16

Regular reporting and review of unusual transactions will help identify:

- Intrusions by unauthorized parties.
- Customer input errors.
- Opportunities for customer education.

Technology: In-House or Outsourced?

The different levels of complexity associated with certain areas involving security, operations, planning, and monitoring have caused many national banks to outsource all or parts of their Internet banking operations. Banks should periodically reassess their sources of technology support to determine whether a given solution continues to fit their business plan and is flexible enough to meet anticipated future needs. Regardless of whether technology services are provided in-house or through a third-party servicer, national banks need to have a strong link between their technology provider and their strategic planning process. This will enable the bank to link new products and services with the existing technology and product mix. There are pros and cons to offering technology-based products and services inhouse versus contracting with a vendor. Larger national banks with substantial resources may choose to purchase computer hardware and operating systems and/or develop the necessary application software in-house. This option may provide the greatest flexibility to customize product offerings. Other banks may choose to purchase a "turnkey" system from a vendor. In this arrangement the vendor typically provides the hardware, operating systems, and applications software necessary to enable the bank to offer the particular product or service to its customers.

The vendor will typically provide the service and maintenance for the turnkey system. A variation is to outsource the service. Using this option, national banks contract with a vendor to operate their Internet banking Web sites at the vendor's location. This option may be especially well suited for banks that do not have the technical expertise to develop this service in-house. However, such banks need to place additional emphasis on their due diligence to ensure that security is not compromised.

Several companies are responding to the developing markets for Web pages, Internet banking applications, and bill presentment and payment services. Although many companies in this market are prosperous and well managed, some are start-up companies with unproven products, services, or track records. National banks need to perform due diligence before selecting a vendor to provide Internet banking services.

They should have a formal service agreement with the vendor that clearly addresses the duties and responsibilities of the parties involved. National banks need to monitor their vendor's operational performance, financial condition, and capability to stay current with evolving technologies. National banks typically fulfill their responsibility to assure their vendors have sound internal controls by obtaining internal or third-party audit reports. Examiners should refer to the *IS internet banking* for a complete discussion of outsourcing issues. Whatever the source of Internet banking technology, products, and services, it is important for the national bank to have personnel with an appropriate level of specialized expertise, consistent with risk, to monitor and manage the business.

Issues in Internet Banking

Financial institutions, their card associations, and vendors are working to develop an Internet payment infrastructure to help make electronic commerce secure. Many in the banking industry expect significant growth in the use of the Internet for the purchase of goods and services and electronic data interchange. The banking industry also recognizes that the Internet must be secure to achieve a high level of confidence with both consumers and businesses.

Sound management of banking products and services, especially those provided over the Internet, is fundamental to maintaining a high level of public confidence not only in the individual bank and its brand name but also in the banking system as a whole. Key components that will help maintain a high level of public confidence in an open network environment include:

- Security
- Authentication
- Trust
- Nonrepudiation
- Privacy
- Availability

Security is an issue in Internet banking systems. The OCC expects national banks to provide a level of logical and physical security commensurate with the sensitivity of the information and the individual bank's risk tolerance. Some national banks allow for direct dial-in access to their systems over a private network while others provide network access through the Internet.

Although the publicly accessible Internet generally may be less secure, both types of connections are vulnerable to interception and alteration. For example, hardware or software "sniffers" can obtain passwords, account numbers, credit card numbers, etc. without regard to the means of access. National banks therefore must have a sound system of internal controls to protect against security breaches for all forms of electronic access. A sound system of preventive, detective, and corrective controls will help assure the integrity of the network and the information it handles. See appendix C for a discussion of online attacks. Firewalls are frequently used on Internet banking systems as a security measure to protect internal systems and should be considered for any system connected to an outside network. Firewalls are a combination of hardware and software placed between two networks through which all traffic must pass, regardless of the direction of flow. They provide a gateway to guard against unauthorized individuals gaining access to the bank's network.

The mere presence of a firewall does not assure logical security and firewalls are not impenetrable: firewalls must be configured to meet a specific operating environment and they must be evaluated and maintained on a regular basis to assure their effectiveness and efficiency. Individuals who are technically competent must perform the installation, configuration, evaluation, and maintenance of firewalls. The specific risks involved may require a broad range of security controls. Appendix A contains a more detailed discussion of firewalls and associated controls.

The *IS internet banking* discusses other logical and physical security controls applicable to Internet banking environments. Examiners should be familiar with these controls before conducting a Internet banking examination.

Authentication is another issue in a Internet banking system. Transactions on the Internet or any other telecommunication network must be secure to achieve a high level of public confidence.

In cyberspace, as in the physical world, customers, banks, and merchants need assurances that they will receive the service as ordered or the merchandise as requested, and that they know the identity of the person they are dealing with. Banks typically use symmetric (private key) encryption technology to secure messages and asymmetric (public/private key) cryptography to authenticate parties. Asymmetric cryptography employs two keys — a public key and a private key. These two keys are mathematically tied but one key cannot be deduced from the other.

For example, to authenticate that a message came from the sender, the sender encrypts the message using their private key. Only the sender knows the private key. But, once sent, the message can be read only using the sender's public key. Since the message can only be read using the sender's public key, the receiver knows the message came from the expected sender. Internet banking systems should employ a level of encryption that is appropriate to the level or risk present in the systems. OCC is aware that stronger levels of encryption may slow or degrade performance and, accordingly, management must balance security needs with performance and cost issues.

Thus, a national bank should conduct a risk assessment in deciding upon its appropriate level of encryption. The OCC does not mandate a particular strength or type of encryption. Rather, it expects management to evaluate security risks, review the cost and benefit of different encryption systems, and decide on an appropriate level of encryption as a business decision. Management should be able to explain the supporting analysis for their decision.

A common asymmetric cryptography system is RSA, which uses key lengths up to 1,024 bits. By using the two forms of cryptography together, symmetric to protect the message and asymmetric to authenticate the parties involved, banks can secure the message and have a high level of confidence in the identity of the parties involved. See appendix B of this for examples of how this technology works.

Biometric devices are an advanced form of authentication. These devices may take the form of a retina scan, finger or thumb print scan, facial scan, or voice print scan. Use of biometrics is not yet considered mainstream, but may be used by some banks for authentication. Examiners should evaluate biometric activities based on management's understanding of risks, internal or external reviews, and the overall performance of these devices. Trust is another issue in Internet banking systems. As noted in the previous discussion, public and private key cryptographic systems can be used to secure information and authenticate parties in transactions in cyberspace. A trusted third party is a necessary part of the process. That third party is the *certificate authority.*

A certificate authority is a trusted third party that verifies identities in cyberspace. Some people think of the certificate authority functioning like an online notary. The basic concept is that a bank, or other third party, uses its good name to validate parties in transactions. This is similar to the historic role banks have played with letters of credit, where neither the buyer nor seller knew each other but both parties were known to the bank. Thus the bank uses its good name to facilitate the transaction, for a fee. *See* OCC Bulletin 99-20, "Certification Authority Services," for more information on this topic.

Banks also may need a way to validate themselves in cyberspace, as theft of identity has taken place. According to GAO testimony (GAO/T-66D-99-34), perpetrators have copied legitimate brokerage-firm Web sites, altered addresses for customers to contact (and send checks), then put the fraudulent Web site back on the Internet. Except for the post office box and possibly the URL, everything on the Web site could appear legitimate. Banks will have to guard against a variety of frauds and scams as banking on the Internet becomes more prominent. A proper mix of preventive, detective, and corrective controls can help protect national banks from these pitfalls. Digital certificates may play an important role in authenticating parties and thus establishing trust in Internet banking systems.

Nonrepudiation is the undeniable proof of participation by both the sender and receiver in a transaction. It is the reason public key encryption was developed, i.e., to authenticate electronic messages and prevent denial or repudiation by the sender or receiver. Although technology has provided an answer to nonrepudiation, state laws are not uniform in the treatment of electronic authentication and digital signatures. The application of state laws to these activities is a new and emerging area of the law.

Privacy is a consumer issue of increasing importance. National banks that recognize and respond to privacy issues in a proactive way make this a positive attribute for the bank and a benefit for its customers. Public concerns over the proper versus improper accumulation and use of personal information are likely to increase with the continued growth of electronic commerce and the Internet. Providers who are sensitive to these concerns have an advantage over those who do not. *See* OCC Advisory Letter 99-6, "Guidance to National Banks on Web Site Privacy Statements," for a more complete discussion of this topic.

Availability is another component in maintaining a high level of public confidence in a network environment. All of the previous components are of little value if the network is not available and convenient to customers. Users of a network expect access to systems 24 hours per day, seven days a week. Among the considerations associated with system availability are capacity, performance monitoring, redundance, and business resumption. National banks and their vendors who provide Internet banking products and services need to make certain they have the capacity in terms of hardware and software to consistently deliver a high level of service.

In addition, performance monitoring techniques will provide management with information such as the volume of traffic, the duration of transactions, and the amount of time customers must wait for service. Monitoring capacity, downtime, and performance on a regular basis will help management assure a high level of availability for their Internet banking system. It is also important to evaluate network vulnerabilities to prevent outages due to component failures. An entire network can become inoperable when a single hardware component or software module malfunctions. Often national banks and their vendors will employ redundant hardware in critical areas or have the ability to switch to alternate processing locations. The latter is often referred to as contingency planning. This topic is covered at length in the *IS*.

In addition to these issues, appendix D contains some discussion points examiners can use in national banks that are contemplating engaging in Internet banking.

ELECTRONIC BILL PAYMENT

From the point of view of Banks, Electronic Bill Payment (EBP) represents something of a threat, in that it could lead to customer attrition and reduce revenue. Among other revenue streams, the following sources of funds for the banks could be affected:

- Float associated with processing in the physical form,
- Cash Management Services

The Banks can protect itself by providing this service to their customers. But EBP also has an important strategic dimension, as it can become an integral part of a bank's portfolio of services. EBP can attract customers to the bank by making transactions more efficient and enabling customers to access their financial information more easily. Moreover, online interactions allow use of such tools as e-CRM to create a more intimate relationship with the customer and promote and deliver other online products and services.

If the Banks do not establish control on EBP, they are likely to loose customers to the new providers of financial services, thus affecting other sources of revenue.

In India, HDFC Bank, ICICI Bank and Citibank are trying setup an EBP portal. ICICI has already started a portal called BillJunction.com. Banks are planning to use the Net for payment of utility bills. They are entering into tie-ups with utilities like MTNL, Airtel, Orange, and BPL Mobile etc. Right now, a customer who's received a bill in the physical form logs into the network in order to make an online payment. In the future, these bills will be sent to customers through the Net.

Consumers and Businesses can derive economic benefit on account of reduction in transaction costs and a reduction in the float resulting from physical processing of the Bills. In addition, many are likely to adopt it mainly for the convenience. They can pay bills electronically in the same way they do today, but by consolidating their bills, they can reduce the effort involved in the whole process. They can also access their account at the same time. They can conveniently access all billers from a single portal that also provides them banking facilities. This would enable them to view their account balance while paying bills. For portals or the intermediaries that consolidate bills from multiple billers at a single online location EBP is a tool to acquire customers and provide them other financial services also. Dominance of the EBP market can lead to an entry into other financial services markets such as credit or debit card payments, or indeed into a much broader range of e-commerce markets, such as payments gateways.

ONLINE BROKERAGE

Online Broking is emerging as another field where traditional service providers are likely to face tough competition from the Dot Coms. In Taiwan and Korea, 30% of the stock trading has already moved online. This is posing a threat to the traditional Full-Service Brokerages. By leveraging the power of the web, Charles Schwab has emerged as a major threat to Full-Service brokers like Merrill Lynch. In order to preempt the moves into these areas by new players, many Banks have already tied up with Online Brokerages.

The Banks have entered the e-trading business. Since many banks are also Depositary participants, they have tied up with e-traders so that a customer is able to buy or sell shares online and make and receive payments through the Net. In India, HDFC Bank has tied up with Investsmart.com and is offering its services to all the clients of the brokerage. ICICI Bank has gone a step ahead and launched ICICIDirect.com. These banks have become exclusive providers of banking and depositary/custodial services to the clients of these online brokerages.

4

Growth in Internet Banking

INTRODUCTION

National banks have significant reasons to develop the technologies that will help them deliver banking products and services by the most cost-effective channels. Many bankers believe that shifting only a small portion of the estimated 19-billion payments mailed annually in the U.S. to electronic delivery channels could save banks and other businesses substantial sums of money. However, national banks should use care in making product decisions. Management should include in their decision making the development and ongoing costs associated with a new product or service, including the technology, marketing, maintenance, and customer support functions. This will help management exercise due diligence, make more informed decisions, and measure the success of their business venture.

Numerous factors — including competitive cost, customer service, and demographic considerations — are motivating banks to evaluate their technology and assess their electronic commerce and Internet banking strategies. Many researchers expect rapid growth in customers using online banking products and services. The challenge for national banks is to make sure the savings from Internet banking technology more than offset the costs and risks associated with conducting business in cyberspace.

Marketing strategies will vary as national banks seek to expand their markets and employ lower cost delivery channels. Examiners will need to understand the strategies used and technologies employed on a bank-by-bank basis to assess the risk. Evaluating a bank's data on the use of their Web sites, may help examiners determine the bank's strategic objectives, how well the bank is meeting its Internet banking product plan, and whether the business is expected to be profitable.

Some of the market factors that may drive a bank's strategy include the following:

Competition — Studies show that competitive pressure is the chief driving force behind increasing use of Internet banking technology, ranking ahead of cost reduction and revenue enhancement, in second and third place respectively. Banks see Internet banking as a way to keep existing customers and attract new ones to the bank.

Cost Efficiencies — National banks can deliver banking services on the Internet at transaction costs far lower than traditional brick-and-mortar branches. The actual costs to execute a transaction will vary depending on the delivery channel used. For example, according to Booz, Allen & Hamilton, as of mid-1999, the cost to deliver manual transactions at a branch was typically more than a dollar, ATM and call center transactions cost about 25 cents, and Internet transactions cost about a penny. These costs are expected to continue to decline.

Geographical Reach — Internet banking allows expanded customer contact through increased geographical reach and lower cost delivery channels. In fact some banks are doing business exclusively via the Internet — they do not have traditional banking offices and only reach their customers online. Other financial institutions are using the Internet as an alternative delivery channel to reach existing customers and attract new customers.

Branding — Relationship building is a strategic priority for many national banks. Internet banking technology and products can provide a means for national banks to develop and maintain an ongoing relationship with their customers by offering easy access to a broad array of products and services.

By capitalizing on brand identification and by providing a broad array of financial services, banks hope to build customer loyalty, cross-sell, and enhance repeat business.

Customer Demographics — Internet banking allows national banks to offer a wide array of options to their banking customers. Some customers will rely on traditional branches to conduct their banking business. For many, this is the most comfortable way for them to transact their banking business. Those customers place a premium on person-to-person contact. Other customers are early adopters of new technologies that arrive in the marketplace. These customers were the first to obtain PCs and the first to employ them in conducting their banking business. The demographics of banking customers will continue to change. The challenge to national banks is to understand their customer base and find the right mix of delivery channels to deliver products and services profitably to their various market segments.

ONLINE DELIVERY OF FINANCIAL PRODUCTS

The Banks have started offering banking services like checking your account status fund transfer, ordering demand drafts and writing out cheques, via the net. Soon these will form only a small part of the total array of services being offered by them. These Banks have embarked on a number of new initiatives to protect their stronghold and to leverage the net. They are offering value-added services to their customers and at the same time are trying to get into B2C and B2B e-commerce. They are even trying to get their finger into various transactions between the Government on one side and the business and the customer on the other. Banks are trying to become a part of the online value chain. For example, they are trying to tie up with corporates so as to become a part of their supply chain and enable electronic transfer of funds between the different components of the Supply Chain. They are doing this by acting as an intermediary between the corporations and their vendors by enabling online transactions at one place.

Some Banks are trying to setup portals for routing payments like Excise Duty and Sales Tax. Not content with that Banks are setting up secure payment gateways to tap the B2C online market.

Banks have taken the application process for personal loans, car loans, and mortgage, online. They plan to offer other financial products like Bonds and Mutual Funds through their financial service portal. This strategy is aimed by pre-empting the entry of new startups into this business.

Another bit of the Net strategy, involves providing infrastructure for B2C as well as B2B e-commerce. Banks are setting up secure payment gateways that will allow online retail shops to obtain instant credit card verifications. Once the buyer hits the pay button at a B2C portal, the buyer's credit card details will get encrypted and travel securely to the Visa or MasterCard approval system through the bank's payment gateway.

The banks are also setting up their own shopping portals. HDFC has a stake in a portal called easy2buy.com where HDFC bank customers can buy using their bank account number. Federal Bank has similar arrangements with Rediff.com and Fabmart.com. ICICI has setup Magiccart.com, an e-tailing site.

At the B2B end, Banks are offering Net Banking service that allows electronic fund transfers among a company, its vendors and dealers. Another service being targeted at this segment is cash management. This will reduce the float, which is present in physical processing of the payments.

The Banks are also trying to integrate their systems with the ERP/Supply Chain system of their clients. This will enable the bank to benefit from the movement towards e-procurement. E-Procurement involves making transactions online and processing the payment electronically.

INTERNET BANKING IN INDIA

The Internet banking is changing the banking industry and is having the major effects on banking relationships. Even the Morgan Stanley Dean Witter Internet research emphasised that Web is more important for retail financial services than for many other industries. Internet banking involves use of Internet for delivery of banking products & services. It falls into four main categories, from Level 1 - minimum functionality sites that offer only access to deposit account data - to Level 4 sites - highly sophisticated offerings enabling integrated sales of additional products and access to other financial services- such as investment and insurance. In other words a successful Internet banking solution offers

- Exceptional rates on Savings, CDs, and IRAs
- Checking with no monthly fee, free bill payment and rebates on ATM surcharges

- Credit cards with low rates
- Easy online applications for all accounts, including personal loans and mortgages
- 24 hour account access
- Quality customer service with personal attention

DRIVERS OF CHANGE

Advantages previously held by large financial institutions have shrunk considerably. The Internet has leveled the playing field and afforded open access to customers in the global marketplace. Internet banking is a cost-effective delivery channel for financial institutions. Consumers are embracing the many benefits of Internet banking. Access to one's accounts at anytime and from any location via the World Wide Web is a convenience unknown a short time ago. Thus, a bank's Internet presence transforms from 'brouchreware' status to 'Internet banking' status once the bank goes through a technology integration effort to enable the customer to access information about his or her specific account relationship. The six primary drivers of Internet banking includes, in order of primacy are:

- Improve customer access
- Facilitate the offering of more services
- Increase customer loyalty
- Attract new customers
- Provide services offered by competitors
- Reduce customer attrition

INDIAN BANKS ON WEB

The banking industry in India is facing unprecedented competition from non-traditional banking institutions, which now offer banking and financial services over the Internet. The deregulation of the banking industry coupled with the emergence of new technologies, are enabling new competitors to enter the financial services market quickly and efficiently.

Indian banks are going for the retail banking in a big way. However, much is still to be achieved. This study which was conducted by students of IIML shows some interesting facts:

- Throughout the country, the Internet Banking is in the nascent stage of development (only 50 banks are offering varied kind of Internet banking services).
- In general, these Internet sites offer only the most basic services. 55% are so called 'entry level' sites, offering little more than company information and basic marketing materials. Only 8% offer 'advanced transactions' such as online funds transfer, transactions & cash management services.
- Foreign & Private banks are much advanced in terms of the number of sites & their level of development.

EMERGING CHALLENGES

Information technology analyst firm, the Meta Group, recently reported that "financial institutions who don't offer home banking by the year 2000 will become marginalized." By the year of 2002, a large sophisticated and highly competitive Internet Banking Market will develop which will be driven by

- Demand side pressure due to increasing access to low cost electronic services.
- Emergence of open standards for banking functionality.
- Growing customer awareness and need of transparency.
- Global players in the fray
- Close integration of bank services with web based E-commerce or even disintermediation of services through direct electronic payments (E-Cash).
- More convenient international transactions due to the fact that the Internet along with general deregulation trends, eliminate geographic boundaries.
- Move from one stop shopping to 'Banking Portfolio' i.e. unbundled product purchases.

Certainly some existing brick and mortar banks will go out of business. But that's because they fail to respond to the challenge of the Internet.

The Internet and it's underlying technologies will change and transform not just banking, but all aspects of finance and commerce. It represents much more than a new distribution opportunity.

It will enable nimble players to leverage their brick and mortar presence to improve customer satisfaction and gain share. It will force lethargic players who are struck with legacy cost basis, out of business-since they are unable to bring to play in the new context.

MAIN CONCERNS IN INTERNET BANKING

In a survey conducted by the Online Banking Association, member institutions rated security as the most important issue of online banking.

There is a dual requirement to protect customers' privacy and protect against fraud. Banking Securely: Online Banking via the World Wide Web provides an overview of Internet commerce and how one company handles secure banking for its financial institution clients and their customers. Some basic information on the transmission of confidential data is presented in Security and Encryption on the Web.

PC Magazine Online also offers a primer: How Encryption Works. A multi-layered security architecture comprising firewalls, filtering routers, encryption and digital certification ensures that your account information is protected from unauthorised access:

- Firewalls and filtering routers ensure that only the legitimate Internet users are allowed to access the system.
- Encryption techniques used by the bank (including the sophisticated public key encryption) would ensure that privacy of data flowing between the browser and the Infinity system is protected.
- Digital certification procedures provide the assurance that the data you receive is from the Infinity system.

Claus Nehmzow, a Principal in the Information Technology Group in London at Booz Allen & Hamilton, writes of some compelling research findings and offers his projections for European banks in The Internet Will Shake Backing's Medieval Foundations.

He believes the low transaction cost will make banking on the Net irresistible, but also that this will require institutions to carefully consider and plan customer relations programs.

- It is believed that everything will be determined by content and context, and where execution will be key. From a customer and service provider perspective, this is where the world is moving-it is going to be real-time, on-line, personalisation for both marketing and the service experience. If existing banks don't want to disappear, it is this challenge of Integration that they need to embrace in order to win and survive. The more things change, the less they change. In the months and years-ahead are going to be how Service Providers integrate and market their offerings across different channels.

  The strategic and executional battles of the future are going to be fought for Channel Integration. What does Channel Integration means? It means that an institution presents an identical face to the customer-be it in the branch, on the web, at an ATM or for that matter, through a sales representative or a broker. An identical face, an identical message. Or better still, messages that reinforce each other. If a sales representative tries to sell you a housing loan, you get e-mail a day later reminding you about the loan. That's called Integrated Sales, which results in incremental economic activity and improved efficiencies of communications.

  Channel Integration across the phone web can clearly lead to a gain of several percentage points of GDP. The beauty of this approach is that one channel does not displace another. They feed on each other to create incremental value for the customer, as well as the institution. The incremental value comes from two distinct sources. Firstly, you reduce inefficiencies. You don't send people junk mail because you know that they are not likely to buy a particular product or service today. That results in net saving for the economy. Secondly, you persuade people at the right time (the right time from the customer's perspective, not from the service provider's perspective) to opt for a tailor made offering. This too increases value. Actually, this has to do with the Internet itself, and more to with the underlying technologies of the Internet which allow incremental efficiency, and empowers the customer to make more enlightened and timely choices.

- Lastly the product range is another issue which becomes important. It will take a technological revolution to make available advanced banking products on the net and given the rate at which the technology is developing we can expect this to happen in near future.

E-FINANCE: QUO VADIS

Internet has touched almost all aspects of our lives. The emergence of e-commerce has revolutionized the way we live, shop, entertain and interact. Therefore, it should not come as a surprise if it tries to influence the way we save and the way we invest. Today, when the customer is king and the service providers are rushing to pay obeisance to the king, financial service providers cannot be left behind. In their quest to differentiate their services and gain competitive advantage over their competitors, the financial service providers are trying to provide their services to the customers in the comfort of their homes. The Internet has emerged as a convenient channel for these service providers.

Living in India, we might find these ideas too far fetched but the truth is that Internet has changed the way these services are delivered, particularly in countries where the Internet penetration is high. The different ways in which Internet is trying to revolutionize the delivery of the financial services and products are given below: -

1. Internet Banking
2. Electronic Bill Payment
3. Online Brokerages
4. Online Delivery of Financial Products like Mortgages

CHALLENGES

One of the challenges before a Bank, which is trying to become e-enabled is that the data is scattered across the countries. Integration of this data is necessary if the banks have to succeed on the net. The second challenge is related to the move towards expanding the basket of financial products being offered by Financial Service providers. In developed countries, Financial Service providers are using the Internet as a media for expanding into new products. Banks are getting into Mutual funds and vice-versa. However, in India, archaic regulations do not allow companies to have a close relationship with the Banks owned by them or to offer products, which are offered by another category of service providers. As a result, companies like ICICI are forced to keep their Banking arms separate from the main company. They are also prevented from offering products, which fall under the purview of Banks. This is a serious impediment for innovation in the financial service sector. Moreover, it prevents Indian Financial Service Providers from exploiting the power of the web.

Given these challenges, only a Bank (or Financial Service provider) which moves fast and tries to capture the first mover advantage can think of succeeding in this sector. Another Key Success Factor will be the Value, which the online operations of the Banks will be offering to the consumer. This is what will differentiate between similar offerings from many providers of financial products and services. Starting now, will give the organization an advantage in terms of the networking it will be able to achieve. This will help it in meeting the first challenge. Banks (or Financial Service providers) should be ready to launch their operations within days of the liberalization of the sector. This will allow them to reach a critical mass and establish themselves in the e-World.

STRATEGIES TO BE ADOPTED BY INDIAN BANKS

Internet banking would drive us into an age of creative destruction due to non-physical exchange, complete transparency giving rise to perfectly electronic market place and customer supremacy.

The question to be asked right now is "What the Indian Banks should do" Whatever is the strategy chosen and options adopted, certain key parameters would determine the bank's success on web:

1. For long term success, a bank may follow:

- Adopting a webs mindset
- Catching on the first mover's advantage

- Recognising the core competencies
- Ability to deal multiplicity with simplicity
- Senior Management initiative to transform the organisation from inward to outward looking
- Aligning roles and value propositions with the customer segments

- Redesigning optimal channel portfolio
- Acquiring new capabilities through strategic alliances.

2. The above can be implemented in four steps:

- Familiarising the customer to new environment by demo version of software on bank's web site. This should contain tour through the features which are to be included. It will enable users to give suggestions for improvements, which can be incorporated in later versions wherever feasible.
- Second phase provides services such as account information and balances, statement of account, transaction tracking, mail box, check book issue, stop payment, financial and customised information.
- The third phase may include additional services such as fund transfers, DD issue, standing instructions, opening fixed deposits, intimation of loss of ATM cards.
- The last step should include advanced corporate banking services like third party payments, utility bill payments, establishment of L/Cs, Cash Management Services etc. Enhanced plan for the customers in future can include requests for demand drafts and pay orders and many more to bring in the ultimate in banking convenience.

All the above strategies will help banks in translating their traditional business model into an Internet one, falling into three main categories

- One stop shop
- Virtual one-stop-shop
- Best of breed supplier.

INTERNET BANKING IN INDIA - GUIDELINES

[RBI has accepted the recommendations of the 'Working Group on Internet Banking' to be implemented in a phased manner. Following recommendations are to be adopted by all banks offering Internet banking services, with immediate effect. These recommendations are applicable, in general, to all forms of electronic banking]

I. Technology and Security Standards:

II. Legal Issues:

III. Regulatory and Supervisory Issues:

INTERNET BANKING - ABBREVIATIONS

ANSI: American National Standards Institute

ASCII : American Standard Code for Information Interchange

ATM : Asynchronous Transfer Mode

CERT: Computer Emergency Response Team

DBA: Database Administrator

DES: Data Encryption Standard

EDI: Electronic Data Interchange

FTP: File Transfer Protocol

GUI: Graphical User Interface

HTML: Hypertext Markup Language

HTTP: Hypertext Transfer Protocol

IC Card: Integrated Circuit Card

ISDN: Integrated Services Digital Network

ISO/OSI: International Organization for Standardization/Open Systems Interconnection

ISP: Internet Service Provider

LAN: Local Area Network

NIST: National Institute for Standards and Technology

FIPS: Federal Information Processing Standards

OSP: Online Service Providers

PIN: Personal Identification Number

POS: Point of Sale

SET: Secure Electronic Transaction

SHTTP: Secure Hypertext Transfer Protocol

SSL: Secure Socket Layer

SMTP: Simple Mail Transfer Protocol

SQL: Structured Query Language

TCP/IP: Transmission Control Protocol/Internet Protocol

URL: Uniform Resource Locator or Universal Resource Locator

WAN: Wide Area Network

web, www: World Wide Web.

RISK MANAGEMENT PRINCIPLES FOR ELECTRONIC BANKING

Continuing technological innovation and competition among existing banking organisations and new entrants have allowed for a much wider array of banking products and services to become accessible and delivered to retail and wholesale customers through an electronic distribution channel collectively referred to as e-banking. However, the rapid development of e-banking capabilities carries risks as well as benefits.

The Basel Committee on Banking Supervision expects such risks to be recognised, addressed and managed by banking institutions in a prudent manner according to the fundamental characteristics and challenges of e-banking services.

These characteristics include the unprecedented speed of change related to technological and customer service innovation, the ubiquitous and global nature of open electronic networks, the integration of e-banking applications with legacy computer systems and the increasing dependence of banks on third parties that provide the necessary information technology. While not creating inherently new risks, the Committee noted that these characteristics increased and modified some of the traditional risks associated with banking activities, in particular strategic, operational, legal and reputational risks, thereby influencing the overall risk profile of banking.

Based on these conclusions, the Committee considers that while existing risk management principles remain applicable to e-banking activities, such principles must be tailored, adapted and, in some cases, expanded to address the specific risk management challenges created by the characteristics of e-banking activities.

To this end, the Committee believes that it is incumbent upon the Boards of Directors and banks' senior management to take steps to ensure that their institutions have reviewed and modified where necessary their existing risk management policies and processes to cover their current or planned e-banking activities. The Committee also believes that the integration of e-banking applications with legacy systems implies an integrated risk management approach for all banking activities of a banking institution.

To facilitate these developments, the Committee has identified fourteen *Risk Management Principles for Electronic Banking* to help banking institutions expand their existing risk oversight policies and processes to cover their e-banking activities.

These *Risk Management Principles* are not put forth as absolute requirements or even "best practice." The Committee believes that setting detailed risk management requirements in the area of e-banking might be counter-productive, if only because these would be likely to become rapidly outdated because of the speed of change related to technological and customer service innovation.

The Committee has therefore preferred to express supervisory expectations and guidance in the form of *Risk Management Principles* in order to promote safety and soundness for e-banking activities, while preserving the necessary flexibility in implementation that derives in part from the speed of change in this area. Further, the Committee recognises that each bank's risk profile is different and requires a tailored risk mitigation approach appropriate for the scale of the e-banking operations, the materiality of the risks present, and the willingness and ability of the institution to manage these risks. This implies that a "one size fits all" approach to e-banking risk management issues may not be appropriate.

For a similar reason, the *Risk Management Principles* issued by the Committee do not attempt to set specific technical solutions or standards relating to e-banking. Technical solutions are to be addressed by institutions and standard setting bodies as technology evolves. However, this Report contains appendices that list some examples current and widespread risk mitigation practices in the e-banking area that are supportive of the *Risk Management Principles*.

Consequently, the *Risk Management Principles* and sound practices identified in this Report are expected to be used as tools by national supervisors and implemented with adaptations to reflect specific national requirements and individual risk profiles where necessary. In some areas, the Principles have been expressed by the Committee or by national supervisors in previous bank supervisory guidance. However, some issues, such as the management of outsourcing relationships, security controls and legal and reputational risk management, warrant more detailed principles than those expressed to date due to the unique characteristics and implications of the Internet distribution channel.

Continuing technological innovation and competition among existing banking organisations and new entrants have allowed for a much wider array of banking products and services to become accessible and delivered to retail and wholesale customers through an electronic distribution channel collectively referred to as e-banking. However, the rapid development of e-banking capabilities carries risks as well as benefits.

The Basel Committee on Banking Supervision expects such risks to be recognised, addressed and managed by banking institutions in a prudent manner according to the fundamental characteristics and challenges of e-banking services. These characteristics include the unprecedented speed of change related to technological and customer service innovation, the ubiquitous and global nature of open electronic networks, the integration of e-banking applications with legacy computer systems and the increasing dependence of banks on third parties that provide the necessary information technology. While not creating inherently new risks, the Committee noted that these characteristics increased and modified some of the traditional risks associated with banking activities, in particular strategic, operational, legal and reputational risks, thereby influencing the overall risk profile of banking.

Based on these conclusions, the Committee considers that while existing risk management principles remain applicable to e-banking activities, such principles must be tailored, adapted and, in some cases, expanded to address the specific risk management challenges created by the characteristics of e-banking activities.

To this end, the Committee believes that it is incumbent upon the Boards of Directors and banks' senior management to take steps to ensure that their institutions have reviewed and modified where necessary their existing risk management policies and processes to cover their current or planned e-banking activities. The Committee also believes that the integration of e-banking applications with legacy systems implies an integrated risk management approach for all banking activities of a banking institution.

To facilitate these developments, the Committee has identified fourteen *Risk Management Principles for Electronic Banking* to help banking institutions expand their existing risk oversight policies and processes to cover their e-banking activities.

These *Risk Management Principles* are not put forth as absolute requirements or even "best practice." The Committee believes that setting detailed risk management requirements in the area of e-banking might be counter-productive, if only because these would be likely to become rapidly outdated because of the speed of change related to technological and customer service innovation.

The Committee has therefore preferred to express supervisory expectations and guidance in the form of *Risk Management Principles* in order to promote safety and soundness for e-banking activities, while preserving the necessary flexibility in implementation that derives in part from the speed of change in this area. Further, the Committee recognises that each bank's risk profile is different and requires a tailored risk mitigation approach appropriate for the scale of the e-banking operations, the materiality of the risks present, and the willingness and ability of the institution to manage these risks. This implies that a "one size fits all" approach to e-banking risk management issues may not be appropriate.

For a similar reason, the *Risk Management Principles* issued by the Committee do not attempt to set specific technical solutions or standards relating to e-banking. Technical solutions are to be addressed by institutions and standard setting bodies as technology evolves. However, this Report contains appendices that list some examples current and widespread risk mitigation practices in the e-banking area that are supportive of the *Risk Management Principles*.

Consequently, the *Risk Management Principles* and sound practices identified in this Report are expected to be used as tools by national supervisors and implemented with adaptations to reflect specific national requirements and individual risk profiles where necessary. In some areas, the Principles have been expressed by the Committee or by national supervisors in previous bank supervisory guidance. However, some issues, such as the management of outsourcing relationships, security controls and legal and reputational risk management, warrant more detailed principles than those expressed to date due to the unique characteristics and implications of the Internet distribution channel.

The *Risk Management Principles* fall into three broad, and often overlapping, categories of issues that are grouped to provide clarity: *Board and Management Oversight; Security Controls; and Legal and Reputational Risk Management.*

5

Significance and Guidance on Internet Banking

INTRODUCTION

Internet banking (or E-banking) means any user with a personal computer and a browser can get connected to his bank -s website to perform any of the virtual banking functions. In internet banking system the bank has a centralized database that is web-enabled. All the services that the bank has permitted on the internet are displayed in menu. Any service can be selected and further interaction is dictated by the nature of service. The traditional branch model of bank is now giving place to an alternative delivery channels with ATM network. Once the branch offices of bank are interconnected through terrestrial or satellite links, there would be no physical identity for any branch. It would a borderless entity permitting anytime, anywhere and anyhow banking. The network which connects the various locations and gives connectivity to the central office within the organization is called intranet. These networks are limited to organizations for which they are set up. SWIFT is a live example of intranet application.

INTERNET BANKING IN INDIA

The Reserve Bank of India constituted a working group on Internet Banking. The group divided the internet banking products in India into 3 types based on the levels of access granted. They are:

(i) Information Only System: General purpose information like interest rates, branch location, bank products and their features, loan and deposit calculations are provided in the banks website. There exist facilities for downloading various types of application forms. The communication is normally done through e-mail. There is no interaction between the customer and bank's application system. No identification of the customer is done. In this system, there is no possibility of any unauthorized person getting into production systems of the bank through internet.

(ii) Electronic Information Transfer System: The system provides customer-specific information in the form of account balances, transaction details, and statement of accounts. The information is still largely of the 'read only' format. Identification and authentication of the customer is through password. The information is fetched from the bank's application system either in batch mode or off-line. The application systems cannot directly access through the internet.

(iii) Fully Electronic Transactional System: This system allows bi-directional capabilities. Transactions can be submitted by the customer for online update. This system requires high degree of security and control. In this environment, web server and application systems are linked over secure infrastructure. It comprises technology covering computerization, networking and security, inter-bank payment gateway and legal infrastructure.

Automated Teller Machine (ATM)

ATM is designed to perform the most important function of bank. It is operated by plastic card with its special features. The plastic card is replacing cheque, personal attendance of the customer, banking hours restrictions and paper based verification. There are debit cards. ATMs used as spring board for Electronic Fund Transfer. ATM itself can provide information about customers account and also receive instructions from customers - ATM cardholders. An ATM is an Electronic Fund Transfer terminal capable of handling cash deposits, transfer between accounts, balance enquiries, cash withdrawals and pay bills. It may be on-line or Off-line. The on-line ATN enables the customer to avail banking facilities from anywhere. In off-line the facilities are confined to that particular ATM assigned. Any customer possessing ATM card issued by the Shared Payment Network System can go to any ATM linked to Shared Payment Networks and perform his transactions.

Credit Cards/Debit Cards

The Credit Card holder is empowered to spend wherever and whenever he wants with his Credit Card within the limits fixed by his bank. Credit Card is a post paid card. Debit Card, on the other hand, is a prepaid card with some stored value. Every time a person uses this card, the Internet Banking house gets money transferred to its account from the bank of the buyer. The buyers account is debited with the exact amount of purchases. An individual has to open an account with the issuing bank which gives debit card with a Personal Identification Number (PIN). When he makes a purchase, he enters his PIN on shops PIN pad. When the card is slurped through the electronic terminal, it dials the acquiring bank system - either Master Card or VISA that validates the PIN and finds out from the issuing bank whether to accept or decline the transactions. The customer can never overspend because the system rejects any transaction which exceeds the balance in his account. The bank never faces a default because the amount spent is debited immediately from the customers account.

Smart Card

Banks are adding chips to their current magnetic stripe cards to enhance security and offer new service, called Smart Cards. Smart Cards allow thousands of times of information storable on magnetic stripe cards. In addition, these cards are highly secure, more reliable and perform multiple functions. They hold a large amount of personal information, from medical and health history to personal banking and personal preferences.

You can avail the following services through E-Banking.

Bill Payment Service

You can facilitate payment of electricity and telephone bills, mobile phone, credit card and insurance premium bills as each bank has tie-ups with various utility companies, service providers and insurance companies, across the country. To pay your bills, all you need to do is complete a simple one-time registration for each biller. You can also set up standing instructions online to pay your recurring bills, automatically. Generally, the bank does not charge customers for online bill payment.

Fund Transfer

You can transfer any amount from one account to another of the same or any another bank. Customers can send money anywhere in India. Once you login to your account, you need to mention the payees's account number, his bank and the branch. The transfer will take place in a day or so, whereas in a traditional method, it takes about three working days. ICICI Bank says that online bill payment service and fund transfer facility have been their most popular online services.

Credit Card Customers

With Internet banking, customers can not only pay their credit card bills online but also get a loan on their cards. If you lose your credit card, you can report lost card online.

Railway Pass

This is something that would interest all the aam janta. Indian Railways has tied up with ICICI bank and you can now make your railway pass for local trains online. The pass will be delivered to you at your doorstep. But the facility is limited to Mumbai, Thane, Nashik, Surat and Pune.

Investing through Internet Banking

You can now open an FD online through funds transfer.Now investors with interlinked demat account and bank account can easily trade in the stock market and the amount will be automatically debited from their respective bank accounts and the shares will be credited in their demat account.

Moreover, some banks even give you the facility to purchase mutual funds directly from the online banking system.

Nowadays, most leading banks offer both online banking and demat account. However if you have your demat account with independent share brokers, then you need to sign a special form, which will link your two accounts.

Recharging your Prepaid Phone

Now just top-up your prepaid mobile cards by logging in to Internet banking. By just selecting your operator's name, entering your mobile number and the amount for recharge, your phone is again back in action within few minutes.

Shopping

With a range of all kind of products, you can shop online and the payment is also made conveniently through your account. You can also buy railway and air tickets through Internet banking.

Advantage of Internet Banking

As per the Internet and Mobile Association of India's report on online banking 2006, "There are many advantages of online banking. It is convenient, it isn't bound by operational timings, there are no geographical barriers and the services can be offered at a miniscule cost."

Through Internet banking, you can check your transactions at any time of the day, and as many times as you want to. Where in a traditional method, you get quarterly statements from the bank. If the fund transfer has to be made outstation, where the bank does not have a branch, the bank would demand outstation charges. Whereas with the help of online banking, it will be absolutely free for you.

Security Precautions

Customers should never share personal information like PIN numbers, passwords etc with anyone, including employees of the bank. It is important that documents that contain confidential information are safeguarded.

PIN or password mailers should not be stored, the PIN and/or passwords should be changed immediately and memorised before destroying the mailers.

Customers are advised not to provide sensitive account-related information over unsecured e-mails or over the phone. Take simple precautions like changing the ATM PIN and online login and transaction passwords on a regular basis. Also ensure that the logged in session is properly signed out.

INTERNET BANKING IN INDIA - GUIDELINES

Reserve Bank of India had set up a 'Working Group on Internet Banking' to examine different aspects of Internet Banking (I-banking). The Group had focussed on three major areas of I-banking, i.e, (i) technology and security issues, (ii) legal issues and (iii) regulatory and supervisory issues. RBI has accepted the recommendations of the Group to be implemented in a phased manner. Accordingly, the following guidelines are issued for implementation by banks. Banks are also advised that they may be guided by the original report, for a detailed guidance on different issues.

I. Technology and Security Standards:

a. Banks should designate a network and database administrator with clearly defined roles as indicated in the Group's report. (Para 6.2.4)

b. Banks should have a security policy duly approved by the Board of Directors. There should be a segregation of duty of Security Officer / Group dealing exclusively with information systems security and Information Technology Division which actually implements the computer systems. Further, Information Systems Auditor will audit the information systems. (Para 6.3.10, 6.4.1)

c. Banks should introduce logical access controls to data, systems, application software, utilities, telecommunication lines, libraries, system software, etc. Logical access control techniques may include user-ids, passwords, smart cards or other biometric technologies. (Para 6.4.2)

d. At the minimum, banks should use the proxy server type of firewall so that there is no direct connection between the Internet and the bank's system. It facilitates a high level of control and in-depth monitoring using logging and auditing tools. For sensitive systems, a stateful inspection firewall is recommended which thoroughly inspects all packets of information, and past and present transactions are compared. These generally include a real time security alert. (Para 6.4.3)

e. All the systems supporting dial up services through modem on the same LAN as the application server should be isolated to prevent intrusions into the network as this may bypass the proxy server. (Para 6.4.4)

f. PKI (Public Key Infrastructure) is the most favoured technology for secure Internet banking services. However, as it is not yet commonly available, banks should use the following alternative system during the transition, until the PKI is put in place:

1. Usage of SSL (Secured Socket Layer), which ensures server authentication and use of client side certificates issued by the banks themselves using a Certificate Server.

2. The use of at least 128-bit SSL for securing browser to web server communications and, in addition, encryption of sensitive data like passwords in transit within the enterprise itself. (Para 6.4.5)

g. It is also recommended that all unnecessary services on the application server such as FTP (File Transfer Protocol), telnet should be disabled. The application server should be isolated from the e-mail server. (Para 6.4.6)

h. All computer accesses, including messages received, should be logged. Security violations (suspected or attempted) should be reported and follow up action taken should be kept in mind while framing future policy. Banks should acquire tools for monitoring systems and the networks against intrusions and attacks. These tools should be used regularly to avoid security breaches. The banks should review their security infrastructure and security policies regularly and optimize them in the light of their own experiences and changing technologies. They should educate their security personnel and also the end-users on a continuous basis. (Para 6.4.7, 6.4.11, 6.4.12)

i. The information security officer and the information system auditor should undertake periodic penetration tests of the system, which should include:

1. Attempting to guess passwords using password-cracking tools.

2. Search for back door traps in the programs.

3. Attempt to overload the system using DDoS (Distributed Denial of Service) & DoS (Denial of Service) attacks.

4. Check if commonly known holes in the software, especially the browser and the e-mail software exist.

5. The penetration testing may also be carried out by engaging outside experts (often called 'Ethical Hackers'). (Para 6.4.8)

j. Physical access controls should be strictly enforced. Physical security should cover all the information systems and sites where they are housed, both against internal and external threats. (Para 6.4.9)

k. Banks should have proper infrastructure and schedules for backing up data. The backed-up data should be periodically tested to ensure recovery without loss of transactions in a time frame as given out in the bank's security policy. Business continuity should be ensured by setting up disaster recovery sites. These facilities should also be tested periodically. (Para 6.4.10)

l. All applications of banks should have proper record keeping facilities for legal purposes. It may be necessary to keep all received and sent messages both in encrypted and decrypted form. (Para 6.4.13)

m. Security infrastructure should be properly tested before using the systems and applications for normal operations. Banks should upgrade the systems by installing patches released by developers to remove bugs and loopholes, and upgrade to newer versions which give better security and control. (Para 6.4.15)

II. Legal Issues

a. Considering the legal position prevalent, there is an obligation on the part of banks not only to establish the identity but also to make enquiries about integrity and reputation of the prospective customer. Therefore, even though request for opening account can be accepted over Internet, accounts should be opened only after proper introduction and physical verification of the identity of the customer. (Para 7.2.1)

b. From a legal perspective, security procedure adopted by banks for authenticating users needs to be recognized by law as a substitute for signature. In India, the Information Technology Act, 2000, in Section 3(2) provides for a particular technology (viz., the asymmetric crypto system and hash function) as a means of authenticating electronic record. Any other method used by banks for authentication should be recognized as a source of legal risk. (Para 7.3.1)

c. Under the present regime there is an obligation on banks to maintain secrecy and confidentiality of customers' accounts. In the Internet banking scenario, the risk of banks not meeting the above obligation is high on account of several factors. Despite all reasonable precautions, banks may be exposed to enhanced risk of liability to customers on account of breach of secrecy, denial of service etc., because of hacking/ other technological failures. The banks should, therefore, institute adequate risk control measures to manage such risks. (Para 7.5.1-7.5.4)

d. In Internet banking scenario there is very little scope for the banks to act on stop-payment instructions from the customers. Hence, banks should clearly notify to the customers the timeframe and the circumstances in which any stop-payment instructions could be accepted. (Para 7.6.1)

e. The Consumer Protection Act, 1986 defines the rights of consumers in India and is applicable to banking services as well. Currently, the rights and liabilities of customers availing of Internet banking services are being determined by bilateral agreements between the banks and customers. Considering the banking practice and rights enjoyed by customers in traditional banking, banks' liability to the customers on account of unauthorized transfer through hacking, denial of service on account of technological failure etc. needs to be assessed and banks providing Internet banking should insure themselves against such risks. (Para 7.11.1)

III. Regulatory and Supervisory Issues:

As recommended by the Group, the existing regulatory framework over banks will be extended to Internet banking also. In this regard, it is advised that:

1. Only such banks which are licensed and supervised in India and have a physical presence in India will be permitted to offer Internet banking products to residents of India. Thus, both banks and virtual banks incorporated outside the country and having no physical presence in India will not, for the present, be permitted to offer Internet banking services to Indian residents.
2. The products should be restricted to account holders only and should not be offered in other jurisdictions.

3. The services should only include local currency products.
4. The 'in-out' scenario where customers in cross border jurisdictions are offered banking services by Indian banks (or branches of foreign banks in India) and the 'out-in' scenario where Indian residents are offered banking services by banks operating in cross-border jurisdictions are generally not permitted and this approach will apply to Internet banking also. The existing exceptions for limited purposes under FEMA i.e. where resident Indians have been permitted to continue to maintain their accounts with overseas banks etc., will, however, be permitted.
5. Overseas branches of Indian banks will be permitted to offer Internet banking services to their overseas customers subject to their satisfying, in addition to the host supervisor, the home supervisor.

Given the regulatory approach as above, banks are advised to follow the following instructions:

a. All banks, who propose to offer transactional services on the Internet should obtain prior approval from RBI. Bank's application for such permission should indicate its business plan, analysis of cost and benefit, operational arrangements like technology adopted, business partners, third party service providers and systems and control procedures the bank proposes to adopt for managing risks. The bank should also submit a security policy covering recommendations made in this circular and a certificate from an independent auditor that the minimum requirements prescribed have been met. After the initial approval the banks will be obliged to inform RBI any material changes in the services / products offered by them. (Para 8.4.1, 8.4.2)
b. Banks will report to RBI every breach or failure of security systems and procedure and the latter, at its discretion, may decide to commission special audit / inspection of such banks. (Para 8.4.3)
c. The guidelines issued by RBI on 'Risks and Controls in Computers and Telecommunications' vide circular DBS.CO.ITC.BC. 10/ 31.09.001/ 97-98 dated 4th February 1998 will equally apply to Internet banking. The RBI as supervisor will cover the entire risks associated with electronic banking as a part of its regular inspections of banks. (Para 8.4.4, 8.4.5)

d. Banks should develop outsourcing guidelines to manage risks arising out of third party service providers, such as, disruption in service, defective services and personnel of service providers gaining intimate knowledge of banks' systems and misutilizing the same, etc., effectively. (Para 8.4.7)

e. With the increasing popularity of e-commerce, it has become necessary to set up 'Inter-bank Payment Gateways' for settlement of such transactions. The protocol for transactions between the customer, the bank and the portal and the framework for setting up of payment gateways as recommended by the Group should be adopted. (Para 8.4.7, 8.4.9.1 – 8.4.9.5)

f. Only institutions who are members of the cheque clearing system in the country will be permitted to participate in Inter-bank payment gateways for Internet payment. Each gateway must nominate a bank as the clearing bank to settle all transactions. Payments effected using credit cards, payments arising out of cross border e-commerce transactions and all intra-bank payments (i.e., transactions involving only one bank) should be excluded for settlement through an inter-bank payment gateway. (Para 8.4.7)

g. Inter-bank payment gateways must have capabilities for both net and gross settlement. All settlement should be intra-day and as far as possible, in real time. (Para 8.4.7)

h. Connectivity between the gateway and the computer system of the member bank should be achieved using a leased line network (not through Internet) with appropriate data encryption standard. All transactions must be authenticated. Once, the regulatory framework is in place, the transactions should be digitally certified by any licensed certifying agency. SSL / 128 bit encryption must be used as minimum level of security. Reserve Bank may get the security of the entire infrastructure both at the payment gateway's end and the participating institutions' end certified prior to making the facility available for customers use. (Para 8.4.7)

i. Bilateral contracts between the payee and payee's bank, the participating banks and service provider and the banks themselves will form the legal basis for such transactions. The rights and obligations of each party must be clearly defined and should be valid in a court of law. (Para 8.4.7)

j. Banks must make mandatory disclosures of risks, responsibilities and liabilities of the customers in doing business through Internet through a disclosure template. The banks should also provide their latest published financial results over the net. (Para 8.4.8)

k. Hyperlinks from banks' websites, often raise the issue of reputational risk. Such links should not mislead the customers into believing that banks sponsor any particular product or any business unrelated to banking. Hyperlinks from a banks' websites should be confined to only those portals with which they have a payment arrangement or sites of their subsidiaries or principals. Hyperlinks to banks' websites from other portals are normally meant for passing on information relating to purchases made by banks' customers in the portal. Banks must follow the minimum recommended security precautions while dealing with request received from other websites, relating to customers' purchases. (Para 8.4.9)

The Reserve Bank of India have decided that the Group's recommendations as detailed in this circulars should be adopted by all banks offering Internet banking services, with immediate effect. Even though the recommendations have been made in the context of Internet banking, these are applicable, in general, to all forms of electronic banking and banks offering any form of electronic banking should adopt the same to the extent relevant.

All banks offering Internet banking are advised to make a review of their systems in the light of this circular and report to Reserve Bank the types of services offered, extent of their compliance with the recommendations, deviations and their proposal indicating a time frame for compliance. The first such report must reach us within one month from the date of this circular. Banks not offering any kind of I-banking may submit a 'nil' report. Banks who are already offering any kind of transactional service are advised to report, in addition to those mentioned in paragraph above, their business models with projections of cost / benefits etc. and seek our post-facto approval.

BANKING & INSURANCE SECTOR

The economic reforms undertaken in the last 15 years have brought about a considerable improvement in the health of banks and financial institutions in India. The banking sector is a very important sector of the Indian economy. The sector has made a marked improvement in the liberalization period. There has been extraordinary progress in the financial health of the commercial banks with respect to capital adequacy, profitability, asset quality and risk management. Deregulation has opened new doors for banks to increase revenues by entering into investment banking, insurance, credit cards, depository services, mortgage, securitization, etc.

The limit for foreign direct investment in private banks has been increased from 49% to 74%. In addition, the limit for foreign institutional investment in private banks is 49%. Liberalization and globalization have created a more challenging environment in the banking sector as well as in the other segments of the financial sector such as mutual funds, Non Banking Finance Companies, post offices, capital markets, venture capitalists, etc.

Now the challenges faced by the sector would be gaining profitability, reinforcing technology, maintaining global standards, corporate governance, sharpening skills, risk management and, the most important of all, to establish 'Customer Intimacy'.

The insurance business is one of the most rapidly growing areas in the financial sector. As an economy grows over the years, insurance sector intensifies and broadens its reach. Every practical and futuristic individual would want himself, his family and his assets to be insured. Insurance deals mainly with life and general insurance. India has a large insurance market commensurate with its population.

The IRDA Act 1999 (Insurance Regulatory and Development Authority of India Act) has given new opportunities to private players to enter into the market on the fulfillment of certain prerequisites. The IRDA is the licensing authority in the sector; the current FDI cap/Equity in the sector stands at 26 percent. There is no doubt the challenges ahead will become tougher with more companies competing both in general and life Insurance. Also mortgage insurance will soon be coming into the industry. New players have contributed to the launch of innovative products, services and value-added benefits. Major foreign players have entered the country and announced joint ventures in both life and non-life areas. These include New York Life, Aviva, Tokio Marine, Allianz, Standard Life, Lombard General, AIG, AMP and Sun Life among others.

Commercial banks are coming up with more and more vacancies, and the banking sector now has more new jobs than any other sector. Right from the branch level to the highest level, there is tremendous range of opportunities available in the sector. Jobs in this sector can be both rewarding and enjoyable, as you get opportunities to learn about business, interact with people and build up clientele. The same is the case with insurance, as it is the fastest growing industry under the financial sector. Both government and private players are currently offering a plenty of jobs in this sector. So, this is great news for you if you are thinking to go into the banking & insurance streams.

SCOPE OF BANKING & INSURANCE SECTORS IN INDIA

The financial sector in India has become stronger in terms of capital and the number of customers. It has become globally competitive and diverse aiming, at higher productivity and efficiency.

Exposure to worldwide competition and deregulation in Indian financial sector has led to the emergence of better quality products and services. Reforms have changed the face of Indian banking and finance. The banking sector has improved manifolds in terms of capital adequacy, asset classification, profitability, income recognition, provisioning, exposure limits, investment fluctuation reserve, risk management, etc.

Diversifying into investment banking, insurance, credit cards, depository services, mortgage financing, securitisation has increased revenues. As large number of players in various fields enter the market, competition would be intensified by mutual funds, Non Banking Finance Corporations (NBFCs), post offices, etc. from both domestic and foreign players. All this would lead to increased sophistication and technology in the sector. Corporate governance would come into the picture and other financial institutions would have to reach global standards. Also the limit for FDI in private banks is increased to 74% and the limit for FII is 49%. There are many challenges ahead for the banking sector such as technology, consumer satisfaction, corporate governance, risk management, etc. and they are redefining their priorities, which are now focused on cost reduction, product differentiation and customer centric services. Some of the major players in this sector are HDFC, ICICI, HSBC, State Bank of India, Punjab National Bank, Ing Vysya, ABN Amro Bank, Centurion Bank, City Bank, etc.

The insurance sector has opened up for private insurance companies with the enactment of IRDA Act, 1999. A large number of companies are competing under both life and general Insurance. The FDI cap/equity in this sector is 26% and the proposals have to be cleared by Insurance Regulatory and Development Authority (IRDA) established to protect the interest of holder of Insurance policy and act as a regulator and facilitator in the industry. Some of the major players in this sector are LIC, Max New York Life Insurance, Bajaj Allianz, ICICI Prudential, HDFC Standard Life, Metlife Insurance, Birla Sun Life Insurance, etc. Various types of policies and instruments are coming up in the market to attract more customers. Most of the population of India is not insured, hence there is a lot of scope in this sector and a number of companies are planning to enter the sector. Every futuristic individual would want himself to get insured.

Capital markets have a long history of over 100 years in India. Bombay Stock Exchange came into existence more than a hundred years ago to remove direct government control. Indian companies are now allowed to raise capital from abroad and Foreign Institutional Investors are allowed to enter the market due to an important policy initiative in 1993. The depository and share dematerialization has enhanced the performance of the capital market reducing processing time and increasing returns. The major players are India Bulls Securities, Kotak, and many more. Many new instruments have been introduced in the market such as index futures, index options, derivatives, including futures and options. Also commodities market is gaining pace. There is a huge potential available in the market and to realize it venture capitalists are coming up with lots of finance. To make use of the human capital, technical skills, cost competitive workforce, research and entrepreneurship VCFs and VCCs are ready to invest in potential projects.

For a stronger and resilient financial system, India needs to move beyond peripheral issues and act maturely by increasing profitability and efficiency, providing better solutions to the customers.

Top Ten In Banking & Insurance Sector

The financial sector in India has become stronger in terms of capital and the number of customers. It has become globally competitive and diverse aiming, at higher productivity and efficiency.

Exposure to worldwide competition and deregulation in Indian financial sector has led to the emergence of better quality products and services. Reforms have changed the face of Indian banking and finance. The banking sector has improved manifolds in terms of capital adequacy, asset classification, profitability, income recognition, provisioning, exposure limits, investment fluctuation reserve, risk management, etc.

MOBILE BANKING IN INDIA

India has about 207 MM (September' 2007 TRAI Data) mobile phone subscribers, a number that is larger than the number of bank accounts or Internet users. Given the mobile tele-density of about 20% and development of secure mobile technology solutions, banks are well-positioned bridge the digital divide and introduce the unbanked sector to the financial mainstream

You may be aware that Reserve Bank of India had set up the Mobile Payments Forum Of India (MPFI), a 'Working Group on Mobile Banking' to examine different aspects of Mobile Banking (M-banking). The Group had focused on three major areas of M-banking, i.e., (i) technology and security issues, (ii) business issues and (iii) regulatory and supervisory issues. A copy of the Group's report is enclosed. RBI has accepted the recommendations of the Group to be implemented in a phased manner. Accordingly, the following guidelines are issued for implementation by banks. Banks are also advised that they may be guided by the original report, for a detailed guidance on different issues. However to start with , we must understand who the various stakeholders are and what there expectation are:

Stakeholders are as follows

(a) Consumers

(b) Merchants

(c) Mobile Network operators

(d) Mobile device manufacturers

(e) Financial institutions and banks

(f) Software and technology providers

(g) Government

Each stakeholder group has the following expectations:

(a) To meet the following Consumer expectations:

- Personalized service
- Minimal learning curve
- Trust, privacy and security
- Ubiquitous – anywhere, anytime and any currency
- Low or zero cost of usage
- Interoperability between different network operators, banks and devices
- Anonymity of payments like cash
- Person to person transfers

(b) To meet the following Merchant expectations:

- Faster transaction time
- Low or zero cost in using the system
- Integration with cxisting payment systems
- High security
- Being able to customize the service
- Real time status of the mobile payment service
- Minimum settlement and Payment time

(c) To meet the following Telecom Network Providers expectations:

- Generating new income by increase in traffic
- Increased Average Revenue Per User (ARPU) and reduced churn (increased loyalty)

- Become an attractive partner to content providers

(d) To meet the following Mobile Device Manufacturers expectations:

- Large market adoption with embedded mobile payment application
- Low time to market
- Increase in Average Revenue Per User (ARPU)

(e) To meet the following Banks expectations:

- Network operator independent solutions
- Payment applications designed by the bank
- Exceptional branding opportunities for banks
- Better volumes in banking – more card payments and less cash transactions
- Customer loyalty

(f) To meet the following Software and Technology Providers expectations:

- Large markets

(g) To meet the following Government expectations

- Revenue through taxation of m-payments
- Standards

The overall security framework should ensure.

- Encrypted messaging / session between consumer's phone and third party service provider / telecom company. Minimum encryption standards to be specified to make the transaction banking grade (E.g. Min 128 bit SSL)
- All subsequent routing of messages to the bank's servers must be with the highest level of security with dedicated connectivity like leased lines / VPNs.
- If any sensitive information is stored in third party systems, banks must ensure that access to this information is restricted with appropriate encryption and hardware security standards.

- All transactions that affect an account (those that result in to an account being debited or credited, including scheduling of such activity) should be allowed only after authentication of the mobile number and the mPIN associated with it. Transactions only for information such as balance enquiry, mini statements, registered payee details, etc may be allowed with either mobile number or PIN.
- Unless fool proof security is used in compiling and deploying the mobile banking applications, the PIN number should not be allowed to be stored in the mobile banking application on the phone. As, generally the application installed on the phone would be developed in Java, it may be possible to decompile it extract the mPIN. Alternatively, the application should be so compiled that it should not be feasible to extract the PIN on decompilation.
- All accounts, credit or debit cards allowed to be transacted through the mobile phones should have the mobile phone number linked to the account, credit or debit card. This mobile number should be used as the second factor authentication for mobile transactions.
- During the transaction, the PIN should not travel in plain text. Doing this, there is risk of the PIN being snooped out of the phone from sent items and also it being exposed at the SMSC level. Also, it may be able to snoop out the PIN during transmission, although, this is very difficult in cellular communications.
- Proper level of encryption should be implemented for communicating from the mobile handset to the mobile payments service provider's server. It has been assumed that proper security checks would be made by the banks to ascertain the security levels of the service providers. This may include PCI DSS certification in addition to bank's own audits.
- Proper system of verification of the phone number should be implemented, wherever possible. This is so as to guard against spoofing of the phone numbers as mobile phones would be used as the second factor authentication.
- It is also recommended that Internet Banking login ids and passwords may not be allowed to be used through the mobile phones. As fraudsters

get more sophisticated, the chances of phishing attacks on mobile phones would become more probable. Allowing Internet banking login id and password usage on the mobile phone may compromise their usage on the Internet banking channel. This restriction may be communicated to the customers through an industry wide effort so as to ensure that Internet banking passwords are not compromised through mobile phones.

- The payment authorisation message from the user's mobile phone should be securely encrypted and checked for tampering by the service provider or the bank. It should not be possible for any interceptor to change the contents of the message.
- Provided the above security recommendations are reviewed, the mobile payment service could use any of the preferred mode of communication viz., SMS, IVRS, WAP/GPRS, USSD and NFC. There are couple of security issues in some of these modes of communications, which are listed below:

  a. SMS is the simplest form of communication, but is vulnerable to tampering. As long as there is a second level of check on the details of the transaction so as to guard against data tampering and the mPIN does not travel in plain text, this mode of communication can be used.

  b. IVRS is also a simple mode of communication and therefore does not have any inbuilt security measures. The system should be capable of encrypting the DTMF tone entries, if required to be stored or transmitted.

  c. USSD communication uses its inbuilt encryption technology to talk between the cell phone and the operator's server. However, the decryption of the information happens at the cell phone operator's server. Vulnerability of data may exists at this point. This information should be re-encrypted and transmitted to the service provider.
- Any of the following modes of user interface may be used, provided the above listed security measures are taken into consideration:

  a. SMS

  b. Menu driven application

c. Menu driven USSD application

d. WAP/GPRS website

- Formats need to be specified for exchange of information between banks. On the debit/credit card front, the exiting ISO 8583 message format may be used for communication between bank switches. However, for account number based mobile transfers, a message format may need to be frozen.
- Banks should designate a network and database administrator with clearly defined roles as indicated in the technology Group's report
- Banks should have a security policy duly approved by the Board of Directors. There should be a segregation of duty of Security Officer / Group dealing exclusively with information systems security and Information Technology Division which actually implements the computer systems. Further, Information Systems Auditor will audit the information systems.
- Banks should introduce logical access controls to data, systems, application software, utilities, telecommunication lines, libraries, system software, etc. Logical access control techniques may include user-ids, passwords, smart cards or other biometric technologies
- At the minimum, banks should use the proxy server type of firewall so that there is no direct connection between the Internet and the bank's system. It facilitates a high level of control and in-depth monitoring using logging and auditing tools. For sensitive systems, a stateful inspection firewall is recommended which thoroughly inspects all packets of information, and past and present transactions are compared. These generally include a real time security alert.
- All the systems supporting dial up services through modem on the same LAN as the application server should be isolated to prevent intrusions into the network as this may bypass the proxy server.
- The information security officer and the information system auditor should undertake periodic penetration tests of the system, which should include:

  o Attempting to guess passwords using password-cracking tools.

- o Search for back door traps in the programs.
- o Attempt to overload the system using DDoS (Distributed Denial of Service) & DoS (Denial of Service) attacks.
- o Check if commonly known holes in the software, especially the browser and the e-mail software exist.
- o The penetration testing may also be carried out by engaging outside experts (often called 'Ethical Hackers')

- Physical access controls should be strictly enforced. Physical security should cover all the information systems and sites where they are housed, both against internal and external threats.
- Banks should have proper infrastructure and schedules for backing up data. The backed-up data should be periodically tested to ensure recovery without loss of transactions in a time frame as given out in the bank's security policy. Business continuity should be ensured by setting up disaster recovery sites. These facilities should also be tested periodically

BUSINESS & LEGAL ISSUES

The following kinds of business applications are envisaged under the purview of this circular. Banks may permit the following transactions to its existing customers. They will encompass three key areas:

- Mobile banking (basic saving account – balance enquiry, bill payment, credit card payment, Draft issuance, Deposit booking, Stop payment request, funds transfer to another bank account including 3rd party transfers, change f personal PIN
- M Commerce (using mobile as a payment instrument either linked to a bank account or through stored value)
- Remittance: Allowing funds transfer between bank accounts, bank to cash(where the beneficiary does not have a bank account) and cash to cash
- Banks may additionally facilitate transactions for their customer's customers (E.g. Bill Payments for their corporate clients and other transactions that facilitate transactional convenience and also the inclusion of the financially excluded into the banking mainstream. Thus

banks may also permit following transactions for non-customers/non-account holders.

i. Small value person-to-person remittances (not exceeding Rs 15,000) including the use of bank branches, ATMs and other 3rd party outlets approved by Banks or Telcos for facilitating cash in / cash out. In such cases, banks may rely on KYC processes performed by other intermediaries (such as Telcos) as detailed in section III A of this circular.

ii. International remittances - i.e. Non resident Indians sending money back home to their families (To be read in conjunction with the MTSS guidelines)

- Considering the legal position prevalent, there is an obligation on the part of banks not only to establish the identity but also to make enquiries about integrity and reputation of the prospective customer. Therefore, even though request for opening a savings / current account can be accepted over Mobile Telecommunication, these should be opened only after proper introduction and physical verification of the identity of the customer.
- From a legal perspective, security procedure adopted by banks for authenticating users needs to be recognized by law as a substitute for signature. In India, the Information Technology Act, 2000, in Section 3(2) provides for a particular technology (viz., the asymmetric crypto system and hash function) as a means of authenticating electronic record. Any other method used by banks for authentication should be recognized as a source of legal risk. Customers must be made aware of the channel risk prior to sign up.
- Under the present regime there is an obligation on banks to maintain secrecy and confidentiality of customers' accounts. In the Mobile-banking scenario, the risk of banks not meeting the above obligation is high on account of several factors. Despite all reasonable precautions, banks may be exposed to enhanced risk of liability to customers on account of breach of secrecy, denial of service etc., because of hacking/ other technological failures. The banks should, therefore, institute adequate risk control measures to manage such risks.

- In Mobile banking scenario there is very little scope for the banks to act on stop-payment instructions from the customers. Hence, banks should clearly notify to the customers the timeframe and the circumstances in which any stop-payment instructions could be accepted.
- The Consumer Protection Act, 1986 defines the rights of consumers in India and is applicable to banking services as well. Currently, the rights and liabilities of customers availing of Internet banking services are being determined by bilateral agreements between the banks and customers.

  Considering the banking practice and rights enjoyed by customers in traditional banking, banks' liability to the customers on account of unauthorized transfer through hacking, denial of service on account of technological failure etc. needs to be assessed and banks providing Mobile banking should consider insuring themselves against such risks, as is the case with Internet Banking.
- Banks may determine their own pricing for the use of these services.
- Banks should get the scheme for facilitating Mobile banking approved by their respective boards / LOMC before offering it to their customers. The LOMC approval must document the extent of Operational and Fraud risk assumed by the bank and the bank's processes & policies designed to mitigate such risk.

KYC Process

Banks are permitted to rely on Financial Intermediaries as recommended by the relaxed KYC guidelines issued vide RBI circular DBOD.NO.AML.BC.28 /14.01.001/2005-06 dated August 23, 2005 A Bank can sponsor the small value remittance service by entering into arrangements with intermediaries in order to manage distribution, technology and scale.

In the same spirit, Banks may partner with Telecom companies, Technology companies etc to facilitate such small value transfers. Banks may rely on introductions from any person on whom KYC has been done and certificates of identification issued by the intermediary. Thus the intermediary can be a Telecom company, another bank or financial institution or a stand alone Trust Company dedicated to the purpose of facilitating such transactions.

It is proposed that in cases where the remitter is the owner of the mobile phone, the Bank relies on the telecom company's KYC and obtains a copy of the registration documents from the telecom company.

In cases where the remitter is not the owner of the mobile phone, a letter of introduction is taken from the owner and the remitter registers with a limited KYC comprising of photograph and address proof. Wherever address proof is not available, the introducer can certify the genuineness of the remitter's address.

Regulatory & Supervisory Issues

As recommended by the Group, the existing regulatory framework over banks will be extended to Mobile banking also. In this regard, it is advised that:

1. Only such banks which are licensed and supervised in India and have a physical presence in India will be permitted to offer Mobile banking products to residents of India. Thus, both banks and virtual banks incorporated outside the country and having no physical presence in India will not, for the present, be permitted to offer mobile banking services to Indian residents.
2. The products should be restricted to account holders only and should not be offered in other jurisdictions.
3. The services should only include local currency products.
4. The 'in-out' scenario where customers in cross border jurisdictions are offered banking services by Indian banks (or branches of foreign banks in India) and the 'out-in' scenario where Indian residents are offered banking services by banks operating in cross-border jurisdictions are generally not permitted and this approach will apply to Internet banking also. The existing exceptions for limited purposes under FEMA i.e. where resident Indians have been permitted to continue to maintain their accounts with overseas banks etc., will, however, be permitted.
5. Overseas branches of Indian banks will be permitted to offer Internet banking services to their overseas customers subject to their satisfying, in addition to the host supervisor, the home supervisor.

Given the regulatory approach as above, banks are advised to follow the following instructions:

a. All banks, who propose to offer transactional services on the Mobile services should obtain prior approval from RBI. Bank's application for such permission should indicate its business plan, analysis of cost and benefit, operational arrangements like technology adopted, business partners, third party service providers and systems and control procedures the bank proposes to adopt for managing risks. The bank should also submit security policy covering recommendations made in this circular and a certificate from an independent auditor that the minimum requirements prescribed have been met. After the initial approval the banks will be obliged to inform RBI any material changes in the services / products offered by them.

b. The guidelines issued by RBI on 'Risks and Controls in Computers and Telecommunications' vide circular DBS.CO.ITC.BC. 10/ 31.09.001/ 97-98 dated 4th February 1998 will equally apply to Mobile banking. The RBI as supervisor will cover the entire risks associated with electronic banking as a part of its regular inspections of banks.

c. Banks should develop outsourcing guidelines to manage risks arising out of third party service providers, such as, disruption in service, defective services and personnel of service providers gaining intimate knowledge of banks' systems and misutilizing the same, etc., effectively.

d. It will become important to set up 'Inter-bank Payment Gateways' for settlement of such transactions. The protocol for transactions between the customer, the bank and the portal and the framework for setting up of payment gateways as recommended by the Group should be adopted fro Mobile Banking

e. Only institutions who are members of the cheque clearing system in the country will be permitted to participate in Inter-bank payment gateways for Internet payment. Each gateway must nominate a bank as the clearing bank to settle all transactions. Payments effected using credit cards, payments arising out of cross border e-commerce transactions and all intra-bank payments (i.e., transactions involving only one bank) should be excluded for settlement through an inter-bank payment gateway.

f. Inter-bank payment gateways must have capabilities for both net and gross settlement. All settlement should be intra-day and as far as possible, in real time.

g. Bilateral contracts between the payee and payee's bank, the participating banks and service provider and the banks themselves will form the legal basis for such transactions. The rights and obligations of each party must be clearly defined and should be valid in a court of law.

h. Banks must make mandatory disclosures of risks, responsibilities and liabilities of the customers in doing business through Mobile, through a disclosure template.The banks should also provide their latest published financial results over the net.

REGULATORY ROLES AND RESPONSIBILITIES OF STAKEHOLDERS

Role of Banks

- Any money exchange i.e. Payments, P2P, remittance, etc – should be executed through Banking instruments & Infrastructure.
- This is to ensure compliance with all financial controls and regulation. Payments can be made by the following
  a. Savings Bank Account/Debit Card
  b. Credit Card Account
  c. Pre-paid Cards
  d. Virtual Cards (Credit & Debit Cards)
- Bank's role should be of providing normal transactional services to customers using the full range of services including Cash, Saving's account, Credit Card, Debit Card and Prepaid Cards services.
- Transactions should be maintained within the banking network and all the stakeholders in transaction processing and should be subject to equal level of scrutiny and regulation as are other bank accounts.
- Transaction settlement should ride on the existing infrastructure for efficient settlement and payment systems.

a. Intra Bank - Transactions involving Bank A/c to Bank A/c funds Transfer should be real time or near real time transactions

b. Inter Bank - Transactions involving Bank A/c to Bank A/c funds Transfer should ride on the NFS or other existing switches available for inter-Bank transactions.

c. Intra Bank – Transactions involving Card A/c (including Credit & Debit Cards) to Merchant/ recipient account should ride on the existing settlement & payment systems available with Banks.

d. Inter Bank – Transactions involving Card A/c (including Credit & Debit Cards) to Merchant/ recipient account should ride on either on India Switch , VISA, MasterCard or any other available switching infrastructure.

- The bank should take responsibility for audit, fraud management, account security etc. under its normal banking license. Banks should ensure that the service operates entirely within the RBI framework.
- Banks should be responsible for ensuring the identity of the sender and the receiver of funds. Banks can design the process of verification of sender and receiver as per the existing guidelines. In case where the existing process of KYC compliance cannot be met, new methods of verification such as mobile based PIN verification and transaction limit fixation can be considered
- In case of m-wallet propositions the pooled funds should be held with a bank so that systemic risk of defaults is minimized.
- Banks may end up playing a limited role in P2P and cash to cash payments other than settler of funds via the pooled account. This should be permissible subject to transaction limits etc.

Role of Telco

- Telcos should provide the KYC and customer history for Banks to offer the services to the customer and full responsibility for fraud management at their outlet as per TRAI guidelines.
- In order to ensure Mobile Payments reaches the critical customer mass, KYC documents required to offer financial products should be made similar to Telco's KYC guidelines.

- Distribution network of Telcos should be used to provide the services of Mobile Payments to maximum possible locations across the country.
- External low-cost hosting at Telco should be explored – Banks will not have to reinvent the technology platform & billing systems for such an offering.
- Policies enabling audit and governance of such a model to be framed.
- Setting up of infrastructure for undertaking Domestic Money Remittances along with Bank's. Domestic Money Remittances using both Telco's dealer network and Bank's Financial infrastructure should piloted along with controls on transaction limit and frequency. Pilot should test the feasibility running such a model for domestic money remittances.

Role of Third Party Payment Processors

- External low-cost hosting at Third party payment processors should be encouraged to have a truly cross-bank , cross-carrier payment system .
- Policies enabling audit and governance of such a model to be framed including a centralized settlement mechanism
- Third party processors should have the responsibility of Fraud management and should have systems and process in place to check and control frauds.

REGULATORY FRAMEWORK SUGGESTED FOR MOBILE PAYMENTS

Payment Account to be used for Mobile Payments e.g. Credit card account, Savings Bank Account, virtual account, Pre-paid account should be similar existing Credit card , Debit Card / bank account issuance framework.

While we can use innovative mechanisms to enable payments through mobile phones, following should be taken into considerations

- RBI's Guidelines and policies on KYC
- RBI's Guidelines and policies on AML
- Financial settlement between the various entities should be undertaken as per the existing Guidelines and processes.

- The messaging system between Application and Bank needs to be regulated and standardized to ensure standard transaction processes and settlement systems.
- Guidelines need to be evolved to ensure complete interoperability of between all the stakeholders of mobile payments. This will lead to the growth of ecosystem and will benefit all the stakeholders.
- Guidelines need to be evolved for allowing domestic money remittances by Cash In and Cash Out at Telco Outlets including usage of Telco's KYC and adherence of AML guidelines.

Telco's role should include providing platform to initiate transactions and carry the messages to the bank's systems

Regulatory Policies and Standards

Service providers, Telcos should have the independence to develop and launch customized applications targeted towards their customer base however messaging system between application and Banks needs to be regulated. This will lead to standardization of the transaction processes and settlement systems. These should include

- Instruction formats for all mobile initiated payments, remittances and banking
- Instruction formats for all mobile initiated payments, remittances and banking
- Security standards for instructions, interfaces, data storage and transactions
- Technology standards and guidelines for various modes of data transfer like SMS, GPRS etc.

Anti Money Laundering control for Telcos especially for proposed services like deposits being accepted and held by Telcos for Funds Transfer and remittances. While Telcos provide an opportunity to reach out to the unbanked and underbanked population of the country, proper regulatory control should be established to ensure conformation to KYC and AML guidelines. The Telcos offering these services should follow bank-approved processes that fulfill the regulatory requirements while performing such transactions. The Bank may appoint payout agents such as the Post Office, other FIs, selective merchants etc

- Sign up for service: Existing or new customer: Bank controlled through regulated KYC
- Transaction: PIN based transactions in terms of domestic transfers.
- Anti Money Laundering: monitoring carried out by the Bank
- Transactions monitoring controlled at the banking end
- Agent appointment responsibility with the bank

Terms and Conditions

Definitions

- 'Bank' refers to IDBI, a banking company incorporated in india under the companies act 1956 and having its registered office at chaturvedi mansion, 2nd floor, 26/4, old palasia, a.b. Road, indore 452 001. The term includes the successors and assigns of IDBI
- Internet Banking is the trade name of the Bank's Internet Banking service which provides access through the internet to account information, account transaction, other products and services as advised by the Bank from time to time to the Bank's customers
- Internet Banking account refers to the user's Savings and/ or Current Account and/ or Fixed Deposit account and/or any other type of account so designated by the Bank to be eligible account(s) for operations through the use of Internet Banking. One of these accounts will be designated as primary account. All other accounts (if any) of the user will be called secondary account(s). The user should be either the account holder and sole signatory or authorised to act alone when there is more than one signatory. An account in the name of a minor or an account in which a minor is a joint account holder, is not eligible to be an Internet Banking account
- User refers to a customer of the Bank or any person authorized to use Internet Banking by the Bank

- Personal information refers to the information about the user obtained by the Bank in connection with the Internet Banking service or for any other services
- Terms refer to terms and conditions for use of Internet Banking as specified in this document
- In this document, all references to the user being referred in masculine gender will also include the feminine gender

Applicability of Terms

These terms form the contract between the user using the i-net banking service and the Bank. By applying for Internet Banking and accessing the service the user acknowledges and accepts these terms. Any conditions relating to the accounts of the customer other than these terms will continue to apply except that in the event of any conflict between these terms and the account conditions, these terms will continue to prevail.

APPLICATION FOR INTERNET BANKING

- The Bank may offer Internet Banking to selected customers at its discretion. Interest in the use of Internet Banking may be registered on-line through the Bank's website. The Bank will forward the Internet Banking application form, a copy of these terms and conditions and the brochure explaining the service to the person who has registered his interest. The acceptance of the registration and the acknowledgement thereof does not automatically imply the acceptance of application for Internet Banking
- The Bank may advise from time to time the internet software such as browsers which are required for using Internet Banking. There will be no obligation on the Bank to support all the versions of these internet software

Internet Banking Service

- The Bank shall endeavour to provide to the user through Internet Banking, services such as enquiry about the balance in his Internet Banking account(s), details about transactions, statement of account, request for issue of cheque-books, request for transfer of funds between accounts of the same user, from user's account to another person's account, bill payment and such other facilities as the Bank may decide to provide from time to time.These facilities shall be offered in a phased manner at the discretion of the Bank. The Bank may also make additions/ deletions to the services offered through Internet Banking at its sole discretion. The availability/ non-availability of a particular service shall be advised through email, web page of the Bank or written communication

- The Bank shall take reasonable care to, ensure the security of and prevent unauthorised access to the Internet Banking service using technology reasonably available to the Bank
- The user shall not use or permit to use Internet Banking or any related service for any illegal or improper purposes

Internet Banking Access

- The user would be allotted one or more Internet Banking user-id(s) and one or more secret password(s) by the bank in the first instance. The user will be required to change the password(s) assigned by the Bank on accessing Internet Banking for the first time. As a safety measure the user shall change the password as frequently thereafter as possible. As an additional safety measure user may be forced to change password(s) whenever Bank wants
- In addition to user-id and password the Bank may, at its discretion, advise the user to adopt such other means of authentication including but not limited to digital certification and/ or smart cards
- The user shall not attempt or permit others to attempt accessing the account information stored in the computers of the Bank through any means other than the Internet Banking service

Password

The user must:

- Keep the user-id and password totally confidential and not reveal the password to any third party

- Choose a password which shall be at least 6 characters long or any number of characters as bank may stipulate time to time and may consist of a mix of alphabets, numbers which must not relate to any readily accessible personal data such as the user's name, address, telephone number, driver license etc. Or easily guessable combination of letters and numbers
- Commit the user-id and password to memory and not record them in a written or electronic form
- Not let any unauthorised person have access to his computer or leave the computer unattended whilst accessing Internet Banking
- If the user forgets theInternet Banking user-id or password, he can request for change of the password by sending a written request to the Bank. The selection of a new password and/ or the replacement of Internet Banking user-id shall not be construed as the commencement of a new contract

JOINT ACCOUNTS

- The Internet Banking service will be available in case of joint accounts only if the mode of operation is indicated as 'either or survivor' or ' anyone or survivor'. For these joint accounts one Internet Banking user-id will be issued to one of the Joint Account holders. Bank has the option to issue additional user-id and password for any type of accounts including Joint Accounts. The other Joint Account holder(s) shall expressly agree with this arrangement and give their consent on the application form for use of Internet Banking . In case any of the joint account holder(s) gives "stop payment" instructions or request to discontinue Internet Banking service in respect of operations through the use of Internet Banking (or in writing) or by some other mode of authorized communication, on any of the Internet Banking -accounts held jointly by them, the Internet Banking service will be discontinued for the user. In case of addition of new name in an existing account, this will automatically apply on him/her.
- Minimum balance and charges

- The user shall maintain, at all times, such minimum balance in Internet Banking account(s), as the Bank may stipulate from time to time. The Bank may, at its discretion, levy penal charges and/or service charges for non-maintenance of the minimum balance. In addition to the minimum balance stipulation the Bank may levy service charges for use of Internet Banking at its discretion. The user authorises the Bank to recover all charges related to Internet Banking as determined by the Bank from time to time by debiting one of user's Internet Banking accounts.
- The Bank may withdraw the i-net banking facility, if at any time the amount of deposit falls short of the required minimum as aforesaid and/ or if the service charges remain unpaid, without giving any further notice to the user and/ or without incurring any liability or responsibility whatsoever by reason of such withdrawal

Funds Transfer

- The user shall not use or attempt to use Internet Banking for funds transfer - as and when the facility is made available - without sufficient funds in the relative i-net banking -account or without a pre-existing arrangement with the bank for the grant of an overdraft
- The Bank will endeavour to effect such funds transfer transactions received through Internet Banking provided there are sufficient funds available in the user's account. In any case , if based on the user instructions, funds are debited from his account by overdrawing the account without without sufficient funds in the relative Internet Banking -account or without a pre-existing arrangement with the Bank for the grant of an overdraft , the account holder will be liable to regularize the account. The Bank shall not be liable for any omission to make all or any of the payments or for late payments due to circumstances beyond the reasonable control of the Bank

AUTHORITY TO THE BANK

- Banking transactions in the user's Internet Banking account(s) are permitted through Internet Banking only after authentication of the user-id and password of the user. The user (alongwith the joint account holder, if any) grants express authority to the Bank for carrying out the banking transactions performed by him through Internet Banking.

The Bank shall have no obligation to verify the authenticity of any transaction received from the user through Internet Banking or purporting to have been sent by the user via Internet Banking other than by means of verification of the user-id and the password

- The display or printed output that is produced by the user at the time of operation of Internet Banking is a record of the operation of the internet access and shall not be construed as the Bank's record of the relative transactions.

  The Bank's own records of transactions maintained through computer systems or otherwise shall be accepted as conclusive and binding for all purposes

- All transactions arising from the use of Internet Banking to operate a joint account, shall be binding on all the joint account holders, jointly and severally

Accuracy of Information

- The user is responsible for the correctness of information supplied to the Bank through the use of Internet Banking or through any other means such as electronic mail or written communication.

  The Bank accepts no liability for the consequences arising out of erroneous information supplied by the user.

  If the user suspects that there is an error in the information supplied to the Bank by him/her, he/she shall advise the Bank as soon as possible. The Bank will endeavour to correct the error wherever possible

- If the user notices an error in the account information supplied to him through Internet Banking or by the use of any of the Internet Banking services, he shall advise the Bank as soon as possible. The Bank will endeavour to correct the error promptly and adjust any interest or charges arising out of the error.

LIABILITY OF THE USER AND THE BANK

- The user shall not be liable for any unauthorised transactions occurring through the use of Internet Banking which can be attributed to the fraudulent or negligent conduct of the employees or agents of the Bank
- If the user has complied with the terms and advises the bank immediately after he suspects that his user-id or password is known to another person and/ or notices an unauthorised transaction in his Internet Banking account, he/she shall not be liable for losses arising out of the unauthorised transactions occurring in the Internet Banking accounts after the receipt of such advice by the Bank
- The user shall be liable for some or all loss from unauthorised transactions in the Internet Banking accounts if he has breached the terms or contributed or caused the loss by negligent actions such as the following:
    - o Keeping a written or electronic record of Internet Banking password
    - o Disclosing or failing to take all reasonable steps to prevent disclosure of the Internet Banking user-id or password to anyone including Bank staff and/ or failing to advise the bank of such disclosure within reasonable time
    - o Not advising the Bank in a reasonable time about unauthorised access to or erroneous transactions in the Internet Banking accounts
    - o The Bank shall not be liable for any unauthorised transactions occurring through the use of Internet Banking which can be attributed to the fraudulent or negligent conduct of the user
    - o The Bank shall in no circumstances be held liable to the user if Internet Banking access is not available in the desired manner for reasons including but not limited to natural calamity, floods, fire and other natural disasters, legal restraints, faults in the telecommunication network or internet or network failure, software or hardware error or any other reason beyond the control of the Bank.

      Under no circumstances shall the Bank be liable for any damages whatsoever whether such damages are direct, indirect, incidental, consequential and irrespective of whether any claim is based on loss of revenue, investment, production, goodwill, profit, interruption of business or any other loss of any character or nature whatsoever and whether sustained by the user or any other person.

Indemnity

The user indemnifies and hold the bank harmless against any loss suffered by the Bank, its customers or a third party or any claim or action brought by a third party which is in any way the result of the improper use of Internet Banking by the user

Disclosure of Personal Information

The user agrees that the Bank or its contractors may hold and process his personal information on computer or otherwise in connection with Internet Banking services as well as for statistical analysis and credit scoring.

The user also agrees that the Bank may disclose, in strict confidence, to other institutions, such personal information as may be reasonably necessary for reasons inclusive of, but not limited to, the following

- For participation in any telecommunication or electronic clearing network
- In compliance with a legal directive
- For credit rating by recognised credit scoring agencies
- For fraud prevention purposes

Bank's Lien

The Bank shall have the right of set-off and lien, irrespective of any other lien or charge, present as well as future on the deposits held in the user's primary account and/ or; secondary account(s) or in any other account, whether in single name or joint name(s), to the extent of all outstanding dues, whatsoever, arising as a result of the Internet Banking service extended to and/ or used by the user.

Proprietary Rights

- The user acknowledges that the software underlying the Internet Banking service as well as other internet related software which are required for accessing Internet Banking are the legal property of the respective vendors. The permission given by the Bank to access Internet Banking will not convey any proprietary or ownership rights in the above software

- The user shall not attempt to modify, translate, disassemble, decompile or reverse engineer the software underlying Internet Banking or create any derivative product based on the software

Change of Terms and Conditions

The Bank has the absolute discretion to amend or supplement any of the terms at any time and will endeavour to give prior notice of fifteen days for such changes wherever feasible except for changes to interest rates and/ or other variations that are subject to market changes. The Bank may introduce new services within Internet Banking from time to time. The existence and availability of the new functions will be notified to the user as and when they become available. The changed terms and conditions applicable to the new Internet Banking services shall be communicated to the user. By using these new services, the user agrees to be bound by the terms and conditions applicable.

Termination of Internet Banking Service

- The user may request for termination of the Internet Banking facility any time by giving a written notice of at least 15 days to the Bank. The user will remain responsible for any transactions made on his Internet Banking account(s) through Internet Banking prior to the time of such cancellation of the Internet Banking servicc
- The Bank may withdraw the Internet Banking facility anytime provided the user is given reasonable notice under the circumstances. If the Internet Banking service is withdrawn by the Bank for a reason other than the breach of the terms and conditions by the user, the Bank's liability shall be restricted to the return of the annual charges, if any, recovered from the user for the period in question
- The closure of all Internet Banking accounts of the user will automatically terminate the Internet Banking service
- The Bank may suspend or terminate Internet Banking facilities without prior notice if the user has breached these terms and conditions or the Bank learns of the death, bankruptcy or lack of legal capacity of the user

Notices

Notices under these terms and conditions may be given by the Bank and the user:

- Electronically to the mail box of either party. Such notices will be regarded as being in writing
- In writing by delivering them by hand or by sending them by post to the last address given by the user and in the case of the bank to the address mentioned in the heading above or any other address as informed by the bank to the user for communication related to Internet Banking
- In addition, the Bank may also publish notices of general nature which are applicable to all users of Internet Banking on its web site. Such notices will have the same effect as a notice served individually to each user

Governing Law

- These terms and conditions and/ or the operations in the accounts of the user maintained by the Bank and/ or the use of the services provided through Internet Banking shall be governed by the laws of the Republic of India and no other nation. The user and the Bank agree to submit to the exclusive jurisdiction of the courts located in Mumbai, India as regards any claims or matters arising under these terms and conditions
- The Bank accepts no liability whatsoever, direct or indirect, for non-compliance with the laws of any country other than the Republic of India. The mere fact that the Internet Banking service can be accessed through internet by a user in a country other than India shall not be interpreted to imply that the laws of the said country govern these terms and conditions and/ or the operations in the Internet Banking accounts of the user and/ or the use of Internet Banking.

General

- The clause headings in this agreement are only for convenience and do not affect the meaning of the relative clause
- The user shall not assign this agreement to anybody else. The Bank may sub-contract and employ agents to carry out any of its obligations under

this contract. The Bank may transfer or assign its rights and obligations under this contract to any other company

ONLINE BANKING:REGULATORY FRAMEWORK IN INDIA

This particular post is a modified version of an abstract prepared for a conference on Online banking. During the research I could found that the literature on regulatory aspect on online baking is very less. I thank Kalpit for working with me for this post.

Shedding the conventional brick and mortar banking style, the Indian banking has entered the new forte of online/internet banking, though of late. This being the transition period, the banking community is facing immense challenge and issues of feasibility also pop-up.

Feasibility of Online Banking in India

The redtapism in public sector banking and lesser consumer base is being attributed to as the reasons for the Indian banks to enter into the online banking this late. With the rapid development in the technological infrastructure (security, confidentiality is being mainly referred to) and the legal framework being better equipped, the online bank has become a feasible mode of banking in India.

Regulatory framework in India has gone a long way forward, with the Information Technology Act 2000 attempting to address a number of e-commerce regulatory issues, address the need for banks to go online and have laid out security measures to be adopted (since online baking is overlapping with e-commerce on most occasions and having to deal with cross-border jurisdictions), and with the comprehensive and forward looking guidelines brought out by the RBI. Along with the favorable scenario in the techno-legal aspect and the increasing internet consumer base has taken the trend of online banking from basic information dissemination service to fund-based transactions on their accounts, hinting at the ample growth prospect of online banking in India.

Challenges

In the Internet banking system, information is considered as an asset and so worthy of protection. However, the present system of authentication does not address the security aspect in full. This calls for an urgent need to acclimatize the whole system.

According to Online Banking Association, member institutions rated security as the most important issue of online banking. There is a dual requirement to protect customers' privacy and protection against fraud. Another major issue is that of Data Protection and the need for a legal and regulatory framework.

Currently, India has no law on data protection. Information security in e-banking presents two main areas of risk: preventing unauthorized transactions and maintaining integrity of customers' transactions. Data protection falls in the latter. Data protection laws primarily aim to safeguard the interest of the individual whose data is handled and processed by others. 'Interests' are usually expressed in terms of privacy, autonomy and/or integrity.

The Information Technology Act, 2000 does not address this issue. India should take cue from nations, which have favored ad hoc enactment of sectoral laws over omnibus legislation. Along with these issues, the contradictory issues present in the Banking Regulations Act, 1949, the Reserve Bank of India Act, 1934 and the Foreign Exchange Management Act, 1999 need also to be looked into.

On the technological front the Indian Internet banking system is facing many hurdles. The problems include operational risks, security risks, system architecture risks, reputational risks and legal risks. Phishing is another issue that needs attention. Experts suggest that simple rules such as not sharing login IDs and passwords with anyone, would keep customers safe.

Future

It would obviously take much time before the online banking could be called a fully alternative banking mode to the conventional one. Legal and cross-border risks can be avoided through proper customer identification devices, information screening techniques, periodic reviews on compliance with various laws, and gaining knowledge of various national laws (applicable) and guide the customers through their cross-border dealings. The compliance part and policy regulation part should be assured by the RBI and the need for a data protection law cannot be denied.

The security issues can be tackled by having the bank's systems technologically equipped to evade operational and security risks. Reputational risks can be prevented by testing of the system before implementation, developing contingency plans (to handle system disruptions, system hackers, security lapses and virus attacks) and creating back-up facilities. Customer education and awareness also need to addressed, as unless the customers are taken into confidence and made comfortable with the working of online banking all the technological development will go in vain.

6

Financial and Banking Sector Reforms

INTRODUCTION

In the last decade, Private Sector Institutions played an important role. They grew rapidly in commercial banking and asset management business. With the openings in the insurance sector for these institutions, they started making debt in the market. Competition among financial intermediaries gradually helped the interest rates to decline. Deregulation added to it. The real interest rate was maintained. The borrowers did not pay high price while depositors had incentives to save. It was something between the nominal rate of interest and the expected rate of inflation.

The last decade witnessed the maturity of India's financial markets. Since 1991, every governments of India took major steps in reforming the financial sector of the country. The important achievements in the following fields is discussed under serparate heads:

- Financial markets
- Regulators
- The banking system
- Non-banking finance companies

- The capital market
- Mutual funds
- Overall approach to reforms
- Deregulation of banking system
- Capital market developments
- Consolidation imperative

Now let us discuss each segment seperately.

FINANCIAL MARKETS REGULATORS

The Finance Ministry continuously formulated major policies in the field of financial sector of the country. The Government accepted the important role of regulators. The Reserve Bank of India (RBI) has become more independant. Securities and Exchange Board of India (SEBI) and the Insurance Regulatory and Development Authority (IRDA) became important institutions. Opinions are also there that there should be a super-regulator for the financial services sector instead of multiplicity of regulators.

The Banking System

Almost 80% of the business are still controlled by Public Sector Banks (PSBs). PSBs are still dominating the commercial banking system. Shares of the leading PSBs are already listed on the stock exchanges. The RBI has given licences to new private sector banks as part of the liberalisation process. The RBI has also been granting licences to industrial houses. Many banks are successfully running in the retail and consumer segments but are yet to deliver services to industrial finance, retail trade, small business and agricultural finance. The PSBs will play an important role in the industry due to its number of branches and foreign banks facing the constrait of limited number of branches. Hence, in order to achieve an efficient banking system, the onus is on the Government to encourage the PSBs to be run on professional lines.

Development Finance Institutions

FIs's access to SLR funds reduced. Now they have to approach the capital market for debt and equity funds.

Convertibility clause no longer obligatory for assistance to corporates sanctioned by term-lending institutions.

Capital adequacy norms extended to financial institutions.

DFIs such as IDBI and ICICI have entered other segments of financial services such as commercial banking, asset management and insurance through separate ventures. The move to universal banking has started.

Non-banking Finance Companies

In the case of new NBFCs seeking registration with the RBI, the requirement of minimum net owned funds, has been raised to Rs.2 crores.

Until recently, the money market in India was narrow and circumscribed by tight regulations over interest rates and participants. The secondary market was underdeveloped and lacked liquidity. Several measures have been initiated and include new money market instruments, strengthening of existing instruments and setting up of the Discount and Finance House of India (DFHI).

The RBI conducts its sales of dated securities and treasury bills through its open market operations (OMO) window. Primary dealers bid for these securities and also trade in them. The DFHI is the principal agency for developing a secondary market for money market instruments and Government of India treasury bills. The RBI has introduced a liquidity adjustment facility (LAF) in which liquidity is injected through reverse repo auctions and liquidity is sucked out through repo auctions.

On account of the substantial issue of government debt, the gilt- edged market occupies an important position in the financial set- up. The Securities Trading Corporation of India (STCI), which started operations in June 1994 has a mandate to develop the secondary market in government securities.

Long-term debt market: The development of a long-term debt market is crucial to the financing of infrastructure. After bringing some order to the equity market, the SEBI has now decided to concentrate on the development of the debt market. Stamp duty is being withdrawn at the time of dematerialisation of debt instruments in order to encourage paperless trading.

The Capital Market

The number of shareholders in India is estimated at 25 million. However, only an estimated two lakh persons actively trade in stocks. There has been a dramatic improvement in the country's stock market trading infrastructure during the last few years. Expectations are that India will be an attractive emerging market with tremendous potential. Unfortunately, during recent times the stock markets have been constrained by some unsavoury developments, which has led to retail investors deserting the stock markets.

Mutual Funds

The mutual funds industry is now regulated under the SEBI (Mutual Funds) Regulations, 1996 and amendments thereto. With the issuance of SEBI guidelines, the industry had a framework for the establishment of many more players, both Indian and foreign players.

The Unit Trust of India remains easily the biggest mutual fund controlling a corpus of nearly Rs.70,000 crores, but its share is going down. The biggest shock to the mutual fund industry during recent times was the insecurity generated in the minds of investors regarding the US 64 scheme. With the growth in the securities markets and tax advantages granted for investment in mutual fund units, mutual funds started becoming popular.

The foreign owned AMCs are the ones which are now setting the pace for the industry. They are introducing new products, setting new standards of customer service, improving disclosure standards and experimenting with new types of distribution.

The insurance industry is the latest to be thrown open to competition from the private sector including foreign players. Foreign companies can only enter joint ventures with Indian companies, with participation restricted to 26 per cent of equity. It is too early to conclude whether the erstwhile public sector monopolies will successfully be able to face up to the competition posed by the new players, but it can be expected that the customer will gain from improved service. The new players will need to bring in innovative products as well as fresh ideas on marketing and distribution, in order to improve the low per capita insurance coverage. Good regulation will, of course, be essential.

Overall Approach to Reforms

The last ten years have seen major improvements in the working of various financial market participants. The government and the regulatory authorities have followed a step-by-step approach, not a big bang one. The entry of foreign players has assisted in the introduction of international practices and systems. Technology developments have improved customer service.

Some gaps however remain (for example: lack of an inter-bank interest rate benchmark, an active corporate debt market and a developed derivatives market). On the whole, the cumulative effect of the developments since 1991 has been quite encouraging. An indication of the strength of the reformed Indian financial system can be seen from the way India was not affected by the Southeast Asian crisis.

However, financial liberalisation alone will not ensure stable economic growth. Some tough decisions still need to be taken. Without fiscal control, financial stability cannot be ensured.

The fate of the Fiscal Responsibility Bill remains unknown and high fiscal deficits continue. In the case of financial institutions, the political and legal structures hve to ensure that borrowers repay on time the loans they have taken.

The phenomenon of rich industrialists and bankrupt companies continues. Further, frauds cannot be totally prevented, even with the best of regulation. However, punishment has to follow crime, which is often not the case in India.

DEREGULATION OF BANKING SYSTEM

Prudential norms were introduced for income recognition, asset classification, provisioning for delinquent loans and for capital adequacy. In order to reach the stipulated capital adequacy norms, substantial capital were provided by the Government to PSBs.

Government pre-emption of banks' resources through statutory liquidity ratio (SLR) and cash reserve ratio (CRR) brought down in steps. Interest rates on the deposits and lending sides almost entirely were deregulated. New private sector banks allowed to promote and encourage competition. PSBs were encouraged to approach the public for raising resources. Recovery of debts due to banks and the Financial Institutions Act, 1993 was passed, and special recovery tribunals set up to facilitate quicker recovery of loan arrears.

Bank lending norms liberalised and a loan system to ensure better control over credit introduced. Banks asked to set up asset liability management (ALM) systems. RBI guidelines issued for risk management systems in banks encompassing credit, market and operational risks.

A credit information bureau being established to identify bad risks. Derivative products such as forward rate agreements (FRAs) and interest rate swaps (IRSs) introduced.

Capital Market Developments

The Capital Issues (Control) Act, 1947, repealed, office of the Controller of Capital Issues were abolished and the initial share pricing were decontrolled. SEBI, the capital market regulator was established in 1992.

Foreign institutional investors (FIIs) were allowed to invest in Indian capital markets after registration with the SEBI. Indian companies were permitted to access international capital markets through euro issues. The National Stock Exchange (NSE), with nationwide stock trading and electronic display, clearing and settlement facilities was established. Several local stock exchanges changed over from floor based trading to screen based trading.

Private Mutual Funds Permitted

The Depositories Act had given a legal framework for the establishment of depositories to record ownership deals in book entry form. Dematerialisation of stocks encouraged paperless trading. Companies were required to disclose all material facts and specific risk factors associated with their projects while making public issues.

To reduce the cost of issue, underwriting by the issuer were made optional, subject to conditions. The practice of making preferential allotment of shares at prices unrelated to the prevailing market prices stopped and fresh guidelines were issued by SEBI.

SEBI reconstituted governing boards of the stock exchanges, introduced capital adequacy norms for brokers, and made rules for making client or broker relationship more transparent which included separation of client and broker accounts.

Buy Back of Shares Allowed

The SEBI started insisting on greater corporate disclosures. Steps were taken to improve corporate governance based on the report of a committee.

SEBI issued detailed employee stock option scheme and employee stock purchase scheme for listed companies. Standard denomination for equity shares of Rs. 10 and Rs. 100 were abolished. Companies given the freedom to issue dematerialised shares in any denomination. Derivatives trading starts with index options and futures. A system of rolling settlements introduced. SEBI empowered to register and regulate venture capital funds.

The SEBI (Credit Rating Agencies) Regulations, 1999 issued for regulating new credit rating agencies as well as introducing a code of conduct for all credit rating agencies operating in India.

Consolidation Imperative

Another aspect of the financial sector reforms in India is the consolidation of existing institutions which is especially applicable to the commercial banks. In India the banks are in huge quantity. First, there is no need for 27 PSBs with branches all over India. A number of them can be merged. The merger of Punjab National Bank and New Bank of India was a difficult one, but the situation is different now. No one expected so many employees to take voluntary retirement from PSBs, which at one time were much sought after jobs. Private sector banks will be self consolidated while co-operative and rural banks will be encouraged for consolidation, and anyway play only a niche role.

In the case of insurance, the Life Insurance Corporation of India is a behemoth, while the four public sector general insurance companies will probably move towards consolidation with a bit of nudging. The UTI is yet again a big institution, even though facing difficult times, and most other public sector players are already exiting the mutual fund business. There are a number of small mutual fund players in the private sector, but the business being comparatively new for the private players, it will take some time.

We finally come to convergence in the financial sector, the new buzzword internationally. Hi-tech and the need to meet increasing consumer needs is encouraging convergence, even though it has not always been a success till date. In India organisations such as IDBI, ICICI, HDFC and SBI are already trying to offer various services to the customer under one umbrella.

This phenomenon is expected to grow rapidly in the coming years. Where mergers may not be possible, alliances between organisations may be effective. Various forms of bancassurance are being introduced, with the RBI having already come out with detailed guidelines for entry of banks into insurance.

The LIC has bought into Corporation Bank in order to spread its insurance distribution network. Both banks and insurance companies have started entering the asset management business, as there is a great deal of synergy among these businesses. The pensions market is expected to open up fresh opportunities for insurance companies and mutual funds.

It is not possible to play the role of the Oracle of Delphi when a vast nation like India is involved. However, a few trends are evident, and the coming decade should be as interesting as the last one.

RESERVE BANK OF INDIA (RBI)

The central bank of the country is the Reserve Bank of India (RBI). It was established in April 1935 with a share capital of Rs. 5 crores on the basis of the recommendations of the Hilton Young Commission. The share capital was divided into shares of Rs. 100 each fully paid which was entirely owned by private shareholders in the begining. The Government held shares of nominal value of Rs. 2,20,000.

Reserve Bank of India was nationalised in the year 1949. The general superintendence and direction of the Bank is entrusted to Central Board of Directors of 20 members, the Governor and four Deputy Governors, one Government official from the Ministry of Finance, ten nominated Directors by the Government to give representation to important elements in the economic life of the country, and four nominated Directors by the Central Government to represent the four local Boards with the headquarters at Mumbai, Kolkata, Chennai and New Delhi. Local Boards consist of five members each Central

Government appointed for a term of four years to represent territorial and economic interests and the interests of co-operative and indigenous banks.

The Reserve Bank of India Act, 1934 was commenced on April 1, 1935. The Act, 1934 (II of 1934) provides the statutory basis of the functioning of the Bank.

The Bank was constituted for the need of following:

- To regulate the issue of banknotes
- To maintain reserves with a view to securing monetary stability and
- To operate the credit and currency system of the country to its advantage.

Functions of Reserve Bank of India

The Reserve Bank of India Act of 1934 entrust all the important functions of a central bank the Reserve Bank of India.

Bank of Issue

Under Section 22 of the Reserve Bank of India Act, the Bank has the sole right to issue bank notes of all denominations. The distribution of one rupee notes and coins and small coins all over the country is undertaken by the Reserve Bank as agent of the Government.

The Reserve Bank has a separate Issue Department which is entrusted with the issue of currency notes. The assets and liabilities of the Issue Department are kept separate from those of the Banking Department. Originally, the assets of the Issue Department were to consist of not less than two-fifths of gold coin, gold bullion or sterling securities provided the amount of gold was not less than Rs. 40 crores in value.

The remaining three-fifths of the assets might be held in rupee coins, Government of India rupee securities, eligible bills of exchange and promissory notes payable in India.

Due to the exigencies of the Second World War and the post-was period, these provisions were considerably modified. Since 1957, the Reserve Bank of India is required to maintain gold and foreign exchange reserves of Ra. 200 crores, of which at least Rs. 115 crores should be in gold. The system as it exists today is known as the minimum reserve system.

Banker to Government

The second important function of the Reserve Bank of India is to act as Government banker, agent and adviser. The Reserve Bank is agent of Central Government and of all State Governments in India excepting that of Jammu and Kashmir. The Reserve Bank has the obligation to transact Government business, via. to keep the cash balances as deposits free of interest, to receive and to make payments on behalf of the Government and to carry out their exchange remittances and other banking operations. The Reserve Bank of India helps the Government - both the Union and the States to float new loans and to manage public debt. The Bank makes ways and means advances to the Governments for 90 days. It makes loans and advances to the States and local authorities. It acts as adviser to the Government on all monetary and banking matters.

Bankers' Bank and Lender of the Last Resort

The Reserve Bank of India acts as the bankers' bank. According to the provisions of the Banking Companies Act of 1949, every scheduled bank was required to maintain with the Reserve Bank a cash balance equivalent to 5% of its demand liabilites and 2 per cent of its time liabilities in India. By an amendment of 1962, the distinction between demand and time liabilities was abolished and banks have been asked to keep cash reserves equal to 3 per cent of their aggregate deposit liabilities. The minimum cash requirements can be changed by the Reserve Bank of India.

The scheduled banks can borrow from the Reserve Bank of India on the basis of eligible securities or get financial accommodation in times of need or stringency by rediscounting bills of exchange. Since commercial banks can always expect the Reserve Bank of India to come to their help in times of banking crisis the Reserve Bank becomes not only the banker's bank but also the lender of the last resort.

Controller of Credit

The Reserve Bank of India is the controller of credit i.e. it has the power to influence the volume of credit created by banks in India. It can do so through changing the Bank rate or through open market operations. According to the

Banking Regulation Act of 1949, the Reserve Bank of India can ask any particular bank or the whole banking system not to lend to particular groups or persons on the basis of certain types of securities. Since 1956, selective controls of credit are increasingly being used by the Reserve Bank.

The Reserve Bank of India is armed with many more powers to control the Indian money market. Every bank has to get a licence from the Reserve Bank of India to do banking business within India, the licence can be cancelled by the Reserve Bank of certain stipulated conditions are not fulfilled. Every bank will have to get the permission of the Reserve Bank before it can open a new branch.

Each scheduled bank must send a weekly return to the Reserve Bank showing, in detail, its assets and liabilities. This power of the Bank to call for information is also intended to give it effective control of the credit system. The Reserve Bank has also the power to inspect the accounts of any commercial bank.

As supereme banking authority in the country, the Reserve Bank of India, therefore, has the following powers:

(a) It holds the cash reserves of all the scheduled banks.

(b) It controls the credit operations of banks through quantitative and qualitative controls.

(c) It controls the banking system through the system of licensing, inspection and calling for information.

(d) It acts as the lender of the last resort by providing rediscount facilities to scheduled banks.

Custodian of Foreign Reserves

The Reserve Bank of India has the responsibility to maintain the official rate of exchange. According to the Reserve Bank of India Act of 1934, the Bank was required to buy and sell at fixed rates any amount of sterling in lots of not less than Rs. 10,000. The rate of exchange fixed was Re. 1 = sh. 6d. Since 1935 the Bank was able to maintain the exchange rate fixed at lsh.6d. though there were periods of extreme pressure in favour of or against the rupee. After India became a member of the International Monetary Fund in 1946, the Reserve Bank has the responsibility of maintaining fixed exchange rates with all other member countries of the I.M.F. Besides maintaining the rate of exchange of the rupee, the Reserve Bank has to act as the custodian of India's reserve of international currencies. The vast sterling balances were acquired and managed by the Bank. Further, the RBI has the responsibility of administering the exchange controls of the country.

Supervisory Functions

In addition to its traditional central banking functions, the Reserve bank has certain non-monetary functions of the nature of supervision of banks and promotion of sound banking in India. The Reserve Bank Act, 1934, and the Banking Regulation Act, 1949 have given the RBI wide powers of supervision and control over commercial and co-operative banks, relating to licensing and establishments, branch expansion, liquidity of their assets, management and methods of working, amalgamation, reconstruction, and liquidation. The RBI is authorised to carry out periodical inspections of the banks and to call for returns and necessary information from them.

The nationalisation of 14 major Indian scheduled banks in July 1969 has imposed new responsibilities on the RBI for directing the growth of banking and credit policies towards more rapid development of the economy and realisation of certain desired social objectives. The supervisory functions of the RBI have helped a great deal in improving the standard of banking in India to develop on sound lines and to improve the methods of their operation.

Promotional Functions

With economic growth assuming a new urgency since Independence, the range of the Reserve Bank's functions has steadily widened. The Bank now performs a varietyof developmental and promotional functions, which, at one time, were regarded as outside the normal scope of central banking.

The Reserve Bank was asked to promote banking habit, extend banking facilities to rural and semi-urban areas, and establish and promote new specialised financing agencies. Accordingly, the Reserve Bank has helped in the setting up of the IFCI and the SFC; it set up the Deposit Insurance Corporation in 1962, the Unit Trust of India in 1964, the Industrial Development Bank of India also in 1964, the Agricultural Refinance Corporation of India in 1963 and the Industrial Reconstruction Corporation of India in 1972. These institutions were set up directly or indirectly by the Reserve Bank to promote saving habit and to mobilise savings, and to provide industrial finance as well as agricultural finance.

As far back as 1935, the Reserve Bank of India set up the Agricultural Credit Department to provide agricultural credit. But only since 1951 the Bank's role in this field has become extremely important. The Bank has developed the co-operative credit movement to encourage saving, to eliminate moneylenders from the villages and to route its short term credit to agriculture. The RBI has set up the Agricultural Refinance and Development Corporation to provide long-term finance to farmers.

CLASSIFICATION OF RBIS FUNCTIONS

The monetary functions also known as the central banking functions of the RBI are related to control and regulation of money and credit, i.e., issue of currency, control of bank credit, control of foreign exchange operations, banker to the Government and to the money market. Monetary functions of the RBI are significant as they control and regulate the volume of money and credit in the country.

Equally important, however, are the non-monetary functions of the RBI in the context of India's economic backwardness. The supervisory function of the RBI may be regarded as a non-monetary function (though many consider this a monetary function).

The promotion of sound banking in India is an important goal of the RBI, the RBI has been given wide and drastic powers, under the Banking Regulation Act of 1949 - these powers relate to licencing of banks, branch expansion, liquidity of their assets, management and methods of working, inspection, amalgamation, reconstruction and liquidation. Under the RBI's supervision and inspection, the working of banks has greatly improved. Commercial banks have developed into financially and operationally sound and viable units.

The RBI's powers of supervision have now been extended to non-banking financial intermediaries. Since independence, particularly after its nationalisation 1949, the RBI has followed the promotional functions vigorously and has been responsible for strong financial support to industrial and agricultural development in the country.

ECONOMIC PERSPECTIVES OF BANKING

According to unconfirmed reports, the Reserve Bank of India (RBI) has approved a proposal from the government to amend the Banking Regulation Act to permit banks to trade in commodities and commodity derivatives. This offer to banks of one more new avenue of speculative investment by removal of a prohibition on commodity trading that has been in existence for long merely furthers the fundamental changes that have been under way in India's banking sector. The, banks seem to be the prime targets of the government's reforming zeal.

Having encouraged foreign acquisition, consolidation and universalisation in the banking system, the Finance Ministry's current thrust seems to be to find a host of new areas of activity for these institutions. These changes impinge upon the nature of the institutions, operations and instruments that constitute the sector. Institutional changes include: a rapid increase in the number of new private sector banks; a process of consolidation of banks that thus far has principally affected the private banking sector but is now being consciously promoted in the public sector as well; privatisation of equity in public sector banks; mergers of banks and other financial institutions, particularly development banking institutions; and the creation of universal banks that are in the nature of financial supermarkets, offering customers a range of products from across the financial sector such as debt products, investment opportunities in equity, debt and commodity markets and insurance products of different kinds.

Implicit in these institutional changes are changes in the operations of the increasingly "universalised" banks. The most crucial change has been an increasing reluctance of banks to play their traditional role as agents who carry risks in return for a margin defined broadly by the spread between deposit and lending rates.

Traditionally, banks accepted small deposits that highly liquid investments protected against capital and income risk. They in turn made large investments in highly illiquid assets characterised by a significant degree of capital and income risk. This made banks crucial intermediaries for facilitating the conversion of savings into investment.

Given this crucial role of intermediation conventionally reserved for the banking system, the regulatory framework that had the central bank at is apex, sought to protect the banking system from possible fragility and failure. That protective framework across the globe involved regulating interest rates, providing for deposit insurance and limiting the areas of activity and the investments undertaken by the banking system. The understanding was that banks should not divert household savings placed in their care to risky investments promising high returns. In developing countries, the interventionist framework also had developmental objectives and involved measures to direct credit to what were "priority" sectors in the government's view.

IN recent years, liberalisation and "denationalisation" have changed all that and forced a change in banking practices in two ways. First, private players are unsatisfied with returns that are available within a regulated framework, so that the government and the central bank have had to dilute or dismantle regulatory measures as is happening in the case of priority lending as well as restrictions on banking activities in India.

Second, even public sector banks find that as private domestic and foreign banks, particularly the latter, lure away the most lucrative banking clients because of the special services and terms they are able to offer, they have to seek new sources of finance, new activities and new avenues for investments, so that they can shore up their interest incomes as well as revenues from various fee-based activities.

In sum, the processes of liberalisation fundamentally alter the terrain of operation of the banks. Their immediate impact is visible in a shift in the focus of bank activities away from facilitating commodity production and investment to lubricating trade and promoting personal consumption. Interest rates in these areas are much higher than that which could be charged to investments in commodity production. According to a study (Consumer Outlook 2004), conducted by market research firm KSA Technopak, Indian consumers are increasingly financing purchases of their dream products with credit that is now on offer, even without collateral. "Personal credit offtake has increased from about Rs.50,000 crores in 2000 to Rs.160,000 crores in 2003, giving an unprecedented boom to high-ticket item purchases such as housing and automobiles," the study reportedly found.

But there are changes also in the areas of operation of the banks, with banking entities not only creating or linking up with insurance companies, but also entering into other "sensitive" markets such as the stock and the real estate. It should be expected that this growing exposure to non-collateralised personal debt and entry into sensitive sectors would increase bank vulnerability to default or failure. The effects on bank fragility became clear after the stock scam of the late 1990s. RBI's Monetary and Credit Policy Statement for the year 2001-2002 had noted:

"The recent experience in equity markets, and its aftermath, have thrown up new challenges for the regulatory system as well as for the conduct of monetary policy. It has become evident that certain banks in the cooperative sector did not adhere to their prudential norms nor to the well-defined regulatory guidelines for asset-liability management nor even to the requirement of meeting their inter-bank payment obligations. Even though such behaviour was confined to a few relatively small banks, by national standards, in two or three locations, it caused losses to some correspondent banks in addition to severe problems for depositors."

INTERESTINGLY, this increase in financial fragility has been accompanied by the emergence of new instruments in the banking sector. Derivatives of different kinds are now traded in the Indian financial system including, crucially, credit derivatives. Most derivatives, financial instruments whose value is based on or derived from the value of something else, are linked to interest rates or currencies. Credit derivatives are based on the value of loans, bonds or other lending instruments.

A working group of the RBI had recommended in 2003 that scheduled commercial banks may initially be permitted to use credit derivatives only for managing their credit risks. But banks were not permitted to take long or short credit derivative positions with a trading intent. Credit derivatives were seen as helping banks manage the risk arising from adverse movements in the quality of their loans, advances, and investments by transferring that risk to a protection seller. Using credit derivatives, banks can (1) transfer credit risk and, hence, free up capital, which can be used in other opportunities; (2) diversify credit risk; (3) maintain client relationships, and (4) construct and manage a credit risk portfolio as per their risk preference.

Banks in India have quickly responded to this opportunity. For example, soon after the introduction of interest rate futures in India, Citigroup concluded three securitisation deals worth Rs.570 crores ($126.6 billion), where yields on government securities or the call money rate, were used as the benchmark for pricing floating rate payments for investors. The underlying receivables arise from a large number of fixed rate loan contracts made for financing commercial vehicles and construction equipment. The risk here is being shared with mutual funds, who are reportedly the major investors.

Even the conservative State Bank of India (SBI) has taken a plunge into the credit derivatives market to cope with the risk arising from its growing loan portfolio.

The bank had recorded a growth of almost Rs.36,000 crores or 25 per cent in its loan portfolio on a year-on-year basis until September 2004, starting from a total loan assets position of Rs.135,000 crores in the corresponding period of the previous year. Of this credit growth, more than 40 per cent had been contributed by retail assets. Credit derivatives offered an opportunity to hedge against the risks being accumulated in this manner. It should be clear that credit derivatives are an industry response to the increasing fragility that comes with the changed nature of banking practices. Derivatives of this kind permit the socialisation of the risks associated with the liberalisation-induced transformation of banking. These trends are in keeping with changes in the international banking industry as well. As The Economist, London, put it: "The world's leading banks decided some years ago that lending is a mugs' game. They began to get rid of their loans, repackaging them and selling them off as securities, or getting others to re-insure their risk."

From the point of view of the banks this effort has been extremely fruitful. Thus, when there was a major melt down in corporate America, as a result of financial fraud and accounting malpractice, leading to the closure of giants like Enron and WorldCom, leading banks that had lent large sums to them appeared unaffected. According to one estimate, loans totalling $34 billion were wiped out through these bankruptcies. But far less amounts showed up as losses in the bank's accounts and, in the second quarter of 2003, Citigroup reported a 12 per cent increase in profits and J.P. Morgan Chase a 78 per cent increase. It should be clear that these losses have to show up somewhere in the accounts of the financial system, but as the Bank of International Settlements (BIS) argued, its not easy to trace them.

"The markets lack transparency about the ultimate distribution of credit risks," it declared. One reason could be that these losses were being borne by insurance companies, which would be treating them like any other casualty loss so that they are not identifiable. The BIS sees this conundrum as being the result of the substantial growth of the practice of credit-risk transfer - the shifting of risk from banks on to the buyers of securities and loans, and on to the sellers of credit insurance. IN sum, the traditional image of the great banks with armoured vaults has little to do with the banks of today. The latter appear to make loans and then pass them on as quickly as possible, pocketing the margin. That allows them to take bigger risks in trading securities, derivatives, and foreign exchange.

But these risks do not go away. At the end of 2002, though non-bank entities accounted for just 10 per cent of the syndicated loan market in the United States, they held 22.6 per cent of the bad or doubtful loans. The same is now happening in India, increasing the fragility of a host of non-bank financial institutions, such as pension funds, mutual funds and life-insurance companies.

Unfortunately, rather than recognise this danger, the Finance Ministry is keen on ensuring changes of the kind described above through a state-directed process of financial engineering. The full implications of the resulting changes would be revealed only in the days to come. But the experience elsewhere provides cause for concern.

INDIAN BANKING SYSTEM: GROWING AT AN ADMIRABLY FASTER PACE

Commendable growth has been witnessed in the financial system of India over the past few years. With a chain of more than 65,000 branches, Indian banking system is one of the largest banking networks in the world.

There has been a considerable growth in the retail-banking sector in India, which makes up for about 1/5th of the overall bank credit. Typically, the retail banking industry encompasses the services such as credit cards, housing loans, educational loans and auto loans etc.

Retail banking has brought in a drastic makeover in the overall banking scenario in India. The exceptional improvement in the banking system in India is a result of strong initiatives taken up by both the government and private companies.

A recent market research report named, "Indian Retail Banking Sector Analysis 2007" published by RNCOS provides an exclusive tour to the entire retail-banking industry of India.

As per the report, "Mainstream banking and retail banking have become one and the same thing for the past several years now. Approximately, 22% of the total outstanding advances were derived from the retail portfolios of the banks in India till March 2004".

"The contribution of retail banking to the overall banking sector has been outstanding. Growing at a rate of 122%, the retail-banking sector of India managed to reach a worth of $67 billion in the year 2005", as per experts at RNCOS. "The retail banking sector in India should reach a worth of $310 billion by the year 2010", anticipate the experts.

Profiles of key players along with the strategies and plans adopted by them for the growth of the industry are also talked about in it.

Besides discussing the present scenario of the financial system in India the report offers a reliable prediction of the market in the years to come. The report is extremely important for the investors and corporates, as it will help them make better strategies for the growth of their business.

INDIAN BANKING SYSTEM IMMUNE

The Indian banking system is better positioned today than ever before in terms of its business and financial health, notes a new CRISIL study. Says Arun Panicker, director, financial sector ratings at CRISIL, "The past few years have seen a continuous improvement in the key indicators of the banks' health, such as asset quality and capital adequacy." This is in alignment with the global banking trends: the performance of the banking sector has improved globally over the past few years.

According to Krishnan Sitaraman, head, financial sector ratings, "CRISIL has ratings outstanding on the debt instruments of 34 scheduled commercial banks; these banks account for 80 per cent of the Indian banking industry's assets. The outlooks, wherever assigned, are stable, on the expectation that the banks' credit will not change materially over the medium term." For the 21 rated public sector banks, CRISIL's ratings reflect the benefits of majority ownership by the government of India, which are expected to continue, and the banks' strong resource profiles.

CRISIL's recent banking sector analyses illustrate these conclusions through the following five commentaries:

- Impact of similarities with mid-90s manageable for banks: There are numerous superficial similarities between the mid-1990s and the mid-2000s, including money supply growth, credit growth, economic growth, industrial growth, and interest rate trends. However, CRISIL sees the underlying indicators pointing towards a substantial improvement in the current overall health of the banking system vis-à-vis the 1990s. Asset quality has improved significantly, with gross NPAs at less than 4 per cent of advances as on March 31, 2006, compared to 19.5 per cent as on March 31, 1995.

Similarly, the capitalisation levels of the scheduled commercial banks has also improved sharply from the mid-1990s, with the aggregate net worth increasing to Rs1,417 billion as on March 31, 2005, from Rs215 billion as on March 31, 1994, leaving them adequately capitalised on a systemic basis even for a stress scenario. Thus, although the deteriorating asset quality in the late 1990s had a severe impact on the banks' balance sheets, CRISIL believes that such a situation is unlikely to recur today.

- Banking sector liquidity manageable at systemic level: CRISIL's analysis reveals that, despite high credit growth rates, systemic liquidity is expected to be manageable in the medium term. In 2005-06 (refers to financial year, April 1 to March 31), the credit extended by the banking sector grew at a rapid 32 per cent, after a significant 26 per cent credit growth in 2004-05. The deposit growth of 15 per cent in 2005-06 was not sufficient to cover this increase. While bank deposits have not been losing out significantly to other sources of savings, the magnitude of credit growth has forced the banks to look to other sources of funds as well.

The gap between deposit growth and credit growth also resulted in some tightness in liquidity in the banking sector during the second half of 2005-06; banks have managed this tightness by selling off investments, and increasing bulk deposits. CRISIL believes that this tightness was a temporary phenomenon, and the aggregate liquidity situation in the banking sector is now manageable. CRISIL's analysis also reveals that a bank deposit growth of 16 per cent in 2006-07 will be sufficient from a systemic perspective to comfortably sustain credit growth of even 25 per cent, given the current structure of banks' balance sheets. Nevertheless, on a case-specific basis, there are banks that have low levels of excess statutory liquidity ratio (SLR) investments; in the absence of corresponding deposit growth, such banks would need bulk borrowings to meet the credit expansion.

- Banking sector asset quality - better than ever before: After a decade of improvement, asset quality in India's banking sector is superior to that of other leading Asian economies such as China, Malaysia and Indonesia. Three years ago, Indian banks were using treasury gains to provide for non-performing assets (NPAs) or write them off; today, however, recoveries are the single most significant route for NPA reduction. CRISIL's simulation of a stressed economic scenario reveals that, even if asset quality were to deteriorate significantly today, the impact on the banking sector would be manageable. This is primarily because of improved capital adequacy, greater diversity in asset portfolio, stronger credit profile of borrowers, and increased risk awareness among banks.
- Banking system adequately capitalised even under Basel-II Framework: CRISIL believes that the incremental capital requirement for the banking sector on the implementation of Basel II norms, and the demands from unprovided-for 'weak assets' are manageable on a systemic basis; 'weak assets' indicate assets that are of an inherently poor credit profile (including speculative exposures, current NPAs and delinquent accounts in case of retail portfolios).

Banks have raised around Rs.150 billion of capital in 2005-06 to finance the high credit growth and ready themselves for Basel II norms.

The flexibility given to banks to raise different forms of capital, permitting the issue of hybrid capital, will help them maintain adequate capital levels on a systemic basis.

- Northbound rates not to hit banks' core profitability: CRISIL expects the core profitability of the banking sector to remain stable despite the increase in cost of funds.

  The banking sector has had a largely stable interest spread, between 2.6 and 3.2 per cent, for more than ten years (even in the increasing interest rate scenario in 1994-96). In 2005-06, there was a decline in the banking sector's core profitability (which excludes non-core aspects such as profits and losses on the investment book).

This was reflected in a lower Net Profitability Margin {NPM which is defined as (Yield on funds deployed) - (Average borrowing costs) - (Operating expense ratio) + (Fee income levels)}.

CRISIL believes the decline in profitability was temporary, as yields on a stock basis are expected to increase from 2006-07, aiding core profitability. CRISIL expects the banking sector's core profitability levels to remain range-bound, with net profitability margins of over 1.50 per cent over the medium term, and loan book expansion being the key driver determining overall profit levels.

STRENGTHENING INDIAN BANKING AND FINANCE: PROGRESS AND PROSPECTS

"We need greater productivity and efficiency to achieve the targets we set for ourselves, whether it be the macro-economic target of achieving 8 per cent growth in the Tenth Plan period or making our banking system strong and efficient and on par with international banks", this was the central message of the inaugural address of Dr. Bimal Jalan, Governor, Reserve Bank of India at the twenty-fourth Bank Economists' Conference.

The Conference was held between December 27 and 29 in Bangalore.

Plan Target not Difficult to Achieve

Referring to the targets set by the Tenth Plan of 8 per cent growth, poverty alleviation and improvement in human development indicator and the cynicism expressed about their achievement, Dr. Jalan unequivocally said, "I believe that the overall macro-economic situation has seldom been better in achieving the targets set by the Tenth Plan. Th e conditions cannot be more appropriate to meet the challenges in both the banking and the real sectors."

Contending that the growth target of 8 per cent envisaged by the Tenth Plan document was not at all difficult to achieve, the Governor pointed out that India had never faced a more favourable situation than it was at present. The Governor said that the conditions were right despite many adverse external factors.

The inflation was low, for instance, despite the most severe drought in the country; India's foreign exchange reserves were at the highest and healthiest level despite a hike in the oil prices, border tensions, global slowdown and tensions prevailing on the Iraq front.

In fact, the reserves were also healthy as they were not built up by increasing external debt, he pointed out. The Indian economy was also nudging towards 5-5.5 per cent growth despite lower agriculture production, slow industrial recovery and a global downturn. There was abundance of liquidity and the interest rates at long and short maturities were the lowest ever despite a high fiscal deficit and a high borrowing requirement of the government. In other words, if domestic and external resources could be a constraint in achieving growth targets, India faced none and therefore the environment was most conducive for growth, he pointed out.

To underscore the positive factors, the Governor recalled the earlier times when the presence of any of the constraints, such as, drought or higher oil prices, would have caused India to face tight liquidity, higher interest rates, high fiscal deficit, scarce foreign exchange and higher exchange controls.

"But today we face none of these and there is no difference of opinion that we are in the best possible situation to achieve the targeted growth", he stated unequivocally.

Increase Productivity and Reduce Costs

The answer to the cynicism despite many favourable conditions lied in low productivity, the Governor said and added that "For every rupee of capital spent by the government or by the private sector, we produce less," he stated. He added that inefficiency in the use of resources, tolerance of waste and slothfulness contributed to low productivity.

"Our savings rate is the highest but our rate of growth is low. Our cost of doing business is relatively high and returns are not commensurate with investments made" the Governor said and added that this was true also of the banking sector which suffers from high cost and low productivity as reflected in high spreads.

The important challenge of managing transformation would, for the banking sector, mean moving from high cost, low productivity and high spread to being more efficient, productive and competitive.

For this, the banks need to address four main areas viz., corporate governance, economic value added, technology upgradation and H RD. Of these, HRD is the more difficult area to tackle. In public sector institutions, there are more challenges to face.

"Taking examination to get into the system is the biggest challenge but once you get in there is no challenge" he observed. Increasing productivity and lowering cost per unit of output were the two biggest challenges faced by India, more specifically the banking and the financial system.

Keep Depositors' Trust

In addition to low productivity, the Governor dwelt upon the other two issues, namely prudential norms and supervision and regulation. He commended the progress made by India's banking and financial system in prudential norms and added that India was contributing at the conceptual level in the international forum and was in fact the chairperson of the committee contributing to the thinking on adoption of BASEL II norms in emerging economies.

Apart from these, India had also made significant progress on transparency, capital adequacy and disclosures. While the achievements were significant,

India lagged behind in management of non-performing assets. He stated that there were two reasons why the banking system should follow international norms. One, concern for depositors' money and second to face international competition.

The Governor pointed out that banking was the only institution that invested other people's money. On capital of 10 rupees they can lend 100 rupees. Bankers must be conscious of this and follow prudential norms of the highest order so that the public money is not threatened. "Banking system's edifice is based on trust, and that should not be eroded" he stressed.

At the international level, the non-adherence to globally accepted prudential norms would result in the international system doubting the repaying capacity of the Indian banks and make them uncompetitive in the international market. The Governor pointed out that no international forum would grudge the time table a country sets out to achieve the global standards.

He added that India was fruitfully participating in all international discussions on these issues and was evolving a framework for consultative process among the emerging economy.

Need for Greater Accountability

The Governor further stated that there are two different trends in area of supervision and regulation. Both, greater stress on supervision and regulation of the banking system and deregulation of financial markets with openness and transparency existed side by side. He also said that two economic factors were special to banking and financial system.

Unlike real sector, the impact of failure in a bank or financial unit has a more pervading effect. When an externality affects a banking unit, the depositors, borrowers and markets feel the impact immedi ately. Secondly, when something goes wrong, the only way to handle this is to take prompt corrective action. Deterioration in a bank or a financial unit does not have a linear course but has multiplying effect. This exponential effect is not seen in the real sector.

This situation can be tackled only by taking prompt corrective action. He said that in India, however, action is often postponed in the name of "doing good". Regulation is weak in some part of bank sector and prompt corrective action lukewarm.

This needs to be corrected by strengthening the legal framework and removing multiple levels of control and specifying a clear-cut supervisory authority. Depoliticisation of bank and bank's accountability of the depositors should be clearly emphasised.

THE CHANGING FACE OF BANKING

THE Indian financial sector is undergoing rapid change. Structural reforms aimed at improving the productivity and efficiency of the economy are apace.

The $28-billion sector, growing at roughly 15 per cent, has displayed remarkable stability over the years even when other markets in the Asian region were facing a crisis. The Indian financial sector has kept pace with the growing needs of its borrowers.

Changing Environment

The most important factor shaping today's world is globalisation. Companies are constantly in search of low-cost markets.

Technology is driving growth in production and productivity and competition is stiff. Secondly, rapid development in communication technology has lead to greater integration of global financial markets, in turn boosting private capital flows and foreign direct investment.

A third factor is the increasing share of emerging market economies in world trade. Another fallout of globalisation is the increase in volatility and vulnerability of markets. This calls for the adoption of international standards and global benchmarks.

Aligning with Global Standards

To strengthen India's banking system in an increasingly competitive environment and guard against financial fragility, financial sector reforms were initiated as part of the economic reforms launched in the country since 1991-92. Significant progress has been made in the past few years to bring the Indian Banking system closer to international standards.

India has adopted international prudential norms and practices with regard to capital adequacy, income recognition, provisioning requirement and supervision and these norms have been progressively tightened over the years.

There has been a steady decline in the level of resource pre-emption from the banking system in the form of CRR (cash reserve ratio) and SLR (statutory liquidity ratio). Interest rates in various segments of financial markets have been deregulated in a phased manner.

The mark-to-market practice for valuation of government securities has been gradually enhanced and further refinement, in line with international best practices, carried out in valuation and classification of investment by banks.

Risk management in banks has been strengthened and measures put in place to mitigate credit and market risks and efforts are on to measure and control operational risk. Banks have been given greater freedom in investing as also raising funds abroad and managing their external liability, subject to prudential guidelines.

In the area of supervision, the Basel core principles for effective banking supervision are being followed. Along with off-site surveillance there is periodic on-site monitoring of the risk profile of banks and their compliance with prudential guidelines and a "CAMELS"-based rating system is being followed. The Reserve Bank of India's regulatory and supervisory responsibility has been widened to include banking institutions and non-banking financial companies.

The end result, is that the Indian banking sector has been considerably strengthened; there is greater transparency and closer convergence of Indian financial system with practices prevailing in international financial markets.

There is special focus on corporate governance and the setting up of specialised board-level panels such as the executive, risk management, audit, compensation, asset-liability management committees, and so on.

The RBI's Standing Committee on International Financial Standards and Codes under the Chairmanship of Dr Y. V. Reddy has identified global standards and codes as part of the efforts to create a sound financial architecture aligned with global practices.

Moving Forward

But there are some areas that need greater attention.

Need to check NPAs: The biggest challenge is the problem of NPAs (non-performing assets). Around 12 per cent of bank credit is locked in NPAs, which means that banks do not earn any interest on NPA accounts. This is a drain on the financial health of banks. If banks have to cut their costs and improve performance, they must reduce their NPAs. The Government has re-promulgated the ordinance to help banks expedite recovery. This calls for strengthening credit appraisal and risk management and developing review and control systems in tune with the changing requirements.

Strengthening internal controls: While the information technology explosion has been beneficial, it has also brought with it some unsavoury side-effects.The increase in frauds and scams in the financial sector is a cause for concern and calls for the strengthening of internal controls of banks and financial institutions.

Focus on Indian economy: Even as banks move closer to international standards, they cannot lose touch with the realities of the Indian economy. In this context, agriculture, small industries/businesses and the services sectors, must be given special consideration and credit flow to the rural sector increased. In an age where the world has become smaller and money moves as quickly as information, achieving global benchmarks is important for global players.

But underlying this is the need to have sound fundamentals. There is no doubt that only banks and financial institutions that are focussed on efficiency, productivity and profitability have a chance to survive in a highly competitive environment and therefore need to equip themselves thoroughly to face the future competition.

THE TRENDS IN INDIAN BANKING

The Indian banking can be broadly categorized into nationalized (government owned), private banks and specialized banking institutions.The Reserve Bank of India acts a centralized body monitoring any discrepancies and shortcoming in the system. Since the nationalization of banks in 1969, the public sector banks or the nationalized banks have acquired a place of prominence and has since then seen tremendous progress.

The need to become highly customer focused has forced the slow-moving public sector banks to adopt a fast track approach. The unleashing of products and services through the net has galvanized players at all levels of the banking and financial institutions market grid to look anew at their existing portfolio offering.

Conservative banking practices allowed Indian banks to be insulated partially from the Asian currency crisis.Indian banks are now quoting al higher valuation when compared to banks in other Asian countries (viz. Hong Kong, Singapore, Philippines etc.) that have major problems linked to huge Non Performing Assets (NPAs) and payment defaults. Co-operative banks are nimble footed in approach and armed with efficient branch networks focus primarily on the 'high revenue' niche retail segments.

The Indian banking has finally worked up to the competitive dynamics of the 'new' Indian market and is addressing the relevant issues to take on the multifarious challenges of globalization. Banks that employ IT solutions are perceived to be 'futuristic' and proactive players capable of meeting the multifarious requirements of the large customers base.

Private banks have been fast on the uptake and are reorienting their strategies using the internet as a medium The Internet has emerged as the new and challenging frontier of marketing with the conventional physical world tenets being just as applicable like in any other marketing medium.

The Indian banking has come from a long way from being a sleepy business institution to a highly proactive and dynamic entity. This transformation has been largely brought about by the large dose of liberalization and economic reforms that allowed banks to explore new business opportunities rather than generating revenues from conventional streams (i.e. borrowing and lending).

The banking in India is highly fragmented with 30 banking units contributing to almost 50% of deposits and 60% of advances. Indian nationalized banks (banks owned by the government) continue to be the major lenders in the economy due to their sheer size and penetrative networks which assures them high deposit mobilization. The Indian banking can be broadly categorized into nationalized, private banks and specialized banking institutions. The Reserve Bank of India act as a centralized body monitoring any discrepancies and shortcoming in the system. It is the foremost monitoring body in the Indian financial sector. The nationalized banks (i.e. government-owned banks) continue to dominate the Indian banking arena. Industry estimates indicate that out of 274 commercial banks operating in India, 223 banks are in the public sector and 51 are in the private sector.

The private sector bank grid also includes 24 foreign banks that have started their operations here. Under the ambit of the nationalized banks come the specialized banking institutions. These co-operatives, rural banks focus on areas of agriculture, rural development etc.

BANKING ON RETAIL

With a jump in the Indian economy from a manufacturing sector, that never really took off, to a nascent service sector, Banking as a whole is undergoing a change. A larger option for the consumer is getting translated into a larger demand for financial products and customisation of services is fast becoming the norm than a competitive advantage.

With the Retail banking sector expected to grow at a rate of 30% [Chanda Kochhar, ED, ICICI Bank] players are focussing more and more on the Retail and are waking up to the potential of this sector of banking.

At the same time, the banking sector as a whole is seeing structural changes in regulatory frameworks and securitisation and stringent NPA norms expected to be in place by 2004 means the faster one adapts to these changing dynamics, the faster is one expected to gain the advantage.

Potential for Retail in India: Is Sky the Limit?

The Indian players are bullish on the Retail business and this is not totally unfounded. There are two main reasons behind this. Firstly, it is now undeniable that the face of the Indian consumer is changing. This is reflected in a change in the urban household income pattern. The direct fallout of such a change will be the consumption patterns and hence the banking habits of Indians, which will now be skewed towards Retail products. At the same time, India compares pretty poorly with the other economies of the world that are now becoming comparable in terms of spending patterns with the opening up of our economy. For instance, while the total outstanding Retail loans in Taiwan is around 41% of GDP, the figure in India stands at less than 5%.

The comparison with the West is even more staggering. Another comparison that is natural when comparing Retail sectors is the use of credit cards. Here also, the potential lies in the fact that of all the consumer expenditure in India in 2001, less than 1% was through plastic, the corresponding US figure standing at 18%.

But how Competitive are the Players?

The fact that the statistics reveal a huge potential also brings with it a threat that is true for any sector of a country that is opening up. Just how competitive are our banks? Is the threat of getting drubbed by foreign competition real? To analyze this, one needs to get into the shoes of the foreign banks. In other words, how do they see us? Are we good takeover targets?

Going by international standards, a large portion of the Indian population is simply not "bankable" - taking profitability into consideration.

On the other hand, the financial services market is highly over-leveraged in India. Competition is fierce, particularly from local private banks such as HDFC and ICICI, in the business of home, car and consumer loans. There, precisely lie the pitfalls of such explosive growth. All banks are targeting the fluffiest segment i.e. the upwardly mobile urban salaried class. Although the players are spreading their operations into segments like self- employed and the semi-urban rich, it is an open secret that the big city Indian yuppies form the most profitable segment. Over-dependence on this segment is bound to bring in inflexibility in the business.

What about the Foreign Giants?

The foreign banks have identified this problem but there are certain systematic risks involved in operating in the Retail market for them.

These include regulatory restrictions that prevent them from expanding their branch network. So these banks often take the Direct Selling Agent (DSA) route whereby low-end jobs like sourcing or transaction processing are outsourced to small regional layers. So now on, when you see a loan mela or a road show showcasing the retail bouquet of an elite MNC giant, you know that a significant commission earned out of any such booking gets ploughed back to our own economy. Perhaps, one of the biggest impediments in foreign players leveraging the Indian markets is the absence of positive credit bureaus. In the west the risk profile can be easily mapped to things like SSNs and this information can be publicly traded.

So all for the Keeping Then?

This will perhaps be the most wrongful inference that can be drawn from the above. We just cannot afford to look inwards and repeat the mistakes that were the side effects of the Nationalization of the Banking System. A growing market can never be an alibi for lack of innovation. Indian banks have shown little or no interest in innovative tailor-made products.

They have often tried to copy process designs that have been tested, albeit successfully, in the West. Each economic culture has its own traits and one who successfully adapts those to the business is the eventual winner. A case in point is the successful implementation of micro-credit networks in Bangladesh. Positioning a bank as a tech-savvy financial vendor in a country where Internet penetration is an abysmal 1.65% can only add to the over-leveraging as pointed out earlier.

The focus of the sector should remain in macroeconomic wealth creation and not increasing the per capita indebtedness that will do little but add to the NPA burden. Retail Banking in India has to be developed in the Indian way, notwithstanding the long queues in front of the teller counters in the Public sector banks!

INDUSTRIAL DEVELOPMENT BANK OF INDIA LTD. (IDBI)

Industrial Development Bank of India (IDBI) is the tength largest bank in the world in terms of development. The National Stock Exchange (NSE), The National Securities Depository Services Ltd. (NSDL), Stock Holding Corporation of India (SHCIL) are some of the institutions which has been built by IDBI. IDBI is a strategic investor in a plethora of institutions which have revolutionized the Indian Financial Markets.

IDBI Bank, promoted by IDBI Group started in November 1995 with a branch at Indore with an equity capital base of Rs. 1000 million.

Main Functions of IDBI

IDBI is vested with the responsibility of co-ordinating the working of institutions engaged in financing, promoting and developing industries. It has evolved an appropriate mechanism for this purpose.

IDBI also undertakes/supports wide-ranging promotional activities including entrepreneurship development programmes for new entrepreneurs, provision of consultancy services for small and medium enterprises, upgradation of technology and programmes for economic upliftment of the underprivileged.

IDBI's Role as a Catalyst

IDBI's role as a catalyst to industrial development encompasses a wide spectrum of activities. IDBI can finance all types of industrial concerns covered under the provisions of the IDBI Act.

With over three decades of service to the Indian industry, IDBI has grown substantially in terms of size of operations and portfolio.

Developmental Activities of IDBI

Promotional Activities

In fulfilment of its developmental role, the Bank continues to perform a wide range of promotional activities relating to developmental programmes for new entrepreneurs, consultancy services for small and medium enterprises and programmes designed for accredited voluntary agencies for the economic upliftment of the underprivileged.

These include entrepreneurship development, self-employment and wage employment in the industrial sector for the weaker sections of society through voluntary agencies, support to Science and Technology Entrepreneurs' Parks, Energy Conservation, Common Quality Testing Centres for small industries.

Technical Consultancy Organisations

With a view to making available at a reasonable cost, consultancy and advisory services to entrepreneurs, particularly to new and small entrepreneurs,

IDBI, in collaboration with other All-India Financial Institutions, has set up a network of Technical Consultancy Organisations (TCOs) covering the entire country. TCOs offer diversified services to small and medium enterprises in the selection, formulation and appraisal of projects, their implementation and review.

Entrepreneurship Development Institute

Realising that entrepreneurship development is the key to industrial development, IDBI played a prime role in setting up of the Entrepreneurship Development Institute of India for fostering entrepreneurship in the country.

It has also established similar institutes in Bihar, Orissa, Madhya Pradesh and Uttar Pradesh. IDBI also extends financial support to various organisations in conducting studies or surveys of relevance to industrial development.

EASY BANKING

This section is fully dedicated to the Tech Banking. A decade before, it was tough to belief that banking secctor will be at a finger tip. Now its possible. A mobile hand set with a connection is the only instrument needed to make a gateway to your banking transaction, the latest innovation of technology.

Apart from the Mobile Banking, including of SMS Banking, Net Banking and ATMs are the major steps taken by the banks in India towards modernisation. With all these devises and systems, there is a complete freedom to experience.

Check your account, transfer your fund, make payments and what more, do anything of everything what has been followed in physical banking since ages. But this time no standing for hours in front of cash counter and no time boundation in withdrawing your own money.

AUTOMATED TELLER MACHINE (ATM)

The first bank to introduce the ATM concept in India was the Hongkong and Shanghai Banking Corporation (HSBC). It was in the year 1987. Now, almost every commercial banks gives ATM facilities to its customers.

The first bank to cross 1,000 marks in installing ATMs in India is ICICI. SBI is following the concept of 'ATMs in Quantity'. But Private Sector Banks have taken the lead. ICICI, UTI, HDFC and IDBI counts more than 50% of the total ATMs in India.

Public Sector Banks are also taking the installation of ATMs seriously for Indian market. They are either setting up their own ATM centres or entering into tie-ups with other banks. The Corporation Bank has the second largest network of ATMs amongst the Public Sector Banks in India.

The Indian banks have also come up with a 'Swadhan' scheme. Under this scheme, the banks can use each other's ATM at a cost, usually Rs. 35 extra from their customers. The main feature of 'Swadhan Card' are as follows:

- No exchange fee charged to change an old ATM card for a Swadhan card.
- Rs. 3,000 fixed as the ceiling on withdrawal.
- Exception made for select customers who can withdraw up to Rs10,000. Still, this is lower than the average withdrawal of Rs15,000 by regular ATMs.
- IBA gives banks the discretion to decide a higher maximum amount for withdrawal.
- Transactions conducted through any of the member banks appear on a bank statement, which is given only by your own bank.
- All transactions conducted in any of the member banks appear on the bank statement, but only your own bank will provide this.

Note :- No overdraft facility is available on Swadhan cards.

How 'Swadhan Card' Works

All informations and transactions are routed among member institutions through a switch. The switch transmits the information and/or data to bank which has issued the card or to its processor, which on the other hand either approves or declines the transaction request and notifies the switch.

The decision of the card-issuing bank's is then routed by the switch to the processor of the ATM, which completes the transaction. The accounts among members are settled and account balances are transmitted at the end of the day to each member institution.

Cost of Setting ATM Center

Approximately Rs.1mn it takes for the setting of an ATM center. Rs.1.2-1.4mn per annum is needed for its maintenance. To keep the cost in equilibrium position, there should be around 250-300 transactions per day per ATM.

To overcome or to reach the break-even point, the banks are always encouraging its customers to use the ATMs. Banks like HDFC and Citibank even charge penalty if a customer visits the branch.

NCR India and HMA Die bold are the main two players in this market to set up ATMs in India. The market, according to them is whopping 100% and they are very optimistic to see 30,000 ATMs in India very soon.

FINANCIAL SERVICES OFFERED BY BANKS

Banks in India have traditionally offered mass banking products. Most common deposit products being Savings Bank, Current Account, Term deposit Account and lending products being Cash Credit and Term Loans. Due to Reserve Bank of India guidelines, Banks have had little to do besides accepting deposits at rates fixed by Reserve Bank of India and lend amount arrived by the formula stipulated by Reserve Bank of India at rates prescribed by the latter. PLR (Prime lending rate) was the benchmark for interest on the lending products. But PLR itself was, more often than not, dictated by RBI. Further, remittance products were limited to issuance of Drafts, Telegraphic Transfers, Bankers Cheque and Internal Transfer of funds.

In view of several developments in the 1990s, the entire banking products structure has undergone a major change. As part of the economic reforms, banking industry has been deregulated and made competitive. New players have added to the competition. IT revolution has made it possible to provide ease and flexibility in operations to customers. Rapid strides in information technology have, in fact, redefined the role and structure of banking in India. Further, due to exposure to global trends after Information explosion led by Internet, customers - both Individuals and Corporates - are now demanding better services with more products from their banks. Financial market has turned into a buyer's market. Banks are also changing with time and are trying to become one-stop financial supermarkets. Market focus is shifting from mass banking products to class banking with introduction of value added and customised products.

Banks in India have traditionally offered mass banking products. Most common deposit products being Savings Bank, Current Account, Term deposit Account and lending products being Cash Credit and Term Loans. Financial market has turned into a buyer's market. Market focus is shifting from mass banking products to class banking with introduction of value added and customized products.

A few foreign & private sector banks have already introduced customized banking products like Investment Advisory Services, SGL II accounts, Photocredit cards, Cash Management services, Investment products and Tax Advisory services. A few banks have gone in to market mutual fund schemes. Eventually, the Banks plan to market bonds and debentures, when allowed. Insurance peddling by Banks will be a reality soon. Banks also offer advisory services termed as 'private banking' - to "high relationship - value" clients.

A few foreign & private sector banks have already introduced customised banking products like Investment Advisory Services, SGL II accounts, Photocredit cards, Cash Management services, Investment products and Tax Advisory services. A few banks have gone in to market mutual fund schemes. Eventually, the Banks plan to market bonds and debentures, when allowed. Insurance peddling by Banks will be a reality soon. The recent Credit Policy of RBI announced on 27.4.2000 has further facilitated the entry of banks in this sector. Banks also offer advisory services termed as 'private banking' - to "high relationship - value" clients.

The bank of the future has to be essentially a marketing organisation that also sells banking products. New distribution channels are being used; more & more banks are outsourcing services like disbursement and servicing of consumer loans, Credit card business. Direct Selling Agents (DSAs) of various Banks go out and sell their products. They make house calls to get the application form filled in properly and also take your passport-sized photo. Home banking has already become common, where you can order a draft or cash over phone/internet and have it delivered home. ICICI bank was the first among the new private banks to launch its net banking service, called Infinity. It allows the user to access account information over a secure line, request cheque books and stop payment, and even transfer funds between ICICI Bank accounts. Citibank has been offering net banking to its Suvidha program to customers.

Products like debit cards, flexi deposits, ATM cards, personal loans including consumer loans, housing loans and vehicle loans have been introduced by a number of banks.

Corporates are also deriving benefit from the increased variety of products and competition among the banks. Certificates of deposit, Commercial papers, Nonconvertible Debentures (NCDs) that can be traded in the secondary market are gaining popularity. Recently, market has also seen major developments in treasury advisory services. With the introduction of Rupee floating rates for deposits as well as advances, products like interest rate swaps and forward rate agreements for foreign exchange, risk management products like forward contract, option contract, currency swap are offered by almost every authorised dealer bank in the market. The list is growing.

Public Sector Banks like SBI have also started focusing on this area. SBI plans to open 100 new branches called Personal Banking Branches (PBB) this year. The PBBs will also market SBI's entire spectrum of loan products: housing loans, car loans, personal loans, consumer durable loans, education loans, loans against share, financing against gold.

LATEST FINANCIAL SERVICES BY BANKS

- Bill Payment
- Shopping
- Ticket Booking
- Prepaid Mobile Recharge
- Card-2-Card FT
- Share Trading

CHANGING PARADIGMS OF THE FINANCIAL SERVICES

Today, financial markets are turbulent, globally. Traditional business models, when businesses were clearly differentiated (Banks conducted banking, insurance companies offered risk covers and securities companies offered investment opportunities), have become the footnotes of the finance literature.

Today, insurance companies are exploring values in the banking and investment products and vice versa . It is no more a bank competing with another bank and insurance company competing with another insurance company, but an insurance company competing with banks and what not. Hence, the most precious word today is the "convergence" of the opportunity zones in financial markets from concept to culmination.

It may be observed that the competitive dynamics of market has changed phenomenally. Today, players in the market compete in one segment and cooperate in other segment. Strategic alliances of the competing banks on the ATM infrastructure is a live example of this. Today, Mutual Funds compete with the Banks on deposits, as they too provide the cheque facility with certain limitations. Revolutionary waves have gone to the extent of providing the ATM facility to the Mutual Funds investors. It is very interesting to observe the competition mounting across the opportunity zones because that encourages people to improve and deliver better values to the market leading to growth of overall productivity of the nation.

Another example here is that of the insurance products. You would observe that the buyer of the insurance products also looks at them as the investment products. This is an issue of conditioning over the period of time and therefore, the customers of the insurance products are both the customers of the risk protection and the investment products. That leads to the insurance sector competing with the other avenues of the investment including banks, financial institutions and investment companies.

Enterprises in the finance are talking about one stop shop offering all the products ranging from commodities to securities to currencies under one roof. Globally, availability of all sorts of financial products (both money market and capital market) on the exchanges is driven by the benefits like transparency, better price discovery, wider dissemination of information and large investing community. Simplification of the customers' life is being priced by the market. Virgin Bank provides all the services to its customers including checking account to savings account to housing loan to car loan to credit card etc...with a single bank account.

ISSUES AND PROSPECTS OF EMERGING FINANCIAL SERVICES IN INDIA

The bank of the future has to be essentially a marketing organisation that also sells banking products. New distribution channels are being used; more & more banks are outsourcing services like disbursement and servicing of consumer loans, Credit card business. Direct Selling Agents (DSAs) of various Banks go out and sell their products.

Products like debit cards, flexi deposits, ATM cards, personal loans including consumer loans, housing loans and vehicle loans have been introduced by a number of banks. The PBBs will also market SBI's entire spectrum of loan products: housing loans, car loans, personal loans, consumer durable loans, education loans, loans against share, financing against gold.

Today, insurance companies are exploring values in the banking and investment products and vice versa. It is no more a bank competing with another bank and insurance company competing with another insurance company, but an insurance company competing with banks and what not.

You may see a real estate products provider having alliance with both banks for the financing and insurance companies for the risk management products, for his customers.

In this paper we also attempt to look at how technology is revamping industrial structure for financial services. We discuss the latest offerings by banks in terms of financial services like Bill Payment, online railway/air ticket booking, mobile phone recharging, Card to Card Funds Transfer, Community Banking Services.

With the competition increasing post 2009 with foreign banks allowed to acquire Indian banks, the major opportunity for Indian banks lies in providing financial Services in Rural Sector via facilities like kiosks and micro-finance services. We discuss microsfinacnce model (of ICICI) and weather finance schemes in this regard.

Some of the latest offerings by banks like Netsafe from HDFC, SBI card scheme, etc have been highlighted in this paper. We have also touched upon the latest facet of outsourcing of financial services.

The problem of limited access to financial services and stable incomes in rural India has been discussed using the concept of weather index insurance.

The philosophy of customer being king is driving the financial markets as well. Accordingly, it is no more customers chasing the products; it is the appropriateness of options chasing the customers. Today, financial institutions are co-designing the products/services with their customers and striving to provide them with global solutions.

FUTURE OF BANKING IN INDIA – CHANGING IMPERATIVES

A healthy banking system is essential for any economy striving to achieve good growth and yet remain stable in an increasingly global business environment. The Indian banking system has witnessed a series of reforms in the past, like deregulation of interest rates, dilution of government stake in PSBs, and increased participation of private sector banks. It has also undergone rapid changes, reflecting a number of underlying developments. This trend has created new competitive threats as well as new opportunities. This paper aims to foresee major future banking trends, based on these past and current movements in the market.

Given the competitive market, banking will (and to a great extent already has) become a process of choice and convenience. The future of banking would be in terms of integration. This is already becoming a reality with new-age banks such as YES Bank, and others too adopting a single-PIN. Geography will no longer be an inhibitor. Technology will prove to be the differentiator in the short-term but the dynamic environment will soon lead to its saturation and what will ultimately be the key to success will be a better relationship management.

OVERVIEW

If one were to say that the future of banking in India is bright, it would be a gross understatement. With the growing competition and convergence of services, the customers (you and I) stand only to benefit more to say the least. At the same time, emergence of a multitude of complex financial instruments is foreseen in the near future (the trend is visible in the current scenario too) which is bound to confuse the customer more than ever unless she spends hours (maybe days) to understand the same. Hence, I see a growing trend towards the importance of relationship managers. The success (or failure) of any bank would depend not only on tapping the untapped customer base (from other departments of the same bank, customers of related similar institutions or those of the competitors) but also on the effectiveness in retaining the existing base.

India has witness to a sea change in the way banking is done in the past more than two decades. Since 1991, the Reserve Bank of India (RBI) took steps to reform the Indian banking system at a measured pace so that growth could be achieved without exposure to any macro-environment and systemic risks. Some of these initiatives were deregulation of interest rates, dilution of the government stake in public sector banks (PSBs), guidelines being issued for risk management, asset classification, and provisioning. Technology has made tremendous impact in banking. '*Anywhere banking*' and '*Anytime banking*' have become a reality. The financial sector now operates in a more competitive environment than before and intermediates relatively large volume of international financial flows. In the wake of greater financial deregulation and global financial integration, the biggest challenge before the regulators is of avoiding instability in the financial system.

RISK MANAGEMENT AND BASEL II

The future of banking will undoubtedly rest on risk management dynamics. Only those banks that have efficient risk management system will survive in the market in the long run. The effective management of credit risk is a critical component of comprehensive risk management essential for long-term success of a banking institution.

Although capital serves the purpose of meeting unexpected losses, capital is not a substitute for inadequate decontrol or risk management systems. Coming years will witness banks striving to create sound internal control or risk management processes.

With the focus on regulation and risk management in the Basel II framework gaining prominence, the post-Basel II era will belong to the banks that manage their risks effectively. The banks with proper risk management systems would not only gain competitive advantage by way of lower regulatory capital charge, but would also add value to the shareholders and other stakeholders by properly pricing their services, adequate provisioning and maintaining a robust financial structure.

'The future belongs to bigger banks alone, as well as to those which have minimised their risks considerably.'

CONSOLIDATION

Consolidation, which has been on the counter over the last year or so, is likely to gather momentum in the coming years. Post April 2009, when the restrictions on operations of foreign banks will go, the banking landscape is expected to change dramatically. Foreign banks, which currently account for 5% of total deposits and 8% of total advances, are devising new business models to capture the Indian market. Their full-fledged entry is expected to transform the business of banking in many ways, which would be reflected in terms of greater breadth of products, depth in delivery channels and efficiency in operations.

Thus Indian banks have less than three years to consolidate their position. Despite the stiff resistance from certain segments, consolidation holds the key to future growth. This view is underpinned by the following:

- Owing to greater scale and size, consolidation can help save costs and improve operational efficiency.
- Banks will also have to explore different avenues for raising capital to meet norms under Basel-II
- Owing to the diversified operations and credit profiles of merging banks, consolidation is likely to serve as a risk-mitigation exercise as much as a growth engine.

Though there is no confirmation yet, speculative signals arising from the market point to the prospect of consolidation involving banks such as Union Bank of India, Bank of India, Bank of Baroda, Dena Bank, State Bank of Patiala, and Punjab and Sind Bank.

Further, the case for merger between stronger banks has also gained ground — a clear deviation from the past when only weak banks were thrust on stronger banks. There is a case being made for mergers between banks with a distinct geographical presence coming together to leverage their respective strengths.

GLOBALIZATION/ OVERSEAS EXPANSION

Growing integration of economies and the markets around the world is making global banking a reality. The surge in globalization of finance has already begun to gain momentum with the technological advancements which have effectively overcome the national borders in the financial services business. Widespread use of internet banking will widen frontiers of global banking, and make marketing of financial products and services on a global basis possible. In the coming years globalization will spread further on account of the likely opening up of financial services under WTO. India is one of the 104 signatories of Financial Services Agreement (FSA) of 1997. This gives India's financial sector including banks an opportunity to expand their business on a quid pro quo basis.

As per Indian Banks' Association report 'Banking Industry Vision 2010', there would be greater presence of international players in Indian financial system and some of the Indian banks would become global players in the coming years. So, the new mantra for Indian banks is to go global in search of new markets, customers and profits.

TECHNOLOGY

There is an imperative need for not mere technology upgradation but also its integration with the general way of functioning of banks to give them an edge in respect of services provided to their constituents, better housekeeping, optimizing the use of funds and building up of MIS for decision making, better management of assets & liabilities and the risks assumed which in turn have a direct impact on the balance sheets of banks as a whole. Technology has demonstrated potential to change methods of marketing, advertising, designing, pricing and distributing financial products and services and cost savings in the form of an electronic, self-service product delivery channel. These challenges call for a new, more dynamic, aggressive and challenging work culture to meet the demands of customer relationships, product differentiation, brand values, reputation, corporate governance and regulatory prescriptions. Technology holds the key to the future success of Indian Banks.

Internet, wireless technology and global straight-through processing have created a paradigm shift in the banking industry. The explosive growth of both the Internet and mobile and wireless technology is revolutionizing the way the financial industry conducts business. The overall wireless technology market is expected to grow profoundly in the coming years.

REGULATIONS

The RBI's approval for banks to raise funds abroad through innovative capital instruments holds great significance. Such fund-raising, which includes preference shares, will, however, not just substitute equity; it could have unintended consequences on the strategies of banks and their profitability. While the cost of raising monies through such instruments is likely to be higher (close to 10 per cent), the consequent higher leverage on equity funds is likely to result in expansion of return on net worth. This is because the same amount of capital supports a higher volume of business, generating higher profits.

Banks are likely to be able to raise long-term preference shares at coupon rates between six per cent and eight per cent. The positive impact on bank profitability could thus be significant.

Preference capital can be used as the currency for acquisition. The advantage for public sector banks is that they no longer need to bother about government stake falling below 51 per cent. Banks such as Dena Bank, Oriental Bank of Commerce and Andhra Bank are most likely to benefit from this move.

SKILLED MANPOWER

There will be a sea change for employees too. Secure jobs will be replaced by contractual appointments, for a specified period of time. The unions will merge into the shadows and bank managements will turn effective. As a result there will be swifter turn over of personnel in banks. But at the same time, skilled personnel from other disciplines will enter banks in increasing numbers. Factors like skills, attitudes and knowledge of the human capital play a crucial role in determining the competitiveness of the financial sector. The quality of human resources indicates the ability of banks to deliver value to customers. Capital and technology are replicable but not the human capital which needs to be valued as a highly valuable resource for achieving that competitive edge.

Business model, which comprises a comprehensive range of business solutions delivered through a unique balance of portfolio and relationship management must be incorporated.

FUTURE CHALLENGES & SUGGESTIONS

Challenges

- Competition
- Customer Retention
- Globalization
- Shrinking Margin

Suggestions

- Strong In-house research & market Intelligence
- Focused marketing- Focus on region-specific campaigns rather than national media campaigns

The growth of the retail financial services sector has been a key development on the market front. Indian banks (both public and private) will not only be keen to tap the domestic market but also to compete in the global market place. New foreign banks will be equally keen to gain a foothold in the Indian market.

FUTURE OF INTERNET BANKING

What will the future of Indian banking and insurance look like? Will the reform in banking and insurance sectors face the same fate as in power and telecom? It is increasingly evident that the economy offers opportunities but no security! Therefore, the future will belong to those who develop good internal controls, checks and balances and a sound market strategy. Business Growth, Cost Efficiency and Evolution are therefore regarded as key drivers which will have to be addressed.

It is by now well recognized that India is one of the fastest growing economies in the world after over a decade of financial and banking sector reforms since 1991. Evidence from across the world suggests that a sound and evolved banking system is required for sustained economic development. India has a better banking system in place vis-à-vis other developing countries, but there are several issues that need to be ironed out.

The course of banking evolution and growth has gone through innumerable twists and turns in the post independence era. Retail banking segment in the banking industry is continuously undergoing innovations, product reengineering, adjustments and alignments. Given the size advantages, diverse customer base and scope for future expansion, there is a need for evolving a systematic approach to retail banking.

Most of the Indian banks have been retail banks in their business composition. The term 'Retail Banking' encompasses various financial products (different types of deposit accounts, housing-consumer-auto and other types of loan accounts, demat facilities, insurance, mutual funds, Credit and Debit Cards, ATM and other technology-based services, stock-broking, payment of utility bills, reservation of railway tickets, etc.,) catering to diverse customer groups, offering a host of financial services, mostly to individuals. Simply speaking, it takes care of the diverse banking needs of an individual. The purpose if this paper is to try and identify the parameters on which the retail banking thrives and try to build insight into *the dynamics of the various parameters* and how they can pose a prospect or a problem in future.

The number of personal loan accounts with Scheduled Commercial Banks (SCBs) in India went up by almost 50 per cent between March 1997 and March 2002, as per CMIE data. Personal loan outstanding, however, went up by more than 130 per cent during the same period. The result was that the average personal loan outstanding increased from Rs. 24,668 in 1997 to Rs. 47,000 in 2002. Housing Loans, which accounted for about 28 per cent of personal loans outstanding in 1997, went up to 40 per cent in 2002. The following table gives a clear picture of the above:

Total personal loans outstanding increased from Rs. 28,000 crores in 1997 to more than Rs. 82,000 crores in 2002. On account of these personal loans, as distinct from loans to agriculture, trade, and industry, shot up from a little more than 20 per cent in 1997 to over 31.2 per cent in 2002. And that too over a period when total SCB outstandings shot up from Rs. 284,000 crore to Rs. Rs. 656,000 crores; an increase of more than 130 per cent. Data on Credit Cards are probably not included, given that there is no evidence that anyone, either in the RBI or in the Ministry of Finance, keeps track of credit cards. This, if true, is surprising news since credit cards account for a large and rapidly growing share of 'money supply', which RBI closely monitors in order to keep inflationary pressures in check.

RBI's Report on Trend and Progress of Banking in India, 2003-04 reveals some new trends in growth of credit. There is an upsurge in retail credit as against corporate advances, which may reveal itself in accumulating non-performing assets in banking sector and may accentuate the indebtedness of households in the medium term. However, with several counter-cyclical measures in place and a vigilant central bank , there is little need for alarm, as per Minna Kumar of Sify Finance in his study titled "Retail lending takes the lead" in November 2004.

Retail lending has been the key profit driver for banks in recent times with retail portfolio constituting 21.5 per cent of the total outstanding advances as on March 2004. On the other hand, stronger corporates strengthened their balance sheets by resorting to sizeable accruals as well as external commercial borrowings.

Current Scenario in Indian Retail Lending: Even though non-performing assets in the banking industry fell from 4.4 per cent in 2003 to 2.9 per cent in 2004, a hike in the percentage of retail lending may also pose a risk of poor asset quality of banks given that bad or 'impaired loans from from 2.5 per cent of total loans outstanding. Of the total retail loans, impaired housing loans constituted 1.9 per cent. The highest was in the consumer durable segment at 6.6 per cent. The retail segment's share in total loans for the period stood at 21.5 per cent, with housing loans constituting 48 per cent of the retail portfolio. The share of the housing loan portfolio out of total loan book of banks has grown from 3 per cent in 1993 to 7 per cent 2004. The following table gives details of Bank Credit to Retail Sector.

Nowadays, retail lending is the buzzword in banks in India. According to RBI's latest monetary policy, out of the total credit flow between April and

August 2004, two-thirds had gone to retail loans. Most banks have retail loans of around 20% of their total lending portfolio and these loans are growing at an unnatural rate of 30 to 35% per annum. Housing loans constitute around 50% of the retail lending portfolio. Despite the fact that the housing loans portfolio grew only at 42% in 2003-04 compared to 55% the previous year, one analyst said "Due to shortage of around 1.9 million housing units, demand for the housing loans may shoot up significantly in the near future".

However, the rate at which the banks are disbursing the housing loans etc., caused concern to the Reserve Bank of India as this might lead to increase of bad loans. In its latest Trend and Progress of Banking in India 2004, RBI mentioned "The rising proportion of retail loans in the total lending portfolio may impair the quality of assets in this segment, thus, increase in the NPAs". To avoid any such bubble in this segment, RBI has increased the risk weightage on Home Loans from 50 to 75% and for Consumer Loans including Personal Loans and Credit Cards, from 100 to 125%. Around 2.5% of the retail loans are bad debts as on March 31, 2004 while this average is at 7.4% for all types of loans. It is even less for Housing Loans at 1.9%, and the obvious conclusion is that Retail Loans are safer. But, to maintain this level of quality and avoid any kind of bubble in the making, banks should adopt sufficient risk management strategies. The following table gives more data on this aspect.

3. The Potential for Retail Banking in India:

An insight into the following paragraphs will justify the immense underlying potential for the Indian retail baking industry.

While the total outstanding retail loans in Taiwan is around *41% of its GDP*, the figure in India stands at *less than 5%*. The comparison with the West is even more staggering. Another situation that is natural when comparing retail sectors is the use of credit cards. Here also, the potential lies in the fact that of the consumer expenditure in India in 2001, *less than 1%* was through plastic, the corresponding US *figure standing at 18%*.

Hence, The Indian players are bullish on the retail business and this is not totally unfounded. *Two primary reasons are as follows*:

It is now undeniable that the face of the Indian consumer is changing. This is reflected adequately in a change in the urban household income pattern.

The direct fallout of such a change will be the consumption patterns and hence the banking habits of Indians, which will now be skewed towards Retail products.

a) Going by international standards, a large portion of the Indian population is simply not "bankable" - taking profitability into consideration. On the other hand, the financial services market is highly over-leveraged in India. Competition is fierce, particularly from local private banks such as HDFC Bank and ICICI Bank, in the business of home, car and consumer loans. There, precisely lie the pitfalls of such explosive growth. All banks are targeting the fluffiest segment i.e. the upwardly mobile urban salaried class. Although the players are spreading their operations into segments like self- employed and the semi-urban rich, it is an open secret that the big city Indian yuppies form the most profitable segment. Over-dependence on this segment is bound to bring in inflexibility in the business. Hence the challenge for various banks is to tap the underlying potential of the tapped and specifically the untapped market by developing sophisticated financial behaviour and spreading the scope to all over the country.

4. Prospects of Retail Banking in India:

The conventional scenario of Banks is fast changing. The Banking Institutions have started revisiting their Visions. Should they have thousands of C class Accounts or a few A and B class Accounts? They have come to the conclusion that it is not economical to service the C class Accounts. Even in India, banks are raising the bar on deposits. Some Banks have even increased the minimum balance in Savings accounts so that they are out of reach of the small man.

Why is this so? This is a natural corollary to the competencies that are being built up at a significant speed in all banks. Examining them one by one will help us know where the banks are heading, in the near future.

4 a. Customer Focus:

All along, the word "Customer" used to denote any person who is having an account with a branch of a Bank or using the services of a Branch. Now, we are seeing a new definition for customer. A customer is no more a customer of the Branch; he is the Customer of the BANK. With the advent of *'AAA Banking' (Anytime, Anywhere,*

Anyhow Banking) the new definition of customer has become relevant. Technology enables the customer to "help himself" through Internet Banking, ATM Banking, Telephone Banking, Online Banking, Mobile Banking, or e-Banking, etc. Moreover the concept like *Know Your Customer (KYC)* reinforced when Reserve Bank of India recently urged banks to improve customer focus as a strategic initiative for effective management of profitability, risk and customer satisfaction as well as customer delight!

4 b. Segment focus:

Banks are obviously for customer service. But banks are finding that they too need to segment and target High Networth Individuals (HNIs) and companies if they have to satisfy the needs of their stakeholders. Therefore, Banks are generally moving towards products that are focused on their targeted end customers. And this target is specifically the high end customers; as they do not find any leverage from the small accounts.

But there is a strong trend in terms of consolidation in terms of the business segmentation. The general pattern of the banks is to cater to all segments – from agriculturists to high net worth individual to corporate banking to international banking. An analysis of the current scenario indicates that in future, each bank will decide on its core competency and cater only to selected segments. For example, the Deutsche Bank in India operates only in the corporate banking and it has turned as a market leader in this segment.

4 c. Product focus:

Banks have been offering various asset products (Loans) and liability products (Deposits), taking the customers' general needs like fixed amount loans or running Cash Credit / Overdraft accounts or Fixed Deposit or Cumulative Deposit or Recurring Deposit as liability products.

Now, the time has come for the Customer to demand a product that is not currently available in the Banker's kitty and the Bank has to literally create customer-specific products. Here comes the Banker in the role of a Financial Engineer.

Financial Services: Then and Now

Old Economy	New Economy
Confined market place	Unlimited market space
Competition between banks	Competition from brands
Limited product line	Extensive product breadth
One-size-fits-all products	Customisation and innovation
Branch-focused	e-Enabled, multi-channel players
Focus on business growth	Focus on revenue growth as well as cost-reduction
Revenues through margin	Revenue generated through fees and value-added services

Existing products and services are changing way for value-added ones thanks to the one-upmanship game among competing banks, sparked off by soaring consumer-demands.

4 d. Technology focus:

As banks face the mutually interdependent forces of competition, regulation, technology, and customer expectations, a picturesque setting for the tremendous upheaval and opportunity emerges. This interdependency, in turn, is built upon mutually dependent technological trends.

- *Increase processing power*
- *Increase in networking*
- *Increase in flexibility in defining business standard:*
- *Increase in modularity of software*

These four trends are impacting irreversibly the business of banking, outsourcing, insourcing, analytics, and payment systems. Given these factors the banks are being more technology focused and driving the use of internet to help meet the requirements of their customers through segmentation.

(i) Internet banking:

The trend in banking is changing from computerization of branches to laying a uniform platform by having core banking solution in all the branches. At the same time, banks are looking at internet banking. While a start has been made in the Internet banking in India, the number of transactions through this mode is extremely negligible (less than 1%). A study group appointed by the RBI has suggested that for Internet banking, there should be robust system keeping a log of all network activities and analyzing the same. RBI has gone on to suggest various technical features essential for having such a robust system. This should be in place within the next 2 years. Hopefully, the retail banks will see a surge/splurge in the usage from 1% to at least 10% in the next couple of years. Passing of Information Technology Act, 2000 gave enough relief to the users assuring of proper use of technology in banking.

(ii) Shared ATMs

Till the year 2003, each bank was interested in opening its own ATMs to provide access and anytime banking to its customers. Cost of Installation of ATM is about Rs. 15 lacs with an additional maintenance cost of Rs.1.5 lacs per month. To break even, 300 transactions are to be put through each ATM per day. The cost of transaction in the branch of the Bank is approximately Rs. 60 while it is Rs. 10 if carried out through an ATM. To take advantage of this lower transaction cost, there is need for banks to induce customers to use more and more ATMs. In view of the huge investment cost of ATMs, Banks have now come to an understanding by which the customer of one Bank can use the ATMs of other Bank/s. This is in the right direction. Already SBI, HDFC Bank, ICICI Bank and others have started offering such a facility at a nominal payment per transaction, for which the customers are readily agreeable.

(iii) Outsourcing

The challenge of managing the diverse services in a networked environment has caused the banks to introspect on what should be considered as their core skills and primary roles.

In future, banks will need to focus on value-differentiating services by keeping in-house their competitive advantages while partnering with others who complement its services-making the argument for best-of-breed integration a necessity.

(iv) In sourcing

In sourcing is a model wherein banks perform operations that are originally done by their customers/other banks. Corporate clients may outsource activities like receivable management, accounting and risk management of corporate investments to banks. New product offerings will emerge as a combination of existing products and the new in sourced activities Banks, with their established processing capacities, are ideal partners for insurance and other financial service firms in their pursuit of customer reach and service provision.

(v) Analytics

As they realize that product and related services by themselves cannot provide sustainable competitive advantage, banks are paying more attention to relationship with their customers and the way they manage risk, determine price, and allocate capital.

Hence, going forward, banks will attempt to augment their behavioral and economic views of the customer, preferably captured at the "Point of Contact" in addition to existing transactional and demographic data (in-house and external). Banks will require use of analytics to effectively manage their customer relationships, conduct detailed analysis that help more accurately model, and predict future customer behaviour and lay a quantified foundation for strategic decision-making.

On the other hand, banks often face the tricky task of asset allocation and pricing. In the last decade, investments in risk management and related systems have increased multifold, albeit made with a compliance objective towards identifying, measuring and funding risk. The future will see increasing investments in risk analytics as part of an integrated framework supporting asset pricing, performance measurement, and asset allocation models.

(vi) Payment systems

In recent years, alternate money transmission avenues, especially the development of electronic money schemes, have been gaining currency. Gradual expansion of Western Union Money Transfer in India through alliances with

Banks, Post Offices, etc., is a thing to note in this direction. While electronic money has the potential to take over from cash for making small-value payments, making such transactions are becoming easier and cheaper for both consumers and merchants. This raises policy issues for central banks in its role as the guardian of the payment network and implementer of the monetary policy. The emergence of peer-to-peer money transmission mechanisms poses a challenge to current role of banks as gatekeepers to traditional payment systems. Robust payment systems, therefore, are a key requirement in maintaining and promoting financial stability with technology playing both a facilitating and disruptive role in them.

(vii) Real Time Gross Settlement (RTGS)

In the last one decade, thanks to continuous thrust on computerization in the banking system, RBI took initiative for bringing in Electronic Funds Transfer (EFT), Electronic Clearing System (ECS), ATMs and Internet Banking. Cross selling of various financial products has been possible due to ATMs and Internet Banking. Investment climate has also geared up in volumes with Dematerialisation facility introduced by setting up of NSDL and CDSL after formation of National Stock Exchange in Mumbai. Clearing Corporation of India Ltd., (CCIL) has also made remarkable impact on funds settlement mechanism. Very soon Cheque Truncation system is going to be spearheaded by RBI in a phased manner.

RTGS is a payment system in which processing and settlement takes place in real-time (continuously). In this system, funds would flow freely from one market to another leading to better integration of the Domestic Financial Markets among themselves, and with International Financial Markets as well. RTGS, as a settlement process will minimize settlement risks by settling individual payments in real time in the books of accounts held by the RBI. RTGS will be a mode for large value Inter-Bank settlement, to be widely used, for enhancing risk control measures, for faster and efficient settlement of liabilities for better customer services for the ultimate users in the value chain.

RTGS would eliminate the time lag between the debit to an account of customer and its corresponding credit to another customer in a different bank. RTGS requires implementation of a 2 Level Gateway- one at the individual bank level and the other at the RBI level. Significant contribution made by Institute for Development and Research in Banking Technology (IDRBT), Hyderabad in this regard is commendable.

4 e. Employee focus:

Earlier, there were premises where the branch of a Bank is located and there were three categories of staff to attend to the customers viz., Supervisory, Clerical and Sub-ordinate staff. With the disappearance of big ledgers and registers, the need for Sub-ordinate staff is also getting reduced.

The role of supervisory staff would increase and not in the sense of controlling the staff working with them but in different areas of delivering competitive services. Awareness about productivity, customer focus, competition, grievance/complaint redressals, market surveys, etc among the bank staff has gone up very high.

The VRS scheme introduced in the year 2000 by the Banks was to reduce the redundant staff consequent to computerization. It is felt that one more VRS would be needed for the Banks to shed their excess flab and make them fit and trim.

Henceforth, the role for clerical staff would have to undergo a change from sitting under the roof in a branch to moving into the field and market various financial services offered by their Bank and not only attract new customers and retain existing clientele but also retrieve the customers lost to competitors. In a nutshell the trend is towards sophisticated well trained customer orientation.

Banking Hours:

Bank hours were fixed so far. Now the fact is that almost all banks are moving towards any time/any where/home banking. Again, a closer look at this will reveal that Banks are moving away from the traditional customer to the customer who is extra busy. Who is this? Again, the high net worth individual and the highly profitable companies. For example ICICI bank has started 8 to 8 banking where the banking hours are 8 a.m. to 8 p.m. looking at this competitive market we may witness *24 hours banking*, very soon.

4 f. Others:

(i) The Basel II effect:

Essentially, the rules evolved by Basel Committee for Bank Supervision (BCBS) and adopted by RBI tell the banks how much capital the banks should have to cover up for the risk that their loans might go bad. The rules set out by Bank for International Settlements (BIS) in 1988 led the banks to differentiate among the customers it lent out money to. Different weightages were given to various forms of assets, with zero percentage weightings being given to cash, deposits with the central bank/govt etc, and 100 per cent weighting to claims on private sector, fixed assets, real estate etc. The summation of these assets gave us the risk-weighted assets. Against these risk weighted assets the banks had to maintain a (Tier I + Tier II) capital of 9 per cent i.e. every Rs100 of risk assets had to be backed by Rs 9 of Tier I + Tier II capital. To put it simply, the Indian banks had to maintain a Capital Adequacy Ratio (CAR) of 9 per cent as at present.

The problem with these rules is that they do not distinguish within a category i.e. all lending to private sector is assigned a 100 per cent risk weighting, be it a company with the best credit rating or company which is in the doldrums and has a very low credit rating. This is not an efficient use of capital. The company with the best credit rating is more likely to repay the loan vis-à-vis the company with a low credit rating. So the banks should be setting aside a far lesser amount of capital against the risk of a Company with the best credit rating defaulting vis-à-vis the company with a low credit rating.

With the rules being revised by BCBS and RBI, BASEL-II norms are to take place in the year 2007, the banks can decide on the amount of capital to set aside depending on the credit rating of the borrowing company.

Credit risk is not the only type that banks face in course of their business. These days, the operational risks that banks face are huge. The various risks that come under operational risk are competition risk, technology risk, casualty risk, crime risk etc. The original BASEL rules did not take into account the operational risks. Besides, there are other risks like Interest Rate Risk, Exchange Risk, etc. As per the BASEL-II norms, banks will have to set aside 15 per cent of net income to protect themselves against operational risks.

So to be ready for the new BASEL rules, the banks all over including in India will have to set aside more capital because the new rules could lead to Capital Adequacy Ratios of the banks falling.

How the banks plan to go about meeting these requirements is something that remains to be seen. A few banks are planning initial public offerings / share issues to have enough capital on their books to meet these new norms. Recent examples are Dena Bank, Punjab National Bank, SBI, Andhra Bank, ICICI Bank, etc.

(ii) Consolidation –the future wave

In the recent past, there has been a lot of talk about Indian Banks lacking in scale and size. The State Bank of India is the only bank from India to make it to the list of Top 100 banks, globally. Most of the PSBs are either looking to pick up a smaller bank or waiting to be picked up by a larger bank. The buzz word in banking circles these days is, in particular, consolidation (mergers) of Public Sector Banks for good although facing stiff resistance from various corners.

The central government also seems to be game about the issue and is seen to be encouraging PSBs to merge or acquire other banks. Global evidence seems to suggest that even though there is great enthusiasm when companies merge or get acquired, majority of the mergers/acquisitions do not really work. So in the zeal to merge with or acquire another bank, the PSBs should not let their common sense take a back seat. Before a merger is carried out cultural issues should be looked into.

A bank based primarily in North India might want to acquire a bank based primarily in South India to increase its geographical presence but their cultures might be very different. So the integration process might become very difficult. Technological compatibility both for software and hardware, besides trained work force, is another issue that needs to be looked into in detail, before any merger or acquisition is carried out.

The banks must not just merge because everybody around them is merging. As Keynes wrote," *Worldly wisdom teaches us that it's better for reputation to fail conventionally than succeed unconventionally*". Banks should avoid falling into this trap.

5. The Problems of Retail Banking in India:

Now, we shall try and look into the challenges that the banking sector in India faces:

5 a. Customer focus:

The retail banks in future will try to aggressively market their products. To market these products, there will be innovative modes to reach customers like SMS, internet, and mobile phones. Some banks are also engaging the services of Direct Selling Agents (DSAs), Franchisees, etc for sourcing and appraisal of loan proposals, issue of Credit Cards, selling of insurance and mutual fund products, etc.

Such methods may some times displease/disturb the customer. Moreover, banks generally pitch on higher levels of service but if the banks do not match up to what they have claimed, this may lead to *unsatisfied customers* and *higher customer attrition rate.*

5 b. Product focus:

The challenge here will be to design and innovate the financial products which cater to the target segment needs. In future, retail banking scenario will see a huge proliferation of products. This will in turn require devising product which is easy to understand and at the same time meet the financial goals of the customers. The problem that lies ahead is to gain a mindshare for one's product given a wide range of products.

5 c. Technology focus:

Technology in India has been in India for over seven years now. But its penetration in the Industry in general and that in the financial services market has been rather uninspiring despite its professed advantages. The surprising aspect that came out from the study was that though the banks were aware of the technology's benefits, they are skeptical about its applicability to their organization. The root cause for this is the astonishing growth that the banks are experiencing at the moment.

Most of the Retail banks are witnessing a tremendous expansion in their customer base: one bank even claim to be adding over 100% customer on y-on-y basis. However, on the other front there is increasing menace of hacking, phishing and farming through which scamsters are creating havoc indulging in cyber crimes on a large scale.

Apart from this, there are many other factors that have undermined the acceptance of Customer Relations Management (CRM). The chart shown below enlists the various factors (and their relative weightages on a scale of 1 to 5) that are believed to have played a role in the sluggish penetration of CRM in the retail-banking sector:

The above chart clearly shows that it is the implementation time that has affected the way people in banks look at CRM the most. In order to further CRM in this segment, it is of paramount importance to reduce the implementation time to minimum possible. This factor makes CRM on Demand (web based CRM services offered by service providers) a particularly attractive alternative. The second important parameter that came out from the study was the cost. To sum up, Indian retail banking players want *less risk and faster returns at lesser costs.*

Since, banks generally can't do with an investment that takes a long time to get running, implementation time figures as the top-most criteria closely followed by initial costs and training required.

5 d. Employee Focus:

In a service based industry the value can be delivered at the moment of interaction with the customers. It is vivid from the above chart that there needs to be focus on the employees and upgrading their skills as they at the front end would be the face of the bank. Hence, training requirement factor figures prominently in the case of banks due to the fact that these banks generally make do with just the required amount of manpower and it is very difficult for them to spare them. That will immediately start affecting their operations.

Banks, in a drive to carry on with tremendous expansion in terms of customer base, need to have requirements of the employees who are well informed about the products as well as have the necessary soft skills to deal and satisfy the customers. In future there may be a problem of getting manpower or in specifics customer care executives with enhanced skills, knowledge and attitude. Hence, it challenges for the bank to *upgrade their existing manpower* and *retain* or lock in the best talents for having competitive edge in terms of human resources.

5 e. Others:

(i) Interest Rate Risk

Interest rate risk can be defined as exposure of bank's net interest income to adverse movements in interest rates. A bank's balance sheet consists mainly of rupee assets and liabilities. Any movement in domestic interest rate is the main source of interest rate risk.

Over the last few years the treasury departments of banks have been responsible for a substantial part of profits made by banks. Between July 1997 and Oct 2003, as interest rates fell, the yield on 10-year government bonds (a barometer for domestic interest rates) fell, from 13 per cent to 4.9 per cent. This will make it difficult to show huge profits from treasury operations. This concern becomes much stronger because a substantial percentage of bank deposits remain invested in government bonds.

Banking in the recent years had been reduced to a trading operation in government securities. Recent months have shown a rise in the bond yields which has led to the profit from treasury operations falling. The latest quarterly reports of banks clearly show several banks incurring losses on their treasury operations. If the rise in yields continues, the banks might end up posting huge losses on their trading books. Given these facts, *banks will have to look at alternative sources of investment.*

(ii) Non-Performing Assets

The best indicator of the health of the banking industry in a country is its low level of NPAs. Given this fact, Indian banks seem to be better placed than they were in the past. A few banks have even managed to reduce their net NPAs to less than one percent (before the merger of Global Trust Bank into Oriental Bank of Commerce, OBC was a zero NPA bank). But as the bond yields start to rise, the chances are the net NPAs will also start to go up. This will happen because the banks have been making huge provisions against the money they made on their bond portfolios in a scenario where bond yields were falling.

Reduced NPAs generally gives the impression that banks have strengthened their credit appraisal processes over the years. This does not seem to be the case. With increasing bond yields, treasury income will come down and if the banks wish to make large provisions, the money will have to come from their interest income, and this in turn, shall bring down the profitability of banks.

The shaping up of newly formed Credit Information Bureau of India Ltd., (CIBIL) is much desired in the years to come so that entire MIS of banks depositors and borrowers is available on line. Credit decisions will be quicker, efficient and of quality both in respect of individuals and institutions.

(iii) Competition

The entry of new generation private sector banks during mid-1990s has changed the entire scenario. Earlier the household savings went into banks and the banks then lent money to corporates. Now they need to sell banking. The retail segment, which was earlier ignored, is now the most important of the lot, with the banks jumping over one another to give out retail loans. The consumer has never been so lucky with so many banks offering so many products to choose from with varying terms and conditions, rates of interest, etc. With supply far exceeding demand it has been a race to the bottom, with the banks undercutting one another. A lot of foreign banks have already burnt their fingers in the retail game and have now decided to get out of a few retail segments completely. Notable examples are Bank Paribas and Oman International Bank in India.

The nimble footed new generation private sector banks have taken a lead on this front and the public sector banks are trying to catch up. The PSBs have been losing business to the private sector banks in this segment. PSBs need to figure out the means to generate profitable business from this segment in the days to come.

6. Conclusion:

Over the last few years, the falling interest rates gave banks very little incentive to lend to projects, as the return did not compensate them for the risk involved. This and a host of other technological, legal, financial, structural changes/developments led to the banks getting into the retail segment in a big way. It also led to a lot of banks playing it safe and putting in most of the deposits they collected into government bonds. Now, with the bond party over and the bond yields starting to go up, the banks will have to concentrate on their core function of lending with reasonable spreads and safety of funds.

Furthermore, the banking sector in India needs to tackle these challenges successfully to keep growing and strengthen the Indian financial system. Moreover the interference of the central government with the functioning of PSBs should stop. A fresh autonomy package for public sector banks has been announced recently. The package seeks to provide a high degree of freedom to PSBs on operational matters. This seems to be the right way to go for PSBs function in a professional manner and face stiff competition from Private and Foreign players. Productivity, Profitability and Pricing of products are at the top of the priority list of the banking system today.

With the economy experiencing respectable growth rates at around 7 – 8 per cent, it is incumbent on the part of the banks to fall in line to offer best quality services to their customers. Retail Banking deals with the lives of a vast majority of the population in the age bracket between 25 and 60 years with disposable incomes. Regulators and Policy makers shall take on their responsibility of facilitating the banks discharge their responsibilities in an efficient manner. Problems enumerated above are not surmountable. The growth of the banking sector will be one of the most important inputs that shall go into making sure that India progresses and becomes a global economic super power.

7

ROLE OF TECHNOLOGY

INTRODUCTION

Technology is also helping market players redefine the way they have been operating in the market. See, today, banks are taking ATM machines to the customers, Availability of the concepts like phone banking, anytime banking etc. has become possible because of the technological developments only.

Strategic alliances between the market participants across the segments is quite apparent in the market. You may see a real estate products provider having alliance with both banks for the financing and insurance companies for the risk management products, for his customers. The goods dealers are providing both the finances and insurance to their customers. The case in example is airline's tickets having insurance embedded in it. Latest and very interesting phenomenon is that Holiday Inn is building a hotel in Texas, wherein entry to the room will be through the credit card. absolutely hassle free check in and check out.

TECHNOLOGY IS REVAMPING INDUSTRIAL STRUCTURE FOR FINANCIAL SERVICES

- Entry of new specialized financial service providers --from direct product providers to so called aggregators
- Entry of non-bank entities (telecoms/utilities)

- Consolidation around recognized brand names
- Emergence of mixed financial and non financial conglomerates
- Globalization of markets and trading systems

TECHNOLOGY: CHANGING FINANCIAL SERVICE PROVISION

Massive cost reductions in technology and communications cost

In particular, the internet :

- reduces processing and labor costs
- allows for new distribution channel
- allows for better and more cost effective

Customer stratification and personalized pricing:

- permits unbundling of financial products and commoditization
- lowers barriers to entry

TECHNOLOGY IS CHANGING THE COMPETITIVE LANDSCAPE

Online Services

The clear trend is movement towards virtual transactions rather than physical. The Internet has impacted the financial services industry in a major way. Today many new players - traditionally in non-finance - are getting into the field and leveraging the World Wide Web. Further, delivery channels of financial services have proliferated and this has resulted in increased customer expectations.

The percentage of credit originating on the Net is increasing. Today a borrower has the power to choose his lender sitting in his premises unlike earlier days when he had to approach a bank manager in person. The emerging trend is electronic bill presentment payment (EBPP) whereby the bank or financial services provider captures various bills - utilities, insurance etc - online and waits for online authorisation from the accountholder to pay the same. Here the consumer does not get a physical bill as it is happening now. Everything is in electronic format. Apart from the comforts offered to the consumer, EBPP results in huge cost savings for the service providers and some utilities in the US actually offer an incentive for switching over to the electronic mode of bill payment. Account aggregation is yet another new trend that is becoming popular among foreign banks. Under this, a bank customer can transact or visit his favourite sites by just logging on to his bank's portal.

BILL PAYMENT

Internet Banking is the most convenient channel to manage and pay your bills anytime. For example, ICICI Bank has tied up with more than 60 organizations across the country to facilitate payment of bills for Utility Companies (Electricity and Telephone) Bills, ICICI Bank credit card, Mobile Phone and Insurance Premium bills.

SHOPPING

Banks have tied up with various organizations to facilitate online shopping for all its Internet Banking Customers.

TICKET BOOKING

Banks provide facility of online railway/air ticket booking, mobile phone recharging, etc.

CARD TO CARD FUNDS TRANSFER

Card to Card Funds Transfer allows to transfer money from your Bank account to any other Visa Debit or Credit Card, anytime, anywhere in India.

COMMUNITY BANKING SERVICES

To Donate, Volunteer, Shop for crafts produced by rural artisans. For instance ICICI has tie-ups with charity organizations like The Cause, GiveIndia, I Volunteer, Infochange.

SHARE TRADING

Banking products now allow investment in Shares, Mutual funds, Derivatives (Futures and Options) and other financial products via cash trading, margin trading, spot trading.

FINANCIAL SERVICES BY BANKS IN RURAL SECTOR

In a phase in the international development endeavour in which ideology is out of fashion, the search is on for practical, workable solutions to the deep-seated challenges of poverty. Micro-credit seems to provide just such a solution.

By delivering financial services at a scale, and by mechanisms, appropriate to poor people, micro-credit can reach them. By providing poor people with credit for microenterprise it can help them work their own way out of poverty. And by providing loans rather than grants the micro-credit provider can become sustainable by recycling resources over and over again. In other words microcredit appears to deliver the 'holy trinity' of outreach, impact and sustainability.

The micro-credit industry has sought to resolve the tensions between a focus on poverty and a commitment to sustainability by integrating them within a matrix defined by two axes, of outreach (or access) and financial sustainability.

The formal financial sector may achieve financial sustainability, but has little outreach to poor clients (quadrant 2). Traditional efforts by non-governmental organizations (NGOs) may reach poor clients, but are often unsustainable (quadrant 4). Good micro-finance practice, on the other hand, combines both outreach and sustainability in the virtuous quadrant 1. Such practice is perhaps most clearly embodied in the micro-finance bank, which marries the best of the formal financial sector in terms of sustainability with the outreach to poor clients of the development NGO.

MICRO FINANCIAL SERVICES INCLUDE FOUR CLASSES OF SERVICES:

1. BASIC BANKING SERVICES: Basic banking services that include savings and withdrawal facilities meet the demand for liquidity whether it be for enterprise purposes or for emergencies. The availability of savings products,the design of which takes into account the cash flows of the poor, would be very crucial to the effective mobilisation of savings. There is also a need to innovate for micro-investment products that enable the poor to maximise returns on their surplus.

2. INSURANCE INCLUDING LIFE, DISABILITY, HEALTH AND ASSETS: The vulnerability of the poor points to insurance being a crucial product.

Existing ways of informal insurance among the poor are: drawing down on savings, reciprocal need-based gift exchange, selling physical assets and diversifying income sources. However, there is only a limited role that these informal mechanisms can play. There is a need for a mechanism to pool, price and trade the risks of the poor and the means to do this would be an insurance product that is able to bring under its fold the poor with varying risk profiles.

3. FINANCE INCLUDING CREDIT, EQUITY AND LEASING: This class of products has great relevance to the promotion of micro-enterprises. Even when these services do not benefit the poorest of the poor directly, they may provide benefits to them through the promotion of economic activity and employment. Equity is an important means of sharing the risk of enterprising poor to engage in ventures with the possibility of high returns.

4. DERIVATIVES: Derivatives are instruments the value of which is derived from the value of an underlying asset. Derivatives enable a buyer and a seller to enter into a contract in the present period to buy/sell at a future date at a pre-determined rate. The principles of a derivative contract appear to have relevance in the context of commodity markets and indices based on weather and other variables that have a bearing on the livelihoods of the poor.

CASE STUDY : ICICI BANK- MICROFINANCE MODEL

UBIQUITY AND LOW COST OUTREACH

1. Shared Services Point of Transaction at the village level
    a. Combining financial and non-financial services
    b. Local partner is either an entrepreneur or an agricultural input service provider
2. Driving down costs of intermediation
    a. Low-cost ATM, use of cards to replace cash
3. The kiosk pilot

a. Through rural internet kiosks in S. India

b. Offer internet banking, investment, remittances, sale of gold coins and insurance products.

EXPANDING THE RANGE OF FINANCIAL SERVICES

1. Aim to provide "complete" market.
2. Weather Insurance a. Launched India's first index based rainfall insurance product which compensates the farmer for loss in yield due to deficient rainfall.
3. Health Insurance.
4. Remittance

   a. Domestic fund transfer facility between urban centers and villages especially to cater to the migrant population.

5. Commodity Derivatives

   a. Enable price discovery and hedging against price risks by small farmers through participation in commodity exchanges with NGO/ MFIs serving as aggregators.

New Products for MFIs and NGOs

1. PARTNERSHIP MODEL

   a. Partner (NGO/MFI) engages in promotional role while ICICI Bank meets the financial needs of the borrowers.

   b. Partner shares the credit risk and is incentivised for good performance of the clients.

2. SECURITISATION

   MFI assigns existing micro-finance receivables to ICICI.

   MFI provides a credit enhancement to ICICI.

   MFI continues to service the portfolio and thus maintain relationships with the clients.

3. ON-TAP SECURITISATION

   ICICI provides advance purchase consideration to

MFI for building portfolio

MFI assigns receivables to ICICI.

MFI provides a credit enhancement to ICICI and collects receivables.

MFI continues to build further portfolio and assign to ICICI.

REGULATION OF FINANCIAL SERVICES

On regulators side, deeper co-ordination has become a respectable word. Creation of the Financial Services Authority by merger of all the regulators in the economy in U.K. has set a precedent in itself. Now, a number of countries, across the globe, are thinking on these lines. Recently, Germany has joined the U.K. through creation of the Financial Services Supervisor, a combined regulatory authority for the banking, securities and insurance. Logic is simple - integration of the opportunities zone demands a flexible, efficient and effective supervisory regime. This can be accomplished either through the effective coordination among the regulators or the creation of single regulatory body. Some economies are choosing the first and some second. Further, financial innovation is becoming ubiquitous. Availability of the financial products, linked to the temperature, earthquake, snow fall, rain fall, hailstorm and what not communicates that there is a huge room for creativity in this area. Today, anything and everything is being traded in the market.

LATEST NEW PRODUCTS BY BANKS NETSAFE FROM HDFC BANK

NetSafe eliminates the need for disclosing the card number while making credit /debit card payments for online shopping and virtually eliminates the risk of cyber fraud. It also saves cardholders from exposing their credit limits or account balances to potential cyber criminals lurking in the anonymity of the web.

To shop online, existing HDFC Bank cardholders can create a virtual card on their existing debit or credit card with a pre-defined limit, valid only for a short time or a single transaction after which the card ceases to exist.

For example, if a customer wishes to buy something from a particular site worth Rs 500, she can create her own NetSafe card where she is allotted a single use card number with a limit of just Rs 500 which is debited to her credit or debit card. In the event that the customer fails to use NetSafe within 24 hours of creating the card, the card simply disappears and the credit limit or amount in account is reverted back to the customer's credit / debit card.

HOW TO REGISTER FOR NETSAFE

* The customer clicks on Register for NetSafe on the home page.
* After agreeing to the terms and conditions, the user is prompted to enter the Debit or Credit Card Number, ATM PIN, and expiry date to identify him.
* Once the customer identity is verified, the customer is directed to the NetSafe enrollment screen to input a few details for enrollment.
* A confirmatory email is sent automatically to the email address given by the customer. The mail content will include the login ID given by the customer.

Even among the young working class the are averse to use credit cards and do feel restricted in using their debt card for transactions over the internet. This gap could be exploited by making a product available like NetSafe.

SBI CARD IN MARCH 2005, LAUNCHED A CREDIT CARD, SBI SOCIAL CARD, THE FIRST AFFINITY CARD in the country to feature four non-governmental organizations (NGOs).

The social card allows the cardholder to donate to the NGOs every time they use it. The card will earn the customers double reward points.

While one half will go to the NGOs. SBI Card will donate 20 per cent of the annual fees or renewal fees to the NGOs. Moreover, customers also have the option to issue standing instructions for a fixed amount to be donated to any of the NGOs.

The non-governmental organisations that have the tie-up with SBI Card are Cancer Patients Aid Association, National Association for the Blind, SOS Children's Villages of India and World Wildlife Fund, India.

NATIONAL SECURITIES DEPOSITORY LTD (NSDL) AND IDBI BANK HAVE LAUNCHED COUNTRY'S FIRST ONLINE DIRECT TAX PAYMENT FACILITY. This facility will enable individuals as well as corporate tax payers, to make payments for income tax, corporation tax, gift tax, tax deducted at source (TDS) etc over internet.

The details entered by the assessee would be validated by NSDL and control would be passed to IDBI bank through a secure payment gateway. The bank will debit the customer account after authentication and completes the payment of tax to the government as an agency bank for which it will be paid a service charge.

IDBI bank also plans to migrate this facility to other channels like mobile phones and ATMs. State Bank of India (SBI), Corporation Bank, Punjab National Bank and Bank of India are expected to soon roll out online direct tax payment facility.

FINANCIAL SERVICES IN RURAL AREAS

1. Kiosk operators to Collect cash from villager and pay
2. Online, the Govt. payments, Telephone bills.
3. Kiosk operator to be an agent for agri-crop loans, Rural Insurance, Health and Crop
4. Rural low cost ATMs at kiosks Works along with the PC already existing with breakthrough pricing envisaged of $ 1000

OUTSOURCING OF FINANCIAL SERVICES

Financial firms have entered into outsourcing arrangements for many years, albeit not to the extent seen in the recent past.

For example, in the securities industry, since the 1970s, firms have outsourced quasi-clerical activity, such as the printing and storage of records. This was undertaken because of the comparative cost savings.

As technology has evolved, outsourcing of information services has become more common.

In the 1980s and 1990s, such deals tended to be large scale and often involved the outsourcing of whole IT divisions primarily based on cost and the importance of remaining up to date with rapidly evolving technology.

GLOBALIZATION OF THE FINANCIAL SERVICES INDUSTRY

- Globalization and technology are fundamentally changing the financial services industry worldwide
- Competition has accelerated and is fierce for "best credits"/corporates in most countries
- New competitors have entered the market
- Margins and fees are narrowing significantly
- Development of securities markets is disintermediating banks

BROAD RANGE OF FINANCIAL SERVICES OFFERED

With time we have seen the changing face of Indian banking which has increased the range of services offered by banks in areas of :

- Mutual Funds
- Insurance
- Debit / Credit Cards
- Retail Loans
- Securitization
- Venture Capital Finance
- Infrastructure Finance
- Financing Export Services
- Financing Social Projects
- Export Credit and Guarantee Services
- IT Enabled Financial Services
- Outsourcing of Financial Services

The Problem of Limited Access to Financial Services and Stable Incomes in Rural India

For the rural poor in India, formal financial services would enable them to maximize returns on their surplus, smooth their consumption, and reduce their vulnerability to risk. However, their financial service needs-which include consumption credit and cash savings are seldom met due to systemic problems in the financial sector and monsoon risk.

Indian banks seek to expand their crop lending to non-irrigated areas but are constrained by monsoon risk. One way to blend index insurance and rural finance is to integrate weather index insurance into loans taken by the farmers.

The objective of the pilot scheme proposed by the World Bank and its partners is to insure farmers against drought risk and allow for continued borrowing and savings throughout drought years. The savings portion of the scheme enables farmers to build collateral, which improves their access to credit and lower interest rates. Eventually the scheme seeks to improve the farmers' creditworthiness to a level where creditors would provide access to consumer credit. The incremental transaction costs are minimized by using smart cards and by packaging the crop loans and risk management with agricultural extension services and crop marketing. The weather index insurance is not a self-standing insurance product, but it is embedded in the loan agreement and then combined with a (forced) savings account.

This scheme can significantly increase access to crop loans and savings mechanisms in rural areas, particularly in rainfed areas.3 Farmers relying on rainfed agriculture in particular do not have access to formal crop finance, because banks perceive the risks as too high for the type of (capped and regulated) interest rate they can charge. Weather risk and moral hazard can tend to be higher for the rainfed farmer.

In the case of monsoon-related crop failure, a culture of low payment morale sets in as the crop failure and resulting default on debts are seen as force majeure. In addition, political pressures for debt forgiveness tend to rise in drought years. This proposed scheme seeks to transfer systemic risk out of the farmer-bank relationship into insurance markets. It can lower the moral hazard problem by removing any excuse for non-repayment in case of monsoon-related crop failure.

The design has four components:

1. monsoon index insurance;
2. a risk management account;

3. weather risk reinsurance; and
4. a smart card

Monsoon Index Insurance

The essential principle of monsoon index insurance is that contracts are written against specific rainfall outcomes (e.g. drought or flood) recorded at a local weather station.

Risk Management Account

The purpose of this component is income stabilization, it is the risk management part based on farmer's individual decisions. The farmer pays half of the overall insurance premium into a risk management account, effectively serving as selfinsurance.

Weather Risk Reinsurance

The monsoon index insurance provider reinsures most of the risk in national and international weather risk markets through traditional excess of loss or quota share treaties. This allows for the global pooling of risk and thereby more competitive "portfolio-adjusted" pricing for the insurer and ultimately for the farmer.

Smart Card

The farmer can access his risk management account through a Smart Card. Initially the card serves as a debit card in agricultural service center hubs, certain points of sale, and at ATMs. Eventually it can be upgraded to a credit card.

Miscellaneous Rural Banking Services

Weather Derivatives

Monsoon derivatives can be a market instrument that can enable them to hedge against an "excess" of rainfall or a "dearth" of the amount of rainfall received in a region over a fixed period of time. The derivative will derive value as a multiple in rupees of the difference in the level of rainfall that fell over a period of time.

Since these contracts can be traded and settled on a national exchange, farmers can hedge their earnings against a "good" or a "bad" monsoon. Different climatic regions of the country can have different rainfall indexes. This can permit farmers in regions which had good rainfall to compensate farmers that received bad rainfall. This can be a market instrument for insuring against the monsoon risk!

ICICI Bank is working in conjunction with ICICI Lombard, the ICICI Group's insurance company, to propose a few pilot cases of indexing interest payments to rainfall measures. The borrower pays a higher interest rate in normal years that comprises the weather index insurance premium, but in case of a severe rainfall deficit and in one case excessive rainfall in critical periods the borrower pays little or no interest on the loan.

A ShubhLabh office starts by "identifying" a set of farmers with good credit history. The farmers sign on for their services for a "consulting" fee: this covers consulting on farming practices, crop advice, sourcing of inputs, pickup of produce, delivery to the final buyer.

The ShubhLabh interfaces with ICICIBank for the financing wrt the fertiliser and seeds firm, as well as for the delivery of produce to the end buyer and payment to the farmer. Offices submit a database of the farmers and their performance on delivery of the produce which is maintained as a database at ShubhLabh.

In the ICICI Bank Farmer Service Center operating model with Mahindra Shubhlabh, (figure 4) ICICI identified an integrated agricultural services provider (IASP) that has a good relationship with the farmer and provides genuine and timely information through extension services. ICICI enters into a tripartite agreement with the IASP and the output buyer. ICICI provides credit to the farmers on the recommendation of the IASP, the farmer pledges its produce to the output buyer, and the IASP provides inputs to the farmer.

Loan processing, disbursement and collection are effectively done by the IASP, while the credit decision remains nominally with ICICI Bank. At the end of the season, the farmers supply the crop to the output buyer and the output buyer deducts the loan amount from the sale proceeds and remits the loan to ICICI Bank in full settlement of the loan amount. The IASP receives a service fee for the loan processing and supervision services (1.5 percent on recovered loans). Currently 45 Shubhlabh offices operate on a franchise basis, financing around 4,000 farmers.

CONCLUSION

Emergence of the areas like credit derivatives, real options, securitizations is paving an entirely fresh set of opportunities for the market. There is a huge room for the structured and synthetic products in the Indian market. The market is in for an exciting phase in terms of the financial innovations. Today, investors are perceived as not just as the investors but buyers of the financial solutions.

Therefore, the philosophy of customer being king is driving the financial markets as well. Accordingly, it is no more customers chasing the products; it is the appropriateness of options chasing the customers. Today, financial institutions are co-designing the products/services with their customers and striving to provide them with global solutions.

8

Domain Name Selection and Registration

INTRODUCTION

Banks should ensure their domain name is registered to them, under their control, and clearly communicated to their customers. In order to avoid customer confusion, banks should consider registering similar domain names. When another entity holds the registration to a similar domain name, banks should consider the risk of customer confusion between the two names.

Where the risk of confusion is unacceptably high, the bank can take actions such as increasing customer education efforts, selecting a different domain name, or seeking to acquire the similar domain name from its owner.

The bank also can dispute the use of the other domain name under the terms of the domain name license agreement. Under those terms, registered domain name owners are required to abide by the policy located at http://www.domainmagistrate.com/dispute-policy.html.

In general, the dispute policy provides for a mandatory administrative proceeding when a domain name is identical, confusing, or similar to trademarks or service marks; is registered to someone with no legal right or legitimate interest in the domain name; or is used in bad faith. For this reason, banks should consider establishing a trademark for their domain names. The bank also may be able to initiate immediate action in federal district court under the recently enacted Anticybersquatting Consumer Protection Act, 15 USC 1125 (d). In the event the similar domain name remains registered to someone other than the bank, the bank should consider surveying the domain periodically to ensure that the use of the domain does not pose an unacceptable risk to the bank or its customers.

CONTROLLING CHANGES TO DOMAIN NAME REGISTRATION

Domain name registration authorities will change registration information upon request. An unauthorized change to the bank's registration information, however, could result in the loss of a bank's on-line identity and a misdirection of its customer communications. To limit the risk of unauthorized changes, banks can select a method of communicating with their domain name registration authority that ensures an adequate degree of authentication. In addition, banks should consider establishing internal procedures to ensure that bank communications with the registration services are authorized.

PROTECTING AGAINST DOMAIN NAME SERVER INTRUSIONS

An intrusion into a domain name server can result in a bank losing its on-line identity, even if a bank carefully selects and protects its domain names. Banks should protect against domain name server intrusions using the guidance provided in the OCC Bulletin 2000-14 "Infrastructure Threats — Intrusion Risks" (May 15, 2000).

SUSPICIOUS ACTIVITY REPORTING

Banks that become aware of identity theft or similar crimes perpetrated in conjunction with the use of similar domain names, unauthorized changes to domain name registrations, or other actions should file a Suspicious Activity Report in accordance with Regulation 12 CFR 21.11 and the instructions of the Suspicious Activity Report form.

Electronic Record Keeping

Federal legislation changed the legal framework for electronic records and will likely result in more banks adopting electronic record retention systems.

Banks can implement electronic record retention systems in many ways to support different business processes.

Some examples of possible electronic record retention systems are loan file imaging, retention of paperless applications and online agreements, and the use of electronic payment systems.

Under the E-SIGN Act (the "Act"), which became effective March 1, 2001, an electronic record can satisfy most legal record retention requirements for contracts or other records (including requirements that a record must be retained in its original form) provided that the electronic record is

- retained in a form that accurately reflects the information in the contract or other record,
- accessible to all persons who are entitled to access the information for the period of time required by law, and
- in a form that allows it to be accurately reproduced for later reference by transmission, printing or otherwise.

An electronic record that meets all of the above general standards will satisfy a legal requirement that a contract or other record (such as a consumer disclosure) must be retained in writing.

However, as discussed below, the general standards under the Act need further development and interpretation before they can be applied with assurance. Moreover, the Act does not resolve all legal or practical issues relating to electronic records to ensure that the records can fulfill their intended purposes and will comply with applicable regulatory requirements other than retention. For example, the Act does not ensure admissibility of electronic records in litigation.

This is important because the practical effect of having electronic records that are not admissible into evidence in judicial proceedings may be to render the electronic contract or record effectively unenforceable. While banks are permitted under E-SIGN to satisfy record retention requirements with electronic record retention systems that comply with the Act, banks will need to carefully plan their implementation and operation of these electronic record retention systems to ensure they meet functional and regulatory requirements.

FUNCTIONAL AND REGULATORY CONSIDERATIONS

The Act does not provide specific definitions for its general, minimum standards of accuracy, integrity, or accessibility. Nevertheless, banks adopting electronic record retention systems should understand and consider the risks resulting from inadequate record retention practices and systems. The failure of banks to maintain adequate record retention systems can create significant reputation, transaction, credit, and compliance risks. Also, the risks and necessary controls associated with different types of electronic record retention systems will vary according to the specific records that are in a particular system and the sensitivity and criticality of those records to the bank or its customers.

Despite the absence of specificity in the Act's standards, an electronic record system of a national bank must have sufficient accuracy, accessibility, and integrity to achieve and accomplish all essential functions and purposes that pertain to the *specific* records that are contained within that particular system. Likewise, the system must have the accuracy, accessibility, integrity, and other attributes needed to comply with regulatory requirements applicable to those specific records. Until more specific standards are developed, banks should design, implement, and operate their electronic records systems so that they are adequate to serve the following purposes and functions according to the nature of the retained records:

- Potential use in litigation support,
- Internal and external audits and controls,
- Bank supervision, and
- Compliance with regulatory requirements.

Each is discussed in greater detail below.

Records needed for litigation

Records that the bank may need to produce or to introduce into evidence in litigation should receive special attention. Without adequate and admissible records, the bank will be unable to enforce its rights and to protect itself against claims in litigation. Thus, if records that support loan or investment transactions are inadmissible, the bank may face credit, transaction, and market risk. Under the "Interagency Guidelines and Standards for Safety and Soundness," Appendix A of 12 CFR Part 30, it is an unsafe and unsound practice if the bank fails to maintain loan documentation that, among other things, ensures that the bank's claims against its borrowers are legally enforceable. Bank management should consult with legal counsel to ensure that electronic record retention systems containing records that the bank may need in litigation are sufficient to ensure admissibility in relevant courts. If an electronic record cannot be admitted into evidence, it is useless in litigation even though it formally satisfies federal record retention requirements.

The Act does not provide any assured standards for admissibility of electronic records. The courts continue to develop precedent on the admissibility of electronic records. However, each new record-retention technology raises issues that must be addressed before the legal uncertainties of record retention systems based on the technology are resolved. Moreover, the standards for admissibility of electronic records can vary from state to state. The standards developed in one state are not binding in another. This lack of uniformity can pose a significant challenge to a bank that wants to establish a single electronic record retention system and is doing business in more than one state. Electronic documents with electronic signatures may pose special retention challenges to ensure their admissibility. National banks should also understand that digital copies of physical documents signed with original manual signatures may face challenges as to authenticity and admissibility if the actual original signature is no longer available.

Records Needed for Internal and External Audits and Controls

Adequate electronic record systems with sufficient accuracy, integrity, and accessibility are also necessary to support controls like internal and external audits. Bank management should consult with internal and external auditors to ensure that electronic record retention systems containing records that the bank may need for such audits are sufficient to support the auditing and control functions. For example, an electronic record retention system with poor integrity due to weak access controls could be subject to falsification and manipulation by insiders seeking to prevent detection of their malfeasance. For this reason, the "Guidelines and Interagency Standards for Safety and Soundness" implicitly require that there be a record retention system (whether paper or electronic) that is adequate to support an appropriate internal auditing system.

Records Needed for Bank Supervision

The ability of the OCC to supervise national banks is dependent upon access to adequate and accurate records. Thus, a national bank that has digitized its records must maintain electronic records that provide OCC staff with prompt and sufficient access to reliable information to permit adequate examination and supervision. 12 USC 481. Moreover, a national bank with electronic record retention systems should maintain records sufficiently complete and accurate to enable the OCC to determine its financial condition and the substance and purpose of transactions that may have a material effect on its financial condition. 12 USC 1818(c)(3). National banks should ensure that any bank electronic record retention system they adopt permits access to electronic records by all persons entitled to access by law. Among other things, the bank should maintain the necessary equipment and software to enable timely OCC access to bank records.

Records Needed to Comply with Laws and Regulations

Inadequate record retention systems may result in compliance violations. Federal rules contain many record retention requirements pertaining to consumer protection (for example, Regulations B, Z, DD), securities activities (for example, 12 CFR 12.3 and 12.4), and Bank Secrecy Act (BSA) compliance (for example, 31 CFR 103.29 and 103.32). Most of these retention laws and regulations do not provide clear instructions on the use of electronic technology or records. If a bank adopts an electronic record retention system to contain records subject to these consumer protection and BSA laws, bank management should ensure that the system is designed and operated so that electronic records will comply with the specific requirements of the applicable laws. For example, electronic record retention systems with unreliable scanning or image capture technology could result in inferior or missing records that would not comply with retention requirements and may subject the bank to regulatory enforcement actions. Moreover, the system must also enable the bank to retrieve and produce records within required timeframes. *See,* for example, 31 USC 5318(k)(2)(which provides that a bank has 120 hours to produce records concerning accounts opened, maintained, administered, or managed in the United States.

INTERNET BANKING EXAMINATION PROCEDURES

General Procedures

The objective of these examination procedures is to determine the adequacy of the institution's policies, procedures, and internal controls as they relate to Internet banking. The extent of testing and procedures performed should be based upon the examiner's assessment of risk. This assessment should include consideration of work performed by internal and external auditors, formal policies and procedures, and the effectiveness of internal controls and management information systems (MIS).

Examiners should use the *FFIEC Information Systems Examination* and related OCC issuances for additional information and guidance as referenced in these procedures.

It may not be necessary to complete all the procedures. When planning, examiners should determine the extent of the bank's reliance on external vendors for Internet banking operations and/or monitoring activities. Procedures to evaluate outsourced activities are incorporated in these general procedures.

Objective: To set the scope for assessing the quantity of risk and quality of risk management in Internet banking.

1. Review the following documents to identify any previously noted problems related to the Internet banking area that require follow-up:
   - Previous examination reports (Asset Management, BIS, Commercial, Compliance, etc.).
   - Supervisory strategy.
   - EIC scope memorandum.
   - Follow-up activities.
   - Work papers from previous examinations.
   - Internal and external audit reports.
   - Correspondence.

(Note: If an examiner is assigned Internal and External Audit, a copy of any significant deficiencies for this area should be obtained from that examiner. If internal and external audit is not part of the overall scope of the examination, review the work performed by the internal and external auditors in this area and obtain a list of any deficiencies noted in their most recent review.)

2. Verify the completeness of requested information with the request list.
3. Obtain other reviews, assessments or system certifications performed by internal/external auditors, consultants, or technology experts contracted by the bank. Note any outstanding deficiencies.
4. Determine whether external vendors are used and what services or products are provided. Examiners should document the major entities responsible for development, operation, and/or support of all or portions of Internet banking systems.
5. Review documentation and conduct early discussions with management to determine:

   (Note: Consultation with examiners responsible for reviewing overall bank information security should be performed and work papers reviewed to avoid any redundancy in reviewing security controls.)

   - How security for Internet banking is addressed.
   - How management supervises Internet banking functions, including those functions that are outsourced.
   - Any significant changes in policies, practices, personnel, or control systems.
   - Any internal or external factors that could affect the Internet banking area.
6. Review the bank's business and strategic plans to determine whether management's plans for the Internet banking business are clear and reflect the current direction of the unit.
7. Determine whether management has incorporated Internet banking as part of contingency and business resumption plans.

8. Gain an understanding of the bank's Internet banking business and disclosures by reviewing the bank's Web site(s).
9. Based on the performance of the previous steps, combined with discussions with the EIC and other appropriate supervisors and examiners, determine the scope and objectives of this examination.
10. As examination procedures are performed, test for compliance with established policies or practices and the existence of appropriate internal control processes. Identify any area with inadequate supervision and/or undue risk, and discuss with the EIC the need to perform additional procedures.

Select from among the following examination procedures the steps that are necessary to meet examination objectives. An examination will seldom require every step to be performed.

QUANTITY OF RISK

Internet Banking Products and Services

Objective: To gain an understanding of the type and volume of the bank's Internet banking product line, transaction flow and settlement processes.

1. Obtain a description or diagram of the configuration of the Internet banking system and its capabilities. Consider hardware, software, points of connectivity to internal systems, and remote access points. To help determine the level of risk, evaluate:
   - How the Internet banking system is linked to other host systems or the network infrastructure in the bank.
   - How transactions and data flow through the network.
   - What type(s) of telecommunications channels and remote access capabilities (direct modem dial-in, Internet access, or both) exist.
2. Identify the current types, volumes, and complexity of retail, wholesale, and fiduciary products and services in the bank's Internet banking product and services line.
3. Review systems and network architecture to identify access points and potential areas of vulnerability.

4. Through discussion with management, note any changes in the type, volume or complexity of products or services expected in the next two years.
5. Evaluate Internet banking marketing strategies to determine whether plans include expansion into new markets, product lines, or other technologies.
6. Obtain from management an overview of transaction and payment services flow and settlement processes and determine whether:
   - Management understands the transaction flow and settlement processes between the parties involved.
   - The bank's settlement responsibilities are clearly defined.
   - Based on the settlement process, the bank assumes additional credit risk caused by settlement time frames.
   - The vendor's policies address uncollected funds, settlement, backup, contingency, customer service, and disaster recovery.
   - There is adequate exception reporting.
7. Review the transaction and payment services products and determine whether adequate control features are built into the systems to ensure authentication of the user, data integrity, and confidentiality of transactions.
8. Determine the extent of the company's use of an Automated Clearing House (ACH) for the Internet banking products and determine whether the bank has adequate ACH controls. (See the *FFIEC Information Systems Examination* for guidance.)
9. Identify key MIS reports provided and whether they are adequate to properly manage Internet banking transaction and payment services activities.
10. Determine whether a risk assessment or audit has been performed on any vendors supporting the transaction or payment services businesses.

COMPLIANCE WITH LAWS, RULES, AND REGULATIONS

Objective: To assess the bank's compliance with applicable banking laws.

1. Determine whether the bank is subject to notification requirements outlined in the Bank Service Corporation Act, section 1867(c)(2). (An example may include banks with investment in or partnerships with Internet service providers).
2. Identify whether the bank is staying informed on legal developments associated with Internet banking.
3. Review the findings from the most recent examinations (asset management, BIS, commercial, compliance, etc.) and the internal/external audit for issues associated with the institution's Internet banking products and services. If applicable, determine whether management has corrected any identified deficiencies.
4. Determine whether the FDIC notice is appropriately displayed and whether uninsured products or services are clearly designated (12 CFR 328).
5. Note whether reporting is in place to identify potential money laundering activities associated with Internet banking businesses.
6. Determine whether Office of Foreign Asset Control (OFAC) identification and reporting capabilities are maintained for Internet banking products and services.
7. As a way to expedite possible litigation and investigation resulting from security breaches, determine whether management has established a warning banner for users, announcing that intruders are accessing a private computer and that unauthorized access or use is not permitted and constitutes a crime punishable by law (18 USC 1030).
8. If the bank is aware of computer-related crimes (*see* AL 97-9, "Reporting Computer-Related Crimes," for guidance), determine whether a suspicious activity report was filed.
9. Determine whether the bank is providing accurate privacy disclosures associated with its Internet banking product line.

QUALITY OF RISK MANAGEMENT

Policy and Strategic Planning

Objective: Determine whether the board of directors has adopted effective policies for Internet banking that are consistent with safe and sound banking practices and are appropriate to the size of the bank and the nature and scope of its operations.

1. Determine whether Internet banking security policies include:
   - Clear lines of responsibility for system security:
     - Review the duties of the security administrator and determine whether they are knowledgeable of internal security policies and controls.
     - Determine whether their authority as security administrator is adequate to dictate controls and enforce policies.
   - Network and data access control.
2. Determine whether Internet banking firewall policies address:
   - Responsibility for firewall maintenance and monitoring.
   - Well-defined access rules.
   - Access rules that dictate what traffic is allowed or forbidden.
3. Determine whether encryption is adequately addressed in the security policy, noting whether the policy includes:
   - Who is responsible for control of encryption processes.
   - How encryption is used.
   - Data classification techniques.
   - Use of encryption to protect transmission of passwords, messages, or data during internal and open network communications sessions.
4. If a public key cryptographic system is used, determine whether private keys are under the control of the bank and determine whether policies and controls have been established that address private key management. Note whether policies or procedures address the following points:
   - Management of keys generated by the bank or a third party.
   - Security of secret or private key storage.
   - Who has access to the keys and how the environment is controlled.
   - If private key escrow arrangements exist, how they are controlled.

- Procedures and practices for proper revocation and reissuance of lost, compromised, or expired keys.
- Storage of keys on a server or computer that have no connection to outside networks.

5. Determine whether policies establish the use of virus detection software and note the products used.
6. Identify whether security policies are periodically reviewed and updated and note whether the board of directors or senior management committee approves the policies.
7. Determine whether the institution has established policies over hypertext links that enable consumers to clearly distinguish:
    - Insured and non-insured financial products.
    - Bank versus non-bank products.
    - When leaving the bank's Web site.

Processes

Objective: Determine whether processes and practices, including internal controls, are effective.

1. Evaluate the bank's short and long term strategies for Internet banking products and services through discussion with management and review of technology plans. Consider the following in assessing the bank's planning process:
    - Whether Internet banking is consistent with the bank's overall mission, strategic goals, and operating plans.
    - The level of oversight provided by the board of directors and senior management.
    - Management's understanding of industry standards to ensure compatibility and interoperability of systems.
    - Whether cost and benefit analyses of Internet banking activities consider start-up, operating, upgrade, customer support, and maintenance costs.

- Management's evaluation of security risks, threats, and vulnerabilities.
- The institution's internal expertise and technical training requirements.
- The status of Y2K compliance issues as they relate to Internet banking systems.
- Management's attention to system security monitoring and testing and performance monitoring.
- Management's knowledge of and adherence to federal and state laws, regulations, and interpretations as they pertain to Internet banking technology and electronic commerce.

2. Determine whether management has an adequate process to periodically evaluate its Internet banking product mix and marketing successes, and links those findings to its strategic planning process.
3. Evaluate the adequacy of the bank's process for performing security risk assessments including whether it:
   - Identifies threats and vulnerabilities associated with Internet banking.
   - Identifies critical applications or data.
   - Defines required security controls.
   - Considers internal expertise and the need for external consultation or support.
4. Evaluate the process the bank employs to ensure reliable and accurate network and data access control.

VENDOR MANAGEMENT

1. Assess management's due diligence activities prior to vendor selection.

   Consider whether:
   - Strategic and business plans are consistent with outsourcing activity.
   - Senior management and the board of directors are involved in outsourcing decisions and vendor selection.
   - Vendor information was gathered and analyzed prior to contract.

   Determine whether management considers:

- Vendor reputation.
- Financial condition.
- Costs for development, maintenance, and support.
- Internal controls and recovery processes
- Service level agreements.
- Vendor and bank management responsibilities.

2. Determine whether the bank has reviews vendor contracts to ensure that the responsibilities of each party are appropriately identified.
3. Determine whether contracts address topics in the "Contracts" section of the *FFIEC Information Systems Examination* . Note whether vendor contracts provide or consider:
   - Description of the work to be performed or service provided.
   - Basis for costs and description of additional fees.
   - Online communications and availability, transmission security, and transaction authentication.
   - Audit rights and responsibilities.
   - Contingency plans for service recovery and data backup and protection provisions.
   - Liability for data and confidential treatment of information.
   - Hardware and software upgrades and price changes.
   - Availability of financial information.
   - Training and problem resolution.
   - Reasonable penalty and cancellation provisions.
   - Prohibition of contract assignment.
4. Determine whether the bank obtains and reviews internal or external audit reports evaluating vendor management processes or specific vendor relationships as they relate to information systems and technology.
5. Determine whether management designates personnel responsible for vendor management. Note management's responsibilities and whether they are held accountable for monitoring activities and services.

6. If the institution is a provider of Internet banking software products, determine whether management has an adequate process to determine who maintains the program source code.
7. If the institution obtains software products from a vendor, determine whether the bank has an adequate process to ensure that software maintained by the vendor is under a software escrow agreement and that the file is confirmed as being current on a regular basis.
8. If the vendor has dial-in capability to the bank's systems for diagnostic or maintenances purposes, determine whether the bank has an adequate process to ensure that the vendor's activities are well controlled and whether fidelity insurance extends to the vendor's employees.

Passwords

1. Assess the adequacy of the process for password administration for Internet banking systems. Consider the following:
   - The adequacy of control and security over the bank's process for issuing passwords to customers.
   - Whether alphanumeric passwords are required.
   - The required length of passwords.
   - Whether passwords have an automatic expiration.
   - If adequate procedures are in place for resetting passwords.
   - If automatic log-off controls exist for user inactivity.
   - Whether excessive failed access attempts by the user disables access.
2. Evaluate the adequacy of the process used to select how passwords are employed to authenticate users including whether:
   - Controls combine passwords with other authentication techniques.
   - Password-only log-in is used for access control and authentication.
   - Password-only log-in is used for public network (Internet) access. If so, determine whether the institution has compensating controls to authenticate users.

Firewalls

1. Evaluate the process management uses to determine the appropriate type of Web site (informational, communicative, or transactional) for the bank's Internet-based banking business.
2. Determine whether the institution has a sound process to ensure adequate control over the path between the Web site and the institution's internal networks or computer systems.
3. Determine the process management employs to ensure that the firewall, if used, prevents unauthorized access to internal networks and computer systems.
4. If the firewall was commercially purchased, determine whether the bank has an adequate process to ensure that the responsibilities of the bank and vendor are well defined.
5. Determine the adequacy of the administration of the bank's firewall configuration and whether it ensures that:
   - Software change control procedures are appropriate.
   - Vendors provide timely fixes or upgrades and whether management implements them in a timely manner.
   - Changes in firewall configuration are tested prior to implementation.
   - Operating system control features have been invoked.
   - Operating system software default settings are adequate.
6. Determine whether the bank has an adequate process for:
   - Conducting penetration testing and certification.
   - Reviewing the qualifications of the company/person performing the certification.
7. Determine whether the bank has an effective process to assess the adequacy of physical controls in place to restrict access to firewall servers and components.
8. Determine whether the institution has an adequate process to identify any remote access, other than through a firewall, and how management monitors and controls that access.

9. Determine the adequacy of the institution's process to restrict access to firewall configuration documentation.

Physical Security

1. Determine whether the bank has an adequate process to address physical security for hardware, software, and data communications equipment associated with the Internet banking system including:
    - Whether the network servers are secured.
    - How the institution prevents unauthorized physical access to equipment.
    - Whether the bank secures vendor owned equipment.
    - If proper physical controls are in place for the data center or other location housing equipment and documentation.

Transaction Verification

1. Determine whether the bank has an adequate process to verify transactions to avoid claims of repudiation by bank customers.

Encryption and Confidentiality

1. Determine whether the bank has an adequate process to select encryption appropriate for its environment and whether the encryption selected is structured upon public, private, or a hybrid encryption system. Note the following:
    - The type of algorithm used and what it is used for.
    - Whether bank uses a proprietary or unknown algorithm.
    - The key length used for encryption, *e.g.,* 56-bit.
    - Whether encryption is used to secure passwords during transmission or storage.
    - Whether encryption is used to protect sensitive stored data.
2. If the bank engages in international banking activity, determine whether the bank is aware of U.S. government exportation policies and related restrictions controlling the exportation and use of encryption technology.

3. Determine whether the bank has an adequate process regarding the collection and use of personal information necessary to protect customer privacy (see AL 99-6).

Virus Detection and Prevention

1. Determine whether the bank has an adequate process regarding virus detection and prevention associated with the Internet banking systems.

   Consider whether:

   - User awareness efforts address viruses.
   - The last risk assessment and/or audit reports identified any deficiencies in virus controls.
   - The frequency with which anti-virus products and definitions are updated and whether the most current version/release is installed.

2. Determine whether the bank has an adequate process regarding virus detection and prevention. Consider whether:

   - Virus detection software distribution is made through downloads from the bank's server.
   - The bank's software distribution process provides for virus detection/ prevention.

Business Resumption and Contingency Planning

1. Determine whether there is an adequate process to develop and review the bank's business impact analysis. Consider whether:

   - Internet banking is viewed as a critical business or product line.
   - Management has reviewed the impact to the bank's reputation if its Internet banking products and services are not operable.

2. Determine whether the bank has an adequate process to develop and test the contingency and business resumption plans for Internet banking products and services including whether:

   - The contingency and business resumption plans provide adequately for recovery.

- Contingency and business resumption plans are appropriately tested on a regular basis.

3. Determine whether the bank has an adequate process in place for Internet banking recovery including whether:
   - Internet banking contingency and business resumption plans are reviewed and updated regularly.
   - Specific personnel and staff are responsible for initiating and managing Internet banking recovery plans.
   - The plan ensures that single points of failure for critical network points are adequately addressed.
   - The plan establishes strategies to recover hardware, software, communication links, and data files.
   - Adequate back up agreements and contracts are in place for external vendors or critical suppliers and if these backup arrangements are tested fully.
   - The response process assures that senior management and the board of directors are made aware of adverse events as dictated by the severity of damage and monetary loss.
   - Outreach strategies are adequate to inform the media and customers of corrective measures.
   - Legal liability issues are contemplated and addressed as part of response processes.
   - Procedures are in place to bring security breaches to the attention of appropriate management and external entities (e.g., Computer Emergency Response Team (CERT), FBI, OCC, etc.).
4. Determine whether the bank has an adequate process to review the results of the most recent contingency and recovery plan testing including whether management:
   - Requires annual testing of recovery processes and systems.
   - Addresses adverse test results in a timely manner.
   - Informs the board or executive management of test results.

Personnel

Objective: Given the size and complexity of the bank, determine whether bank management and personnel display acceptable knowledge and technical skills to manage Internet banking.

1. Through discussions with management, determine their level of technical knowledge and assess the adequacy of that knowledge for the size and scope of the bank's Internet banking operations.
2. Assess technology related training programs and security awareness efforts including whether:
   - Management provides timely technical training opportunities.
   - Management measures the effectiveness of security awareness.
   - Bank staff and Internet banking users are aware of security responsibilities and bank policies.
   - Management relies, solely or in part, on external vendors for technical expertise.

Controls

Objective: Determine whether management has instituted controls that are appropriate to the type and level of risks arising from Internet banking.

Digital Signatures and Certificate Authorities (CA)

1. Determine whether management requires use of digital signatures to authenticate the bank, users, and transactions.
2. Determine whether digital signatures are issued, managed, and/or certified by an external vendor.
3. If the bank is acting as its own certificate authority note:
   - Whether the digital signature system is open or closed.
   - Whether the bank has written policies and procedures for issuance, renewal, and revocation of certificates.
   - How the institution establishes and verifies credentials of subscribers.
   - Whether administrative reporting systems are adequate to provide for directory lookup and auditing (i.e., time stamping).

- Whether the CA facility or area is adequately secured including whether:
  - Controls are in place to protect servers housing CA information and directories.
  - Contingency plans accommodate customer needs in case of system failure or disaster.
  - The bank has addressed the legal implications of providing a CA function.
  - The CA conforms to established standards (*e.g.*, NIST or IETF).
  - An audit process is in place.
- Whether limitations have been established for certificates such as:
  - The number of transactions.
  - The type of transactions.
  - Expiration dates.
- Whether the CA establishes classes of certificates based on message or transaction sensitivity.
- Whether the bank is staying current on applicable laws.
- Whether the bank periodically performs a cost/benefit analysis of the business.

Biometric Devices

1. Determine whether the institution uses biometric devices for authentication purposes.
2. Determine whether a risk assessment, audit, or cost/benefit analysis has been performed of biometric devices used for authentication purposes.
3. Determine whether acceptable biometric tolerances and policies have been established for authenticating the transaction to be processed.
4. Obtain and review management reports that address statistical performance of the biometric authentication devices in service.

Monitoring

1. Discuss with management the techniques used to monitor the security of Internet banking systems. Obtain and review sample reports such as:
   - Penetration test scope and results.
   - Security violation information.
   - Real-time intrusion detection reports.
   - Reports depicting security breaches or system intrusion.
2. Determine whether security analysis software is used and note its capabilities.
3. Determine whether management conducts or has employed outside vendors to conduct penetration testing. Assess whether:
   - An objective party performs penetration testing.
   - Persons performing the tests are appropriately bonded.
   - Penetration testing is performed at least annually or at an acceptable frequency based on management's risk analysis and risk tolerance.
   - Test information and documentation is strictly controlled.
4. Determine how management monitors and detects internal or external network intrusion including whether:
   - Monitoring software is used to track real-time network traffic.
   - A qualified individual is responsible for regularly monitoring network traffic.
   - Activity logs are maintained and reviewed on a regular basis.
   - Intrusion detection techniques allow for immediate notification of network administrators or security personnel.
   - Security policies define reportable events.
   - Processes are incorporated to assure appropriate levels of management, directors, and external authorities are notified.
5. Determine through review of reports or inquiries of management whether the bank has experienced any of the following occurrences. If so, document in work papers:

- Any alteration of the bank's home page.
- Any unauthorized access from external or internal sources.
- Financial damage incurred as a result of any unauthorized intrusion. If losses have been sustained, determine if the bank filed a suspicious activity report per OCC Advisory Letter 97-9, "Reporting Computer-Related Crimes."

6. Determine whether management has emergency response procedures and evaluate whether they are effective in handling an unauthorized intrusion. Discuss and document controls for remote access including whether:
   - Security policies address remote access.
   - Staff is aware of policies and adherence is monitored.
   - Audit logs are maintained to monitor remote access.

Performance Monitoring

1. Determine how management monitors system performance (e.g., transaction volume, response times, availability/downtime, capacity reports, and customer service logs and complaint summaries).
2. Determine how management projects future systems needs to ensure continued availability of the network to meet customer demands.

Customer Support

1. Evaluate the role and quality of customer service and support for Internet banking products and services.
2. Review the organization and responsibilities of the customer support function.
3. Determine whether the customer support service is outsourced. If so, note the responsibilities of the vendor and determine how management monitors customer problems, demands, or complaints.
4. Determine whether customer service levels have been established. If so, determine how management monitors adherence to service levels.
5. Determine how management assesses the adequacy of customer service.

6. Through reviews of problem logs or customer service reports and discussion with management, determine whether deficiencies exist in the process.
7. Determine whether customer service is considered in Internet banking growth projections and resource planning.

Software Distribution

1. Determine whether program change controls exist and whether they are adequate to prevent unauthorized software alterations including whether:
   - Approval procedures exist to initiate program changes and whether they are at critical points throughout the development process.
   - Procedures are followed for emergency and temporary software fixes, and new releases.
   - Change control documentation provides adequate audit trails and support for software changes.
2. Evaluate version control and software distribution procedures associated with Internet banking applications including:
   - The adequacy of software distribution (automatic download, user initiated download, or manual delivery).
   - Whether adequate controls are in place to guard against virus infection during distribution and to ensure the integrity of software.
   - Whether software testing is performed prior to distribution.

Audit

1. Determine whether the scope of internal or external audit coverage includes Internet banking.
2. Determine whether a risk assessment or audit has been performed on key management practices. Review applicable reports.
3. Determine whether internal audit is or was involved in planning and implementing the Internet banking system.
4. If available, obtain internal or external audit reports (including Type II SAS 70 reviews) that evaluate vendor management processes or specific vendor relationships as they relate to information systems and technology.

5. Obtain management reports or conduct interviews with management to determine whether vendor controls have been evaluated. Determine whether management has considered the adequacy of:
   - Security controls and reporting including whether management understands and has evaluated security for access control, user authentication, and data privacy.
   - Security monitoring activity including whether the vendor performs real-time intrusion detection and penetration testing of offsite or in-house networks.
   - Service levels and the vendor's ability to meet negotiated standards.
   - Testing activity by the vendor prior to product distribution.
   - Virus detection processes.
   - Contingency planning and business resumption plans.
6. If the bank outsources its Internet banking processing, determine the name of the vendor(s) employed and whether the bank has obtained and reviewed the regulatory agency examination report of the vendor.
7. Determine whether the audit function reviews the consistency between the bank's disclosed security and privacy standards and actual bank practices.

Internet Service Providers (ISP)

1. Determine whether the bank relies on a third party Internet service provider (ISP) to support access to Internet banking services. If so, note whether management's supervision of the vendor includes:
   - Determining whether performance meets service level agreements.
   - Requiring the ISP to monitor bank Internet links and report to them when these links are down or unavailable.
   - Determining the ISP's contingency planning and business recovery capabilities.
   - Identifying whether the ISP has adequate support staff.
   - Determining whether the bank is subject to differing service access types that may cause less than acceptable support.

- Determining whether the ISP provides bank-defined filtering or establishes its own firewall-filtering parameters.
- Determining whether the ISP has sound controls over changes to the bank's Internet address.
- Assessing the soundness of the ISP's financial condition.
- Reviewing the ISP's security standards and practices.

2. Determine whether the bank has alternate data communications paths in the event the primary ISP is unable to handle the bank's Internet traffic due to a malfunction or inadequate capacity.

Conclusion Procedures

Objective: Communicate findings and initiate corrective action on violations and other deficiencies.

1. Prepare a summary memorandum detailing the results of the Internet banking examination. Draft conclusions on:
   - The quantity of risk.
   - The quality of risk management.
   - The direction of risk.
   - The extent to which risk management practices affect aggregate risk.
2. Also address in the summary memorandum:
   - Appropriateness of strategic and business plans.
   - Adequacy and adherence to policies.
   - Adequacy of MIS.
   - Compliance with applicable laws, rules, and regulations.
   - Adequacy of internal controls.
   - Recommended corrective action regarding deficient policies, procedures, practices, or other concerns.
   - The institution's Internet banking prospects.
   - Other matters of significance.

3. Discuss examination findings and conclusions with the EIC. If necessary, compose "Matters Requiring Board Attention" (MRBA). MRBAs should cover practices that:
   - Deviate from sound fundamental principles and are likely to result in financial deterioration if not addressed.
   - Result in substantive noncompliance with laws or regulations.

   MRBA should discuss:
   - Causes of the problem.
   - Consequences of inaction.
   - Management's commitment to corrective action.
   - The time frame and person(s) responsible for corrective action.
4. Discuss findings with management including conclusions regarding applicable risks. If necessary, obtain commitments for corrective action.
5. As appropriate, prepare a Internet banking comment for inclusion in the report of examination.
6. Write a memorandum specifically stating what the OCC should do in the future to effectively supervise Internet banking in this bank. Include supervisory objectives, time frames, staffing, and workdays required.
7. Update the electronic information system and any applicable report of examination schedules or tables.
8. Update the examination work papers in accordance with OCC guidance.

Firewalls and Associated Controls

The purpose of this appendix is to provide background material on the *fundamentals of firewalls and their use in banking and electronic commerce.*

Examiners and other readers of this section should familiarize themselves with the *FFIEC Information Systems Examination* (*IS*) chapters on Security and Networking. This discussion assumes a knowledge of the content of the *IS* , specifically the section dealing with networks.

Management needs to understand the capabilities and functionality of the firewall and make sure that their systems are configured appropriately for the bank's business needs. Ongoing monitoring of the firewall ensures that the appropriate functions and utilities are activated to protect the institution and prevent attacks against known system weaknesses.

Institutions that do not have the expertise to design, install, and test firewalls should seriously consider engaging professionals to perform this function.

Due care should be exercised when selecting the vendors to perform these functions and sound internal controls should be in place along with audits to verify the vendor's activities with the firewall. The institution should periodically engage an independent source to test the firewall for weaknesses. This includes annual, or more frequently as circumstances warrant, penetration testing to ensure controls are appropriate to the type and level of risk arising from the institution's Internet banking products and services.

A firewall is hardware and software placed between two networks. The intent is for all network traffic, regardless of the direction of flow, to pass through this firewall. The firewall then can check all traffic to make sure it is authorized and prevent unwanted traffic from entering the system. The firewall also can check the traffic to determine whether it contains any unauthorized attachments, such as viruses. Firewalls need to be efficient to catch any traffic that is unauthorized in order to prevent potential harm to the institution.

Network isolation is a function of firewalls. A domain name server converts publicly known addresses into internal addresses that are not publicly known. This is sometimes referred to as a "bastion host." The feature prevents intruders from gaining access to internal names and addresses on the bank's internal network. External devices attempting to access internal addresses are suspect and should be screened out.

Address screening is another of the functions of a firewall. This function is used to filter-out messages with inappropriate source addresses. For example, this function would screen out messages with internal system addresses. Messages that have not gone through a domain name server should not have internal addresses and would be suspect. Such traffic should not be allowed to pass through the firewall.

Application screening is a firewall function used to prevent inappropriate instructions from entering the system or an unauthorized access to the administrator level of the server. A "proxy server" is a device used to test the system's "rules" to prevent deviations from the established rules.

Message flow inspection or state full inspection is a function of a firewall used to detect inappropriate responses by the system. The system creates a database and looks for inappropriate responses by a server to messages or inquiries. For example, if a request asks for account balance information and the response is to transfer funds, the "state full inspection" will recognize an inappropriate response and terminate the session.

Other controls normally work in tandem with firewalls. These controls include logical access controls and physical security. The reason these controls are important is that insiders represent the greatest threat to bank computer systems and data communications networks. Various studies reflect that nearly 70 percent of intrusions originate within the organization. Insiders have knowledge of the system or network and may have the opportunity to originate an unauthorized transaction either by accident or intent. Access to systems, networks, and information should be on a "need-to-know" basis. Banks also need to provide protection from employee ignorance such as sharing passwords and running outside software without virus checking.

A logical access control includes a user identification and a password. An individual's user ID might be J. Examiner. But each user should also have a unique password composed of at least 6-8 alphanumeric characters; more is better. It is important to avoid using passwords that are easily discerned. Names, addresses, or words found in the dictionary, any language, spelled forward or in reverse should be avoided. One option is to use mnemonics — something that is easy to remember but difficult to guess. An example of a mnemonic is the following phrase; "Examiners are curious, bright people." The mnemonic is EACBP. By adding some numbers and/or special characters, a password can be created that is easy to remember but difficult to discern. *See* OCC Bulletin 98-38 "Technology Risk Management: Internet Banking" and the *IS internet banking* for a more complete discussion of logical access security and controls.

Physical security also is an important control function in protecting a bank's data communications networks and internal accounting systems. Network hardware should be stored in secure locations so that it is accessible only to authorized personnel. This is a preventive control to protect the bank's assets and protect the institution from transaction, reputation, and strategic risk. Personal computers connected to a network should have sound logical access controls. This includes a password feature to access the network and time-out password controls to protect the network when a particular PC is unattended, even for brief periods of time.

Banks should consider the feasibility of centrally controlled modem pools. Controlling the placement and access to modems attached to a bank's network will help the bank limit access to only authorized individuals. Banks should specifically guard against unauthorized modems that employees may attach to their PCs which are connected to the bank's data communication network. These unauthorized modems can be targets of "random dialing" efforts and can be a vulnerable entry point into the bank's network.

Time of day controls can be used to restrict access to a bank's network to certain, preauthorized times. The objective is to limit the opportunity for afterhours access except as authorized by the network administrator. Decisions on this type of control will be based on the types of business the bank is engaged in and the need for access to its internal networks.

Well-defined policies will help a bank develop a sound system of controls and ultimately reduce the vulnerability to penetration. Well-defined control objectives will help the systems administrator or vendors to properly configure the firewall. Such policies also will give auditors a standard to measure against when performing tests. Some considerations for bank firewall policies include:

- Communicating the bank's policy with respect to monitoring employee use of data communications networks, including electronic mail and the Internet.
- Requiring virus checking for all diskettes or downloads from other than authorized sources. Even diskettes received from other employees can be contaminated with a virus and should be scanned before use, especially on a PC connected to the bank's network.

- Determining the bank's policy for the access to PCs and the bank's network after hours for uses that are not related to work.
- Informing employees of the consequences of violating the institution's network usage policies.
- Limiting access to and use of administrator level capabilities of the firewall hardware and software.
- Requiring periodic review of the vulnerabilities of the bank's firewalls from known threats including, penetration testing.
- Regularly logging and reviewing all activity.

Sophisticated auditing techniques are appropriate to determine whether effective policies are in place and whether the system of controls over the bank's networks are working as intended. The controls and audits of firewalls need to be performed on a regular basis. Firewall systems are dynamic and need regular reviews to ensure protection from newly identified vulnerabilities and system weaknesses.

Once the internal or external auditor gains a sound understanding of the bank's network configuration and types of business, he or she may decide to perform various tests to ensure the soundness of logical access controls. This might include testing default settings to determine whether only authorized firewall functions are permitted.

The auditors might use audit software to scan the activity logs looking for anomalies or unusual activity. They might review the screening of employees who developed or installed the network.

The auditors might also review the frequency of password changes for employees authorized access to a bank's data communications network. Depending on the level of Internet banking employed, the bank will want to consider engaging outside experts to review their security measures and offer recommendations for enhancements.

This type of review should be considered at least annually for transaction systems and somewhat less frequently for communicative and informational systems.

Examiners will find a more complete discussion of these issues in the *IS*

Cryptography

This appendix provides background material on the fundamentals of cryptography and the uses of encryption in banking and electronic commerce. Business, including banking, is shifting from paper based or physical processes to electronic based or digital processes.

This includes retail delivery of products and services, electronic data interchange, wholesale funds transfer, clearing, settlement, and Internet banking. Bank managers will need to engineer sound controls into these new business models to manage risk. While all of this is taking place, the basic needs for data privacy, trust, and verification will continue in the digital world as it has in the physical world. Encryption offers possible solutions.

Different Kinds of Encryption

Two different kinds of encryption exist with two separate purposes. One purpose is to keep information private. The other is to verify the identity of parties in a transaction. Both kinds of encryption are typically used together to both protect messages and validate the parties involved.

Each is governed by industry standards. Vendors provide the encryption technology as software products or as part of specific hardware devices. These two fundamental types of encryption are symmetric and asymmetric. Symmetric, also known as secret key cryptography, requires both the sender and receiver to have the same key (the integers that drive the encryption algorithm). The diagram on the following page shows how the process works. The sender encrypts the message and the receiver decrypts the message using the same key.

One of the most commonly used systems of this type is the Data Encryption Standard, or DES. The U.S. Government adopted this IBM- developed technology in 1977. It is widely used and operates on a minimum 56 bit (binary digit) base key. Some institutions will use Triple-DES where the message is encrypted three times to enhance its resistance to decoding.

Sender Receiver

The disadvantages are that key administration is complex, requiring both parties to maintain absolute control over exchanging keys, it does not include a separate authentication mechanism, and there is no non repudiation (undeniable proof of participation of the sender and receiver). In addition, some cryptographic systems are subject to export restrictions from the U.S. government.

Asymmetric, also known as public/private key cryptography, employs two keys. As noted in the following diagram, in order to secure a message the sender performs the encryption using the recipient's public key.

However, the receiver can only read the information using their private key. Often the literature refers to this technology as two key cryptography. A popular public key technology is RSA. Ron Rivest, Adi Shamir, and Leonard Adleman developed RSA in 1977.

The primary use of RSA is for authentication and the secure exchange of encryption keys and digital signatures. Key length can vary from 40 to 1,024 bits.

Sender Receiver

Some of the advantages of public key cryptography over private key cryptography are that it simplifies key administration. For example, there is no requirement for a prior relationship between the sending and receiving parties. In addition, the key lengths can be much longer than DES. According to the vendors, this makes public key cryptography stronger. It also provides for non repudiation. The major disadvantage is that public key is much slower than private key cryptography. Thus, it is used primarily to authenticate messages rather than encrypt an entire message.

How Encryption Works in Practice

Encryption may be used to both secure the message and authenticate the sender. The normal approach is to use the asymmetric and symmetric encryption technologies in tandem. Symmetric encryption is typically used for encrypting large volumes of information and asymmetric encryption is for authentication.

This is because the symmetric technology is up to 10,000 times faster than the asymmetric technology. The following is an example of how this works: If FNB wants to send a secure message to its correspondent, FNB needs to do two things. First, FNB needs to make sure the message is secure. FNB might do this by using DES or Triple DES (symmetric or secret key) to encrypt the message.

Second, FNB will authenticate themselves thus providing an assurance to the correspondent that the message came from FNB. FNB does this by using a hash function (a mathematical function derived from the message) to create a message digest from the text. Using RSA (asymmetric or public/private key), FNB then encrypts the message digest using its RSA private key. The correspondent can only read the encrypted message digest using FNB's public key. Thus, the recipient knows the message came from FNB.

When the correspondent receives the message, the correspondent then uses FNB's public RSA key to decrypt the message digest. The correspondent compares the decrypted hash total to one they have independently calculated from the message. If the hash totals agree, the correspondent has a high level of assurance that the message came from FNB and that nothing was lost or tampered with during transmission. The correspondent can then use the DES key to decrypt the text of the message.

Not every message needs the security or privacy provided through encryption. In addition, some countries will not allow encrypted messages to travel across their borders. Message authentication can be used in these situations. Message authentication is a technique used to attach a digital signature to a transmission. In the example below, if the correspondent wants to send a message to FNB but the correspondent is located in a country that does not permit message encryption, the correspondent can use message authentication to assure FNB that the message came from them. From the text of the message, the correspondent will first use a hash function to create a message digest. Next, the correspondent will use their private key to encrypt the message digest to create a digital signature. The encrypted message digest can only be read using the correspondent's public key. Accordingly, FNB will use the correspondent's public key to decrypt the message digest and compare the hash total to one they have independently calculated. If they agree, FNB has a high level of assurance that the message came from the correspondent and that, even though the message was sent in clear text, nothing was lost or tampered with during transmission.

Unencrypted Text Hash Function Message Digest RSA Encryption Digital Signature This is the same process for adding the digital signature for the encrypted DES message above. However, when used with an unencrypted or clear text message, the process is called message authentication. This process is sometimes referred to as a digital envelope, a digital message protected by a digital signature.

Types of Online Attacks

Banks and service providers need to guard against various types of online attacks. The object of an attack may vary. Attackers may try to exploit know vulnerabilities in particular operating systems. They also may try repeatedly to make an unauthorized entry into a Web site during a short time frame thus denying service to other customers.

Types of attacks may include:

- Sniffers — Also known as network monitors, this is software used to capture keystrokes from a particular PC. This software could capture logon IDs and passwords.
- Guessing Passwords — Using software to test all possible combinations to gain entry into a network.
- Brute Force — A technique to capture encrypted messages then using software to break the code and gain access to messages, user ID's, and passwords.
- Random Dialing — This technique is used to dial every number on a known bank telephone exchange. The objective is to find a modem connected to the network. This could then be used as a point of attack.
- Social Engineering — An attacker calls the bank's help desk impersonating an authorized user to gain information about the system including changing passwords.
- Trojan Horse — A programmer can embed code into a system that will allow the programmer or another person unauthorized entrance into the system or network.
- Hijacking — Intercepting transmissions then attempting to deduce information from them. Internet traffic is particularly vulnerable to this threat.

Discussion Points

There are several topics examiners can discuss with bankers who are considering engaging in Internet banking for the first time. These talking points will help the examiner determine if fundamental risk issues are under consideration. C Strategic Plans — The proposed Internet banking business should be a good fit with the institution's strategic business direction and customer demographics.

- Hosting — One of the major decisions a national bank will have to make is whether to host the service in-house or through an outsourcing arrangement.
- Functionality — A needs analysis can help the bank determine what products and services should be a part of the new Internet banking business. This should be an on-going process to ensure the bank remains current with Internet banking technology, products, and services.
- User Department — The bank's user departments should be involved in the outsourcing vendor or software vendor selection process as these individuals will have to work with the system on a daily basis once it is operational.
- Impact on Earnings and Capital — Bank management should have a projection of the expected impact on earnings and capital of the new Internet banking business.
- Security — Bank management needs to understand security issues associated with Internet banking products and services. Security issues include how the bank or its outsourcer will authorize users, prevent data interception and unauthorized alteration, and deal with intrusions.
- Internal Controls and Audit — Management should determine whether the controls and audit processes are adequate to enable the identification, measurement, and monitoring of risk associated with the Internet banking business.
- Legal Requirements — Various legal requirements, including compliance issues, need to be understood before initiating an Internet banking business. Since many legal issues are undecided, management will need to monitor developments.

- Vendor Management — If the bank is researching outsourcers, the analysis should include consideration of potential vendors' financial conditión, years in the business, and future plans.
- Contingency planning — Whether provided by the bank or outsourcer, management should have an understanding of contingency planning as part of the due diligence process.
- Insurance — A review of insurance coverage may be in order especially if the hosting of the Web site has been outsourced.
- Consultants — The bank should ensure they have the proper level of expertise to make this business decision. The board and senior management may need to enhance their understanding of technology issues. If the expertise is not available in-house, the bank should consider engaging outside expertise.

Since these are dynamic discussion points, examiners should periodically reference the Bank Technology Division Intranet site for updates.

CUSTOMER IDENTITY THEFT: E-MAIL RELATED FRAUD THREATS

PURPOSE

This alert is intended to raise awareness of an increasingly common Internet fraud called "phishing" and encourages banks to educate their customers, strengthen monitoring systems, and enhance response programs to reduce the potential risk to their organizations and customers.

BACKGROUND

The FBI's Internet Fraud Complaint Center (IFCC) reports a steady increase in complaints involving unsolicited e-mails directing consumers to a phony "customer service" Web site or directly asking for customer information. These scams are contributing to a rise in identity theft, credit card fraud, and other Internet-based frauds. E-commerce customers, including bank customers, have fallen victim to these scams.

Phishing involves sending customers a seemingly legitimate e-mail request for account information, often under the guise of asking the customer to verify or reconfirm confidential personal information such as account numbers, social security numbers, passwords, and other sensitive information. In the e-mail, the perpetrator uses various means to convince customers that they are receiving a legitimate message from someone whom the customer may already be doing business with, such as a bank. Techniques such as a false "from" address or the use of seemingly legitimate bank logos, Web links, and graphics may be employed to mislead the customer. After gaining the customer's trust, the perpetrator attempts to convince the customer to provide personal information and provides one or more methods for the customer to communicate that information back. For example, the e-mail might include a link to the perpetrator's Web site that contains a form for entering personal information. Like the e-mail, the Web site is designed to trick the customer into believing it belongs to the bank. Alternatively, the e-mail might simply include an embedded form for the customer to complete. The ultimate goal of this fraud is to use the customer information to gain unauthorized access to a customer's bank or financial accounts or to engage in other illegal acts.

Risk Mitigation for E-mail-related Frauds

Banks should implement appropriate controls consistent with the security process described in the Federal Financial Institutions Examination Council's (FFIEC) "Information Security Booklet." Management should consider the following actions to help prevent, detect, and respond to the threat from e-mail-related frauds:

Prevention

- Provide notices on Web sites reminding customers that the bank will never request confidential information through e-mail and to report any such requests to the bank.
- Print warnings and notices on customer statements or other paper mailings.
- Improve authentication methods and procedures to protect against the risk of user ID and password theft from the customer through e-mail and other frauds. Authentication methods solely reliant on shared secrets (e.g., passwords) are more susceptible to phishing schemes than stronger authentication methods.

- Review and, if necessary, enhance practices for protecting confidential customer data.
- Maintain current Web site certificates and describe how the customer can authenticate the bank's Web pages by checking the properties on a secure Web page.
- Refer customers to or use Federal Trade Commission (FTC) resources to develop educational brochures to explain the red flags and risks of identity theft.
  - FTC, "How Not to Get Hooked by the 'Phishing' Scam," July 2003
  - FTC, "ID Theft: When Bad Things Happen to Your Good Name," September 2002

Detection

- Monitor accounts individually or in aggregate for unusual account activity such as address or phone number changes, large or a high volume of transfers, and unusual customer service requests.
- Monitor for fraudulent Web sites using variations of the bank's name.
- Establish a toll-free number for customers to verify requests for confidential information or to report suspicious e-mails.
- Train customer service staff to refer customer concerns regarding suspicious e-mail request activity to security staff.

Response

- Incorporate notification of known e-mail-related frauds into the response program to alert customers of fraudulent requests for information and to caution them against responding.
- Establish a process to notify Internet service providers, domain name issuing companies, and law enforcement to shut down fraudulent Web sites and other Internet resources that are being used to facilitate phishing or other fraudulent e-mail practices.
- Increase suspicious activity monitoring and employ additional identity verification controls.

- If fraud is detected in connection with customer accounts, the bank should report the fraud and consider offering its customers assistance consistent with the comprehensive guidance on reporting and customer assistance given in OCC Advisory Letter 2001-4, "Identity Theft and Pretext Calling."

In the event your institution is a victim of an e-mail-related scam, you should promptly notify your OCC supervisory office. As appropriate, you should also report the event to law enforcement by filing a Suspicious Activity Report.

Protecting Internet Addresses of National Banks

This alert highlights the need for banks to carefully select and protect their Internet addresses. Recently, several banks discovered Internet Web sites with Internet addresses similar to the addresses of their national bank Web sites. This confusing situation resulted in some bank customers mistakenly transmitting confidential information to these other similar Web sites.

Banks and others establish Internet addresses by registering a domain name through a domain name registration authority. Domain name registration information typically consists of the name of the registered owner, contact information, and technical information necessary to operate the domain naming system. Since domain name registration services are primarily concerned with establishing unique names, they do not impose restrictions on the registration of similar names.

A hypothetical example of a domain name is examplebank.com, which can coexist with examplebank.net and examplebank.org. Country suffixes also can be used to create similar names, (e.g., examplebank.de for Germany). Although the prefix of "www" is often used to denote a Web address (e.g., www.examplebank.com), it is possible to include "www" in a domain (e.g., www.wwwexamplebank.com). To avoid customer confusion, banks should consider the following actions in establishing and monitoring Internet addresses.

IMPLEMENTATION CONSIDERATIONS

National banks should conduct proper planning and due diligence before acquiring or developing an electronic record retention system. An effective planning process will include representation from all affected areas in the bank, including management and personnel from the relevant business lines, information technology, operations, audit, legal, and compliance. The electronic record retention system should be fully consistent with the bank's general corporate records management program. Management should assess the risks and objectives associated with the new electronic system and consider the potential effect on current business processes and internal controls. As part of this risk assessment, national banks should consult with knowledgeable legal counsel before undertaking any systematic digitalization of their records. This will help ensure that the electronic records comply with the requirements of the E-SIGN Act and, when appropriate, will satisfy applicable standards for admissibility into evidence. National banks should be especially careful regarding digitization of records that are likely subjects of litigation, such as consumer compliance, asset management, and loan records. Bank management should also consider consulting with their audit and compliance personnel when planning and developing a new electronic record retention system. After assessing the risks of an electronic records system, bank management will need to establish the necessary business and control requirements and conduct due diligence to compare the various options against those requirements. As part of the planning and due diligence process, OCC encourages national banks to consider the general points described below:

Security

The failure to properly secure and protect bank electronic record retention systems that contain confidential customer information will violate the minimum security standards imposed under section 501(b) of the Gramm-Leach-Bliley Act. *See* 12 CFR Part 30, Appendix B. However, the security device utilized must not prevent accessibility of the record to those legally entitled to it, including OCC examiners. Bank management should confirm that its record systems are properly secure from unauthorized access and data alteration, and this aspect of the systems should be adequately tested. The record systems architecture should be fully documented, and the systems adequately indexed.

Internal Controls

When appropriate because of the nature of the records stored in the system, national banks should implement effective internal controls to protect electronic record retention systems from unauthorized access and alteration, including associated business and information management practices. Internal controls include methods such as segregation of duties, physical and logical access controls, retention requirements, documentation of changes to records, elimination of write-access to records after capture, encryption for transmission and storage, software integrity checks, and equipment and record media disposal procedures. The effectiveness of these controls should be subject to audit review.

Back-up and Recovery

A national bank with an electronic records retention system with inadequate back-up and recovery processes may find that its records are inaccessible following an emergency. Thus, national banks should ensure that their electronic records are sufficiently backed up so that recovered records will meet the same accuracy and integrity standards as the primary electronic versions. National banks should assess whether they have a consistent process for periodic record back-up that stores the records in a secure off-site location with proper access controls, and for periodically testing their ability to recover the records.

Record Destruction and Disposal

Record destruction and disposal should generally occur only in accordance with a systematic and well-documented procedure and an approved records retention and disposition schedule. Among other things, the bank's procedures for disposal of electronic records should contain provisions for suspending records destruction if warranted by litigation or regulatory requests. This procedure should also comply with the guidelines and rules on safeguarding customer information previously issued to implement section 501(b) of the Gramm-Leach-Bliley Act. 12 CFR Part 30, Appendix B. Additionally, the procedure must conform to OCC's requirements issued under Section 216 of the Fair and Accurate Credit Transactions (FACT) Act, Pub. L. No. 108-159, requiring "any person that maintains or otherwise possesses consumer information ... derived from consumer reports ... to properly dispose of any such information or compilation." The OCC and the other federal banking agencies will implement section 216 of the FACT Act by amending the existing 501(b) guidelines.

Retention Periods and Content

Electronic record retention systems of national banks should also comply with all requirements imposed by statute or regulation for the mandated retained records. Thus, management should seek to establish a period of retention appropriate to the specific record and consistent with applicable legal, regulatory, fiscal, and administrative requirements. As part of its evaluation of an electronic records retention system, bank management should determine which electronic messages and communications to retain. This determination will depend on whether a particular e-mail or electronic message is a "record" for purposes of the particular record retention requirement or whether the bank may need it later for business or litigation purposes.

Thus, banks should look to the content of particular messages rather than their format or technology. If the e-mail were considered a "record" or would be retained for business purposes because of its content if it had been received or sent in paper, then it should also be retained as a "record" even though it is in electronic form. This is consistent with the general approach in developing law to impose "record" requirements that are technology neutral. See, for example, the E-SIGN Act and Sarbanes-Oxley Act of 2002, Pub. L. 107-204 (especially section 802 on retention of auditor work papers). The process should ensure that both the content of the message and sufficient information about its attributes, such as the source, destination, date, and time, are retained for authenticity purposes.

Change Management

A national bank's plan for its electronic records systems should provide for continuing accessibility despite future changes in technology that will require that record systems be updated and that records be migrated to the updated systems. National banks should assess and test the impact on the integrity and accessibility of their electronic records that may be caused by any changes in their systems or those of their service provider. Banks should consider change management controls that address risks to electronic record systems before, during, and following a change.

For many consumers, electronic banking means 24-hour access to cash through an automated teller machine (ATM) or Direct Deposit of paychecks into checking or savings accounts. But electronic banking now involves many different types of transactions. Electronic banking, also known as electronic fund transfer (EFT), uses computer and electronic technology as a substitute for checks and other paper transactions. EFTs are initiated through devices like cards or codes that let you, or those you authorize, access your account. Many financial institutions use ATM or debit cards and Personal Identification Numbers (PINs) for this purpose. Some use other forms of debit cards such as those that require, at the most, your signature or a scan. The federal Electronic Fund Transfer Act (EFT Act) covers some electronic consumer transactions.

Electronic Fund Transfers

EFT offers several services that consumers may find practical:

- *Automated Teller Machines or 24-hour Tellers* are electronic terminals that let you bank almost any time. To withdraw cash, make deposits, or transfer funds between accounts, you generally insert an ATM card and enter your PIN. Some financial institutions and ATM owners charge a fee, particularly to consumers who don't have accounts with them or on transactions at remote locations. Generally, ATMs must tell you they charge a fee and its amount on or at the terminal screen before you complete the transaction. Check the rules of your institution and ATMs you use to find out when or whether a fee is charged.
- *Direct Deposit* lets you authorize specific deposits, such as paychecks and Social Security checks, to your account on a regular basis. You also may pre-authorize direct withdrawals so that recurring bills, such as insurance premiums, mortgages, and utility bills, are paid automatically.
- *Pay-by-Phone Systems* let you call your financial institution with instructions to pay certain bills or to transfer funds between accounts. You must have an agreement with the institution to make such transfers.
- *Personal Computer Banking* lets you handle many banking transactions via your personal computer. For instance, you may use your computer to view your account balance, request transfers between accounts, and pay bills electronically.

- *Point-of-Sale Transfers* let you pay for purchases with a debit card, which also may be your ATM card. The process is similar to using a credit card, with some important exceptions. While the process is fast and easy, a debit card purchase transfers money - fairly quickly - from your bank account to the store's account. So it's important that you have funds in your account to cover your purchase. This means you need to keep accurate records of the dates and amounts of your debit card purchases and ATM withdrawals in addition to any checks you write. Your liability for unauthorized use, and your rights for error resolution, may differ with a debit card.
- *Electronic Check Conversion* converts a paper check into an electronic payment at the point of sale or elsewhere, such as when a company receives your check in the mail. In a store, when you give your check to a store cashier, the check is processed through an electronic system that captures your banking information and the amount of the check. Once the check is processed, you're asked to sign a receipt authorizing the merchant to present the check to your bank electronically and deposit the funds into the merchant's account. You get a receipt of the electronic transaction for your records. When your check has been processed and returned to you by the merchant, it should be voided or marked by the merchant so that it can't be used again. In the mail-in situation, you should still receive advance notice from a company that expects to process your check electronically.

Be especially careful in telephone transactions, which also could involve e-checks. A legitimate merchant should explain the process and answer any questions you may have. The merchant also should ask for your permission to debit your account for the item you're purchasing or paying on. However, because telephone e-checks don't occur face-to-face, you should be cautious with whom you reveal your bank or checking account information. Don't give this information to sellers with whom you have no prior experience or with whom you have not initiated the call, or to sellers who seem reluctant to discuss the process with you.

Not all electronic fund transfers are covered by the EFT Act. For example, some financial institutions and merchants issue cards with cash value stored electronically on the card itself. Examples include prepaid telephone cards, mass transit passes, and some gift cards. These "stored-value" cards, as well as transactions using them, may not be covered by the EFT Act. This means you may not be covered for the loss or misuse of the card. Ask your financial institution or merchant about any protections offered for these cards.

Disclosures

To understand your legal rights and responsibilities regarding your EFT account, read the documents you receive from the financial institution that issued your "access device." That is, a card, code or other means of accessing your account to initiate electronic fund transfers. Although the means varies by institution, it often involves a card and/or a PIN. No one should know your PIN except you and select employees of the financial institution. Before you contract for EFT services or make your first electronic transfer, the institution must tell you the following information in a form you can keep.

- A summary of your liability for unauthorized transfers.
- The telephone number and address of the person to be notified if you think an unauthorized transfer has been or may be made, a statement of the institution's "business days" (which is, generally, the days the institution is open to the public for normal business), and the number of days you have to report suspected unauthorized transfers.
- The type of transfers you can make, fees for transfers, and any limits on the frequency and dollar amount of transfers.
- A summary of your right to receive documentation of transfers, to stop payment on a pre-authorized transfer, and the procedures to follow to stop payment.
- A notice describing the procedures you must follow to report an error on a receipt for an EFT or your periodic statement, to request more information about a transfer listed on your statement, and how long you have to make your report.
- A summary of the institution's liability to you if it fails to make or stop certain transactions.
- Circumstances under which the institution will disclose information to third parties concerning your account.

- A notice that you may be charged a fee by ATMs where you don't have an account.

In addition to these disclosures, you will receive two other types of information for most transactions: terminal receipts and periodic statements. Separate rules apply to passbook accounts from which pre-authorized transfers are drawn. The best source of information about those rules is your contract with the financial institution for that account. You're entitled to a terminal receipt each time you initiate an electronic transfer, whether you use an ATM or make a point-of-sale electronic transfer. The receipt must show the amount and date of the transfer, and its type, such as "from savings to checking." When you make a point-of-sale transfer, you'll probably get your terminal receipt from the salesperson.

You won't get a terminal receipt for regularly occurring electronic payments that you've pre-authorized, like insurance premiums, mortgages, or utility bills. Instead, these transfers will appear on your periodic statement. If the pre-authorized payments vary, however, you should receive a notice of the amount that will be debited at least 10 days before the debit takes place.You're also entitled to a periodic statement for each statement cycle in which an electronic transfer is made. The statement must show the amount of any transfer, the date it was credited or debited to your account, the type of transfer and type of account(s) to or from which funds were transferred, and the address and telephone number for inquiries. You're entitled to a quarterly statement whether or not electronic transfers were made. Keep and compare your EFT receipts with your periodic statements the same way you compare your credit card receipts with your monthly credit card statement. This will help you make the best use of your rights under federal law to dispute errors and avoid liability for unauthorized transfers.

Errors

You have 60 days from the date a periodic statement containing a problem or error was sent to you to notify your financial institution. The best way to protect yourself if an error occurs - including erroneous charges or withdrawals from an account, or for a lost or stolen ATM or debit card - is to notify the financial institution by certified letter, return receipt requested, so you can prove that the institution received your letter. Keep a copy of the letter for your records. If you fail to notify the institution of the error within 60 days, you may have little recourse. Under federal law, the institution has no obligation to conduct an investigation if you've missed the 60-day deadline.

Once you've notified the financial institution about an error on your statement, it has 10 business days to investigate. The institution must tell you the results of its investigation within three business days after completing it and must correct an error within one business day after determining that the error has occurred. If the institution needs more time, it may take up to 45 days, in most situations, to complete the investigation - but only if the money in dispute is returned to your account and you're notified promptly of the credit. At the end of the investigation, if no error has been found, the institution may take the money back if it sends you a written explanation. An error also may occur in connection with a point-of-sale purchase with a debit card. For example, an oil company might give you a debit card that lets you pay for gas purchases directly from your bank account. Or you may have a debit card that can be used for various types of retail purchases. These purchases will appear on your periodic statement from the bank. In case of an error on your account, however, you should contact the card issuer (for example, an oil company or a bank) at the address or phone number provided by the company. Once you've notified the company about the error, it has 10 business days to investigate and tell you the results. In this situation, it may take up to 90 days to complete an investigation. If no error is found at the end of the investigation, the institution may take back the money if it sends you a written explanation.

Lost or Stolen ATM or Debit Cards

If your *credit card* is lost or stolen, you can't lose more than $50. If someone uses your ATM or *debit card* without your permission, you can lose *much more.* If you report an ATM or debit card missing to the card issuer before it's used without your permission, you can't be held responsible for any unauthorized withdrawals. If unauthorized use occurs before you report it, the amount you can be held responsible for depends upon how quickly you report the loss to the card issuer.

- If you report the loss within two business days after you realize your card is missing, you won't be responsible for more than $50 for unauthorized use.

- If you fail to report the loss within two business days after you realize the card is missing, but do report its loss within 60 days after your statement is mailed to you, you could lose as much as $500 because of an unauthorized transfer.
- If you fail to report an unauthorized transfer within 60 days after your statement is mailed to you, you risk unlimited loss. That means you could lose all the money in your account and the unused portion of your maximum line of credit established for overdrafts.

If you failed to notify the institution within the time periods allowed because of an extenuating circumstance, such as lengthy travel or illness, the issuer must reasonably extend the notification period. In addition, if state law or your contract imposes lower liability limits, those lower limits apply instead of the limits in the federal EFT Act. Once you report the loss or theft of your ATM or debit card, you're no longer responsible for additional unauthorized transfers occurring after that time. Because these unauthorized transfers may appear on your statements, however, you should carefully review each statement you receive after you've reported the loss or theft. If the statement shows transfers that you did not make or that you need more information about, contact the institution immediately, using the special procedures provided for reporting errors.

Limited Stop-Payment Privileges

When you use an electronic fund transfer, the EFT Act does not give you the right to stop payment. If your purchase is defective or your order is not delivered, it's as if you paid cash. That is, it's up to you to resolve the problem with the seller and get your money back. There is one situation, however, when you can stop payment. If you've arranged for regular payments out of your account to third parties, such as insurance companies, you can stop payment if you notify your institution at least three business days before the scheduled transfer. The notice may be oral or written, but the institution may require a written follow-up within 14 days of the oral notice. If you fail to provide the written follow-up, the institution's responsibility to stop payment ends. Although federal law provides only limited rights to stop payment, individual financial institutions may offer more rights or state laws may require them. If this feature is important to you, you may want to shop around to be sure you're getting the best "stop-payment" terms available.

Other Rights

The EFT Act protects your right of choice in two specific situations regarding use of electronic fund transfers: First, the Act prohibits financial institutions from requiring you to repay a loan by electronic transfer. Second, if you're required to receive your salary or government benefit check by EFT, you have the right to choose your institution.

Suggestions

If you decide to use EFT, keep these tips in mind:

- Take care of your ATM or debit card. Know where it is at all times; if you lose it, report it as soon as possible.
- Choose a PIN for your ATM or debit card that's different from your address, telephone number, Social Security number, or birthdate. This will make it more difficult for a thief to use your card.
- Keep and compare your receipts for all types of EFT transactions with your periodic statements. That way, you can find errors or unauthorized transfers and report them.
- Make sure you know and trust a merchant before you share any bank account information or pre-authorize debits to your account. Be aware that some merchants use electronic processing of your check if you sign a receipt authorizing the transaction.

Glossary

Access Control Entry (ACE) : Each access control list has an associated ACE, which lists the permissions that have been granted or denied to the users or groups listed in the ACL.

Access Control List (ACL): List of security identifiers that allow only certain processes to be activated.

Access Products Products that allow consumers to access traditional payment instruments electronically, generally from remote locations.

Access Tokens Objects containing the security identifier of a running process. The access token is checked against each object's ACL to determine whether or not appropriate permissions are granted.

Automated Clearing House An automated clearing and settlement system (ACH) for recurring payments. Most ACH systems are operated by the Federal Reserve Banks.

Administrative Alerts When a computer generates an alert, the message is sent to a predefined list of users. These messages relate to server and resource use; they warn about problems in areas such as security and access, user sessions, server shutdown because of power loss (with UPS), directory replication, and printing.

Alerter Service Notifies selected users and computers of administrative alerts that occur on a computer. Algorithms Mathematical formulas used to encrypt and decrypt messages. These encryption formulas can reside in software or specialized hardware devices.

Alpha Test The first stage of testing a new software product, carried out by the manufacturer's technical staff.

Alternative Payment Systems Payment systems such as those based on stored value cards, electronic currency, and debit or credit cards. These are alternative avenues to deliver traditional banking and related products and services.

American National A standard-setting organization; it is the U.S. Standards Institute (ANSI) representative to the International Standards Organization (ISO).

American Standard Code A standard code for representing characters as numbers that for Information Interchange is used on most microcomputers, computer terminals, and printers.

Applet A small application program that is designed to do a small, specific job.

Application A computer program or set of programs that perform the processing of records for a specific function.

Asymmetric Cryptography Is also known as public/private key cryptography. A private key encrypts the data and a public key decrypts the information.

Asymmetric cryptography is slower than symmetric technology and is used primarily for message authentication purposes.

Asynchronous Transfer Mode Method of transmitting bits of data one after another with a start bit and a stop bit to mark the beginning and end of each data unit.

Auditability The degree to which transactions can be traced and audited through a system.

Audit Policy Defines the type of security events that are logged for a domain or for individual computers; determines what the operating system will do when the security log becomes full. Audit policy can track the success or failure of specified security events.

Authentication 1) The process which assures the receiver of a digital message of the identity of the sender. It also is used to validate the integrity of the message. 2) The process of proving the claimed identity of an individual user, machine, software component or any other entity. Authoring Software Software used to produce multimedia or hypertext presentations by linking sounds, music, visuals, and text.

Authorization The process of determining what types of activities are permitted. Usually, authorization is in the context of authentication: once you have authenticated a user, he or she may be authorized different types of access or activity.

Backdoor A hole or access point left, by design, in the program by the original programmer or developer. Usually used by programmers to simplify the program-testing procedures; however, on occasion, programmers forget to close these holes or are not aware of other holes created by the original backdoor.

Bandwidth The transmission capacity of a computer channel or communications line.

Bastion Host A firewall system that has been designed to resist attack, and which is installed on a network in such a way that it is expected to potentially come under attack. Bastion hosts are often components of firewalls, or may be "outside" web servers or public access systems.

Baud Rate Measurement of data transfer speed.

Beta Test The second stage of a new software product that is almost ready for market, typically carried out by volunteers in a wide variety of settings such as those in which the finished product will be used.

Biometrics A method of verifying an person's identity by analyzing a unique physical attribute.

BIT A binary digit (0 or 1) used in the representation of a number, letter, or special character.

Bridge In local area networks, a device that enables two networks, even ones dissimilar in topology, wiring, or communications protocols, to exchange data.

Browser A computer program that enables the user to retrieve information that has been made publicly available on the Internet; also that permits multimedia (graphics) applications on the World Wide Web.

Bundled Software Software that is sold in combination with hardware.

CERT See Computer Emergency Response Team

Certifying Authority A trusted third party that confirms a person's identity by certifying that the transaction belongs to the stated party. The certifying authority must be recognized, trusted, and protected from fraud and abuse. A certifying authority issues a digital certificate signed by their private key. It can be verified by decrypting the certificate using the authority's public key.

Chip An electronic device consisting of circuit elements on a single silicon chip. The most complex circuits are microprocessors, which are single chips that contain the complete arithmetic and logic units of computers.

Chip Card Also known as an integrated circuit (IC) card. A card containing one or more computer chips or integrated circuits for identification, data storage, or special-purpose processing used to validate personal identification numbers, authorize purchases, verify account balances, and store personal records.

Cipher Text An encrypted message that outsiders cannot read.

Clearing The process of transmitting, reconciling, and, in some cases, confirming payment orders prior to settlement, possibly including netting of instructions and the establishment of final positions for settlement.

Clearing House A central location or central processing mechanism through which financial institutions agree to exchange payment instructions. The institutions settle for items exchanged at a designated time, based on the rules and procedures of the clearing house.

Clearing System A set of procedures whereby financial institutions present and exchange data and/or documents relating to funds or securities transfers to other financial institutions.

Client-server Network A network that dedicates certain computers called servers to act as service providers to computers called clients.

Closed Network A data communications network that is used for a specific purpose, such as a payment system, and to which access is restricted (also referred to as a private network).

Code Computer programs, written in machine language (object code) or programming language (source code).

Computer Emergency Located at Carnegie-Mellon University, this Response Team (CERT) incident response team offers advisories that contain useful, specific security information.

Cyber Mall A set of electronic or digital storefronts linked through a common Web site.

Cyberspace A popularized term that refers to the part of society and culture that exists in networked computer systems rather than in any particular physical location.

Cryptography The art/science of keeping messages secret from outsiders.

Data Encryption Standard DES is a well-known symmetric encryption standard that the U.S. Government endorsed in 1977.

Developed by IBM, it operates off of a 56-bit base key.

Data Integrity The property that data meet with a priority expectation of quality and that the data can be relied upon.

Dedicated Assigned to only one function.

Default Shares Resources shared by default when the operating system is installed.

Denial- of- Service Attack An attempt to overwhelm a server with requests so that it cannot respond to legitimate traffic.

Design Phase The phase of systems development during which the problem solution that was selected in the Study Phase is designed. The design includes the allocation of system functions; the design of inputs, outputs, and files; and the identification of system and component requirements.

Design Specification A baseline specification that defines how to construct a computer-based business system.

Development Phase The phase in which the computer-based system is constructed from the "blueprint" prepared in the Design Phase. Equipment is acquired and installed. All necessary procedures, manuals, and other documentation are completed. Personnel are trained, and the complete system is tested for operational readiness.

Dial-up The ability of a remote user to access a system by using private or common carrier telephone lines.

Dial-up Client A computer with a temporary connection to the Internet. Digital Referring to communications processors, techniques, and equipment where information is encoded as a binary "1"or "0".

Digital Certification A process to authenticate (or certify) a party's digital signature; carried out by trusted third parties.

Digital Envelope A digital message protected by a digital signature.

Digital Signature: (1) A mathematical encryption technique that associates a specific person with a given computer file and indicates that the file has not been altered since that person signed it; should not be confused with making an electronic representation of a written signature. (2) A message digest encrypted using asymmetric cryptography. This is used to verify that a message came from the expected sender.

Domain A group of computers and devices on a network that are administered as a unit with common rules and procedures.

Domain Controller The server that authenticates domain logins and maintains the security policy.

Domain Name An alphanumeric name for a Web site that includes both the online address and online name.

Domain Name Service A network service that translates (DNS) external Internet addresses into numerical Internet network addresses. Download To transmit a file or program from a central computer to a smaller computer or to a remote site.

Dynamic Host Configuration Method of automatically assigning addresses to client computers on a network.

Electronic Benefits The electronic delivery of government Transfer (EBT) benefits using plastic cards.

Electronic Data Interchange The transfer of information between (EDI) organizations in machine readable form.

Electronic Document The digital or computer equivalent of paper documents.

Electronic Money Monetary value measured in currency units stored in electronic form on an electronic device in the consumer's possession. This electronic value can be purchased and held on the device until reduced through purchase or transfer.

Electronic Purse A stored value device that can be used to make purchases from more than one vendor.

Feasibility Analysis The process of determining the likelihood that a proposal will fulfill specified objectives.

File Transfer Protocol A standard way of transferring files from one (FTP) computer to another on the Internet.

Firewall A system or combination of hardware and software solutions that enforces a boundary between two or more networks.

Gamma Test The third stage of software testing completed before release.

Gateway 1) A computer that performs protocol conversion between different types of networks or applications. 2) A computer that serves as a router, a format translator, or a security filter for an entire network.

Gopher A computer program, and an accompanying data transfer protocol, for reading information that has been made available to users on the Internet.

Graphical User Interface A way of communicating with a computer by (GUI) manipulating icons and windows with a "mouse."

Group Identifiers Security identifiers that contain a set of permissions given to a given group of users. All of the users in that group have the permissions granted to that group.

Groups Security identifiers to which users can be assigned membership for the purpose of applying a broad set of group permissions to the user. This allows for better management and control over large security environments.

Groupware Software that allows a group of users to work on the same data through a network by facilitating file sharing and other forms of communication.

Hacker A computer operator who breaks into a computer without authorization, for malicious reasons, just to prove it can be done, or other personal reasons.

Hardware Compatibility A listing of all hardware devices supported by the operating system.

Hash Function Used to create a message digest. The sender of a message uses a hash function to derive a calculation from a particular message.

Heterogeneous Networks Networks consisting of a variety of computer systems. Typically, these types use the TCP/IP (transmission control protocol/Internet protocol) network communication protocol to get these systems operating together. Managing a heterogeneous network is difficult since each operating system has its own security system. How these operating systems interact as a whole will determine the effectiveness of the security system.
Home Banking Banking services that allow a customer to interact with a financial institution from a remote location by using a telephone, television set, terminal, personal computer, or other device to access a telecommunication system which links to the institution's computer center.

Home Page A screen of information made available to users through the Internet or a private Intranet; it is the "main page" that users are expected to read first in order to access the other pages that comprise the Web site.

Host Also known as a host computer that is the primary or controlling computer in a computer network, generally involving data communications or a local area network.

Hypertext Electronic documents that present information that can be connected together in many different ways, instead of sequentially.

Hypertext Markup A set of codes that can be inserted into text files to indicate special Language (HTML) typefaces, inserted images, formatting, and links to create Web pages.

Hypertext Transfer Protocol HTTP is a standard method of publishing information as hypertext in HTML format on the Internet.

Icon A small picture on a computer screen that represents a particular object, operation, or group of files.

IDEA International Data Encryption Algorithm.

IETF Internet Engineering Task Force: a standardssetting organization.

Incident Response Team A team of computer experts (internal or external) organized to protect an organization's data, systems, and other assets from attack by hackers, viruses, or other compromises.

Integrated Circuit Card A plastic card in which one or more integrated circuits are embedded (also called a chip card).

ISDN Integrated Services Digital Network. A type of all-digital telephone service that can transmit digital data as well as voice, without a modem.

ISO/OSI An international standard-setting organization. ANSI is the U.S. representative.

Internet A worldwide network of computer networks (commonly referred to as the Information Superhighway).

Internet Information Software used to serve higher-level Internet Server protocols, like HTTP and FTP for clients using Web browsers.

Internet Service Provider An entity that provides access and/or services (ISP) related to the Internet, generally for a fee.

Interoperability The compatibility of distinct applications, networks, or systems.

Intranet A private network that uses the infrastructure and standards of the Internet and World Wide Web, but is cordoned off from the public Internet through firewall barriers.

Kernel The core process of a preemptive operating system, generally consisting of a multitasking scheduler and the basic security services.

Key 1) The integers that drive the encryption algorithm. 2) A secret value or code used in an encrypting algorithm known by one or both of the communicating parties.

Local Area Network (LAN) A network that connects several computers that are located nearby (in the same room or building), allowing them to share files and devices such as printers.

Lock and Key Protection A protection system that involves matching a key or password with a specific access requirement.

Logging The storing of information about events that occurred on the firewall or network.

Logon Script Command files that automate the logon process by performing utility functions such as attaching to additional server resources or automatically running different programs based on the user account that established the logon.

Long File Name (LFN) A filename longer than the MS-DOS allowed eight plus extension. In Windows NT, windows 98/95, OS/2, Unix, and Linux, for example.

Magnetic Stripe Used on debit, credit, and identification cards to store encoded information read by card readers; less secure than computer chip cards.

Memory Card An integrated circuit (IC) card capable of storing information only.

Message Digest A value created from a hash function. This value is known as the message digest. The receiver can verify the value to determine whether any changes were made to the message during transmission.

Middleware Facilitates the client/server connections over a network and allows client applications to access and update remote databases and mainframe files.

Multimedia The combining of different elements of media (i.e., text, graphics, audio, video) for display and control from a personal computer.

Multiprocessing Using two or more processors simultaneously to perform a computing task. Normally a hardware level capacity to perform this function: C Asymmetrically: Certain processors are assigned certain threads independent of the load they create. C Symmetrically: Threads are dynamically assigned to processors according to an equitable scheduling scheme.

Multitasking The ability of a processing unit to switch rapidly among threads of execution.

Multitasking divides processor time among threads as if each thread ran on its own slower processor. These systems allow two or more applications to run at the same time and can provide a greater degree of service to applications than single-tasking operating systems.

National Institute for Established within the Department of Standards Technology Commerce to develop technical, management, physical, and administrative standards and guidelines for the cost effective security and privacy of sensitive information in federal computer systems. NIST issues the Federal Information Processing Standards (FIPS).

National Security Agency Responsible for government and/or military (NSA) information security.

National Telecommunications A government agency charged with Information Administration safeguarding personal information on U.S. citizens.

Navigation Moving through a complex system of menus or help files.

Network A group of computers connected by cables or other means and using software that enables them to share equipment and exchange information. A system of software and hardware connected in a manner to support data transmission.

New Technology (NT) A Microsoft operating system. Node Any device, including servers and workstations, connected to a network. Also, the point where devices are connected. Nonrepudiation The undeniable proof of participation by both the sender and the receiver in a transaction.

It is the reason public key encryption was developed, i.e., to authenticate electronic messages and later prevent denial or repudiation by the sender or receiver.

Nonrepudiable Transactions Transactions that cannot be denied after the fact.

NT File System (NTFS) A secure, transaction-oriented file system developed for Windows NT allowing assignment of permissions and shares with access limited to properly authenticated users. Object A self-contained entity that contains its own data and the functions necessary to manipulate the data. NT's security system controls access to objects and the audit system logs them.

Off-line Equipment or devices that are not in direct communication with the central processor of a computer system, or connected only intermittently.

Online Equipment or devices that are currently capable of communicating with one relevant computer system.

Online Scrip Debit accounts on the Internet or other major computer network.

Online Service Providers Closed network services that provide access (OSP) to various computer sites or networks for a fee.

Open Network A data communications network to which access is not restricted.

Operation Phase The phase in which changeover from an old system to a new system occurs. The system is then operated and maintained. System performance is audited, and change to the system is managed.

Operating System 1) A collection of services that form a foundation upon which applications run. Examples include: MS-DOS: A simple I/O service provider with a command shell and Windows NT: A sophisticated, preemptive, multitasking, multiprocessing application platform. 2) A program that controls a computer and makes it possible for users to enter and run their own programs.

Ownership The owner of a file or directory has control of that file or directory and can change its permissions. By default, the user who creates the file or directory owns it.

Packet Switching A data transmission method that routes packets along the most efficient path and allows a communication channel to be shared by multiple connections.

Password A unique word or string of characters that a programmer, computer operator, or user must supply to satisfy security requirements before gaining access to the system or data.

Password Cracker A software program designed to conduct an automated brute force attack on the password security controls of an information system by "guessing" user passwords.

Password Sniffer A software program that is illicitly inserted somewhere on a network to capture user passwords as they pass through the system. Payment System A financial system that establishes the means for transferring money between suppliers and users of funds, usually by exchanging debits or credits between financial institutions.

Performance Specification A baseline specification that describes what a computer-based business system is to do. It is completed at the conclusion of the study phase.

Penetration Testing Using automated tools to determine a network's vulnerability to unauthorized access.

Permission A rule associated with an object to regulate which users can access the object and in what manner.

Personal Identification A sequence of digits used to verify identify. Number (PIN)

Personal User Profile A profile created by the administrator and assigned to a user. This records changes the user makes to their operating system or network environment settings. This is saved when the user logs off, and is loaded when the user logs on.

PGP Pretty Good Privacy data encryption algorithm.

Piggyback A means of gaining unauthorized access to a system through another user's legitimate connection.

Plain Text An unencrypted message.

Point-to-Point Tunneling Supports a secure, multi-protocol private network across the Protocol Internet. Makes use of authentication and encryption to secure communications. Windows NT supports this function by its remote-access service (RAS).

Policies General controls that enhance the security of an operating environment. For example, policies could affect restrictions on password use and rights assignments and determine which events will be recorded in the security log.

Priority A level of execution importance assigned to a thread. In combination with other factors, the priority level determines how often that thread will get computer time according to a scheduling algorithm.

Privacy-Enhanced Mail An Internet standard for secure electronic mail. The standard adds several security services to the Internet electronic mail messages: message origin authentication; message integrity; nonrepudiation of origin; and message confidentiality.

Private Branch Exchange A computer system that drives the internal telephone (PBX) system in an organization. The PBX is connected to the telephone company and possibly other networks.

Protocols 1) A standardized set of rules that define how computers communicate with each other. 2) An established rule of communication adhered to by the parties operating under it.

Proximity Cards Cards that can be read from a short distance; mainly used for security and vehicle identification.

Public Key Cryptography A two-key method of cryptography where a non-public key is used to encode and a second, publicly available key is used to decode.

Public Law 100-235 Computer Security Act of 1987; assigned the National Institute of Standards and Technology with the responsibility for developing standards and guidelines for federal computer systems processing unclassified data.

Real Time Monitoring The monitoring of activity as it occurs rather than storing the data for later review.

Registry A database repository for information about a computers configuration, including the hardware, installed software, environment settings, and other information.

Remote Access Letting off-site users access a central network. Remote Payment A payment carried out through the sending of payment orders or payment instruments.

Remote Procedure Calls A network interprocess communication mechanism that allows an application to be distributed among many computers on the same network.

Repudiation The denial by one of the parties to a transaction of participation in all or part of Internet Banking 82 that transaction or of the content of the communication.

Requests for Comments The set of standards defining the Internet protocols by the Internet Engineering Task Force and available in the public domain on the Internet. RFCs define the functions and services provided by each of the many Internet protocols. Compliance with the RFCs significantly enhances cross-vendor compatibility.

Router A computer system in a network that stores and forwards data packets between local area networks and wide area networks.

RSA A public key (asymmetrical) encryption methodology. It was invented in 1976 by Ron Rivest, Adi Shamir, and Leonard Adleman.

RSA is used as a supplement to DES. It provides for secure key exchanges and digital signatures. Key lengths can vary from 40 to 1,024 bits.

Scalability The ability of a system to support high-growth enterprise applications. These applications are typically large-scale, mission-critical in nature. Examples include supporting widely used online banking activities, hosting popular Web sites, maintaining large data warehouses, and administering large e-mail systems.

Scattering The process of mixing the integrated circuit (IC) chip components so that they cannot be analyzed easily.

Search Engines Software programs that are capable of locating specified information or Web sites on the Internet.

Searchware Software used to search through a database.

Secure Hypertext Provides secure communication mechanisms between an HTTP Transfer Protocol clientserver pair.

Security Accounts Manager The module of the NT executive that authenticates a user name and password against a database of accounts, generating an access token that includes users' permissions.

Secure Socket Layer (SSL) A protocol for providing data security during transmission using data encryption, server authentication, and message integrity.

Security Identifiers (SIDs) Unique codes that identify a specific user or group to the NT security system. SIDs contain a complete set of permissions for that user or group.

Security Policies The security policy consists of the Account, User Rights, Audit, and Trust Relationships policies, and are managed with User Managers for Domains.

Server 1) A computer dedicated to servicing requests for resources from other computers on a network. Servers typically run network operating systems. 2) A computer that provides services to another computer (the client).

SET A set of standards jointly developed by Visa, MasterCard, and several technologies companies to facilitate secure credit card transactions over the Internet. Secure Electronic Transactions is a standard developed by VISA and MasterCard. SET uses public key cryptography and requires merchants and consumers to have authentication keys to conduct online transactions. The purpose is to secure transactions over open networks such as the Internet.

Settlement An act that discharges obligations with respect to funds or securities transfers between two or more parties.

Settlement system A system used to facilitate the settlement of transfers of funds.

Simple Mail Transfer A protocol used to transfer electronic mail between computers on the Internet.

Smart Card A card with a computer chip embedded, on which financial, health, educational, and security information can be stored and processed.

Social Engineering Posing as managers, technicians, or other employees to gain access to computer resources either directly by corporate or by obtaining access codes or access from authorized users.

Specification Documents that contain basic detailed data.

Spoofing An attempt to gain access to a system by posing as an authorized user.

Standards The rules under which analysts, programmers, operators, and other personnel in an information service organization work.

Stored Value Card A card that stores prepaid value by magnetic stripe or computer chip.

Structured Query Language A query language used to manipulate large (SQL) databases.

Structured Walk-Through A technical review performed to assist the technical people working on a project. It is one of a series of reviews that should be a planned part of system design and development activities.

Study Phase The phase during which a problem is identified, possible solutions are studied, and recommendations are made with regard to committing the resources required to design a system.

Subnet Mask A number mathematically applied to addresses to determine which addresses are a part of the same subnetwork as the computer applying the subnet mask.

Switch A type of bridge that can move several packets at the same time.

Symmetrical A private or secret key cryptography methodology that uses the same key to both encrypt and decrypt messages. DES is an example of this type of technology.

Systems Analysis The performance, management, and documentation of the four phases of the life cycle of a business system: study, design, development, and operation.

System Flowchart A flowchart diagraming the flow of work, documents, and operations in a data processing application.

System Integrity The quality that a system has when it performs its intended function in an unimpaired manner, free from deliberate or inadvertent manipulation of the system.

System Policy A policy used to control what a user can do and the environment of that user. System policies can be in Windows NT, applied to a specific user, group, computer, or all users. System policies work by overwriting current settings in the registry with the system policy settings.

System Specification A baseline specification containing all the essential computer-based business system documentation. It is completed at the end of the Development Phase.

Systemic Risk The risk that the failure of one participant in a funds transfer system, or in financial markets, to meet its required obligations will cause other participants or financial institutions to be unable to meet their obligations when due.

Tamper-evident The capacity of devices to show evidence of physical attack.

Tamper-proof The proven capacity of devices to resist attacks.

Tamper resistant The capacity of devices to resist physical attack up to a certain point.

Telecommunications Data transmission between a computing system and remotely located devices by telephone lines, cable, or wireless technology.

Telnet A protocol that permits users to access a remote terminal or another computer through a network; widely used on the Internet.

Thread A list of instructions running in a computer to perform a certain task. Each thread runs in the context of a process, which embodies the protected memory space and the environment of the threads. Multi-threaded processes can perform more than one task at the same time.

Threat Monitoring The analysis, assessment, and review of audit trails and other data collected for the purpose of searching out system events that may constitute violations or attempted violations of system security.

Throughput The total amount of useful work performed by a data processing system during a given period of time.

Topology The arrangement of nodes usually forming a star, ring, tree, or bus pattern.

Traceability The degree to which transactions can be traced to the originator or recipient (also referred to as auditability).

Transport Control Protocol Also Internet protocol (TCP/IP). A standard format for transmitting data in packets from one computer to another, on the Internet and within other networks. TCP deals with the construction of the data packets, while IP routes them from machine to machine.

Trap Door A concealed and unauthorized entrance into a computer operating system, designed by the programmer.

Trojan Horse A program that appears to perform a useful function and sometimes does so quite well but also includes an unadvertised feature, which is usually malicious in nature.

Truncation Dropping off part of a character string either to conserve space or because of limited space.

Trusted Computer System A system that employs sufficient assurance measures to allow its use for simultaneous processing of a range of sensitive or classified information.

Trusted Relationship Links between domains that enable passthrough validation, in which a user has only one user account in one domain, yet can access the entire network. A trusting domain honors the log in validation of another trusted domain.

A key weakness with these systems is that a hacker may try to gain access to a lesser secured system to take advantage of its trust relationship with other computers.

Trusted Third Party A reputable entity that authenticates one or more parties to an electronic transaction. The authentication process generally involves the issuance and administration of digital certificates.

Uninterruptible Power Provides power to a system in case of a Supply (UPS) power outage.

UNIX A multitasking, kernel-based operating system developed by AT&T in the early 1970s and provided, originally, free to universities as a research operating system. Because of its availability and ability to scale down to microprocessor-based computers, UNIX became the standard operating system of the Internet and its attendant network protocols and is the closest approximation to a universal operating system that exists. Most computers can run some variant of the UNIX operating system.

Uniform Resource Locator A way of specifying the location of available or Universal Resource information on the Internet.

Locator (URL) Upload To transmit a file to a central computer from a smaller computer or a remote location.

Usenet A set of many news groups distributed by the Internet.

User Manager for Domains A tool used to manage security for a domain or an individual computer. Administers user accounts, groups, and security policies.

Virtual Corporations Corporations that have no official physical site presence, and are made up of diverse geographically dispersed or mobile employees.

Virus A program with the ability to reproduce by modifying other programs to include a copy of itself. It may contain destructive code that can move into multiple programs, data files, or devices on a system and spread through multiple systems in a network.

Vulnerability A weakness in system security procedures, system design, implementation, internal controls, etc., that could be exploited to violate system security.

War-Dialing Dialing every number on an institution's telephone exchange looking for the existence of authorized or unauthorized modems on which to launch an attack.

Web Page Information presented through a Web browser in a single view.

Web Site A Web page or set of Web pages designed, presented, and linked together to form a logical information resource and/or transaction initiation function.

Wide Area Network (WAN) A communications network that covers a wide geographic area, such as state or country, using high speed long distance lines or satellites provided by a common carrier.

Win 16 The set of application services provided by the 16-bit versions of Windows 3.1 and Windows for Workgroups 3.11 Win 32 The set of applications services provided by the 32-bit versions of Windows 95 and NT.

Windows NT The portable, secure, 32-bit, preemptive multitasking member of the Windows operating system family. This system includes peer networking services, server networking services, Internet client and server services, and a broad range of utilities.

Windows NT Server The Windows NT Server provides centralized management and security, advanced fault tolerance, and additional connectivity.

Windows 95 A 32-bit version Windows for medium-range, Intel-based computers. This system includes peer networking services, Internet support, and strong support for older DOS applications and peripherals.

Workgroup A collection of computers that are grouped for viewing purposes. Each workgroup is identified by a unique name.

Workstation A powerful personal computer.

World Wide Web A subnetwork of the Internet through which (Web, WWW) information is exchanged by text, graphics, audio, and video.

Worm A program that scans a system or an entire network for available, unused space in which to run. Worms tend to tie up all computing resources in a system or on a network and effectively shut it down.

Bibliography

Ariel Buira: *Challenges to the World Bank and IMF: Developing Country Perspectives*, London, Anthem Press, 2003.

Bhagwati, J.: *Trade, Balance of Payments and Growth: Essays in Honor of C. P. Kindleberger*, Amsterdam, North-Holland Publishing Company, 1971.

Bhuleshkar, Vasant: *Indian Economy in the World Setting*, Bombay, Himalaya, 1988.

Bouman, F.J.A.: *Small, Short and Unsecured: Informal Rural Finance in India*, Delhi, Oxford University Press, 1989.

Connolly, M.: *The International Monetary System: Choices for the Future*, New York, Praeger, 1983.

Cooley, Thomas F.: *Frontiers of Business Cycle Research*, Princeton University Press, 1995.

Downs, Anthony: *An Economic Theory of Democracy*, New York, Harper and Row, 1957.

Gerald, K.: *The Less Developed Countries in the International Economy*, Cambridge, Cambridge University Press, 1975.

Greer, Douglas F.: *Industrial Organization and Public Policy*, MacMillan Publishing Company, 1992.

Guhan, S.: *The World Bank's Lending in South Asia*, Washington, Brookings Institution, 1995.

Hauft, Ottomar: *Distribution of Stock of Money*, Effingham, London, 1892.

Hoshii, Iwao: *A Financial History of the New Japan*, Kodansha International Ltd., Lokyo, 1972.

Jha, P.R.: *Agriculture and Economic Development*, New Delhi, Ashish, 1988.

Le Prestre, Philippe: *The World Bank and the Environmental Challenge*, London, Associated University Presses, 1989.

Magliveras, Konstantinos D. *Banks, Fraud and Crime*, Lloyd's of London Press, London, 2000.

McCallum, J. : *Global Disequilibrium*, London, MacMillan, 1992.

Michael Connolly, *The International Monetary System: Choices for the Future*, New York, Praeger, 1983.

Ottomar, H.: *Distribution of Stock of Money,* Effingham, London, 1892.

Paul, Kegan : *Money and the Mechanism of Exchange,* Oxford, London, 1890.

Peet, Richard, Born, Beate: *Unholy Trinity: The IMF, World Bank, and WTO*, New York, Zed Books, 2003.

Polak, J.J. : *The New International Monetary System*, New York, Columbia University Press, 1978.

Raj, K.N.: *New Economic Policy*, Delhi, Oxford University Press, 1986.

Ranade, Sudhanshu: *Rural Banking Adrift*, Bombay, Jaico Publishing House, 1984.

Rao, M.G. and R.J. Chelliah: *Survey of Research in Indian Fiscal Federalism*, National Institute of Public Finance and Policy, New Delhi, 1991.

Robert Z. Aliber: *The International Market for Foreign Exchange*, New York, Praeger, 1969.

Savla, Sandeep: *Money Laundering and Financial Intermediaries*, The Hague and Boston, Kluwer Law International, 2001.

Seligman, E. R. A. : *Currency Inflation and Public Debts,* New York, 1922.

Sinha, R.K.: *Economic Development since Independence*, New Delhi, Deep and Deep, 1988.

Vines, David and Christopher Gilbert: *The IMF and its Critics: Reform of the Global Financial Architecture*, Cambridge, Cambridge University Press, 2004.

Wolfe, J.N.: *Value, Capital and Growth*, Chicago, Edinburgh University Press. 1968.

Index

N

O

P

R

S

T

V

□□□